The Bedside Guardian 2015

The Bedside Guardian 2015

EDITED BY MALIK MEER

guardianbooks

Published by Guardian Books 2015

2 4 6 8 10 9 7 5 3 1

First published in Great Britain in 2015 by
Guardian Books
Kings Place, 90 York Way
London N1 9GU

www.guardianbooks.co.uk

A CIP catalogue record for this book is available from the British Library

ISBN 978-1783-56115-5

Cover design by Two Associates
Typeset by seagulls.net

Printed and bound in Great Britain
by CPI Group (UK) Ltd, Croydon CR0 4YY

Contents

SPRING

SUMMER

Foreword: The Year the People Yelled 'Fire!'

NAOMI KLEIN

What do we do when our political leaders treat profound moral crises as if they are nothing extraordinary? Nothing to see here, move along?

What if a supposedly ho hum phenomenon is actually an existential threat to our species? How do we wrench the script away from those in power and sound the alarm?

In the final months of his editorship, Alan Rusbridger publically struggled with this question in a memorable essay that kicked off the *Guardian*'s special coverage of the climate crisis. 'Changes to the Earth's climate rarely make it to the top of the news list,' he wrote. 'The changes may be happening too fast for human comfort, but they happen too slowly for the newsmakers – and, to be fair, for most readers ... There may be untold catastrophes, famines, floods, droughts, wars, migrations and sufferings just around the corner. But that is futurology, not news, so it is not going to force itself on any front page any time soon.'

At the end of the hottest year on record – one marked by serial disasters, as well as armed conflicts exacerbated by drought – it's getting tough to view climate change as futurology. Yet Rusbridger's central point holds: this is a complex, slow motion crisis.

And with politicians loath to put it front and centre, how can the warming of our world compete with the many other pressing issues that scream daily for our attention?

Rusbridger's solution was simple: don't wait for politicians to treat climate as crisis. Instead, just do it. And so climate crisis suddenly appeared on the front page of the paper and the website, 'even though nothing exceptional happened on this day. It will be there again next week and the week after.'

Most extraordinary about the *Guardian*'s coverage has been its strong focus on fossil fuel divestment, based on research showing that oil, gas and coal companies have several times more carbon in their proven reserves than is compatible with keeping warming below 2 degrees Celsius – something our governments have pledged to do. Just a few years ago, the fact that fossil fuel companies were frantically searching out more carbon despite the fact that the climate system is destabilising was treated as an utterly normal part of the market system. Nothing remarkable. Not a story.

But then a relatively small group of activists drew the line and said 'no'. They redefined the frenetic quest for more carbon as immoral behavior, perpetuated by, as author and activist Bill McKibben put it, 'a rogue industry'. And they said it must be stopped.

When the *Guardian* launched its #Keepitintheground series, throwing the full weight of its reporting, graphics and film departments behind what had previously been a grassroots campaign, things started changing very quickly. Suddenly all kinds of people came out of the woodwork to say that they, too, supported divestment – from Prince Charles to Ed Davey, then minister for energy and climate change. Even a former chairman of Shell declared divestment a 'rational approach'.

Most significantly, since September 2014, the number of organisations around the world that have decided to divest has doubled. And in the 10 weeks following the launch, global main-stream press coverage of divestment shot up by a third. This is the result of a huge amount of grassroots activism, to be sure, but the impact of the *Guardian*'s leadership has been unmistakable.

All of this speaks to the fact that politicians aren't the only ones with the power to declare an emergency. Large and organised social movements have that power too. So, too, do major news organisations. Looking back at many of the significant stories of 2015, this phenomenon emerges as a defining theme: some ephemeral line is crossed and suddenly an activity that had been regarded as unremarkable is vociferously rejected as intolerable.

And when that happens, the *Guardian* is the news organisation most reliably on the side of the people who are sounding the alarm. Telling the most compelling stories, digging up the most damning facts, and publishing the most heart-stopping photography.

Though it began in 2013, this bottom-up declaration of a national emergency is what the Black Lives Matter movement has been doing in US streets without pause. Many analysts have wondered what sparked this uprising, since the number of police killings in the United States appears not to have risen significantly in recent years. Nothing has really changed, they insist, so what's all the marching about?

But that misses the point entirely: what has changed, thanks to the rise of the movement, is the idea that 'normal' levels of state violence are normal at all. Police violence has been redefined, in the streets, as both a scandal and an emergency. 'For the last couple of years the brutal banality of daily life for some people in this country has become visible and undeniable to those who have no immediate connection to it,' writes Gary Younge in a searing essay included in this collection. 'But nothing new has happened. There has been no spike in police brutality. What's new is that people are looking.'

To help expose this 'brutal banality', this year the *Guardian* launched 'The Counted', a detailed, crowdsourced database tracking US police killings. It amounts to 'the most thorough public accounting for deadly use of force' in the country. (As of September, this year's harrowing tally was approaching 850.) And it once again shows the power of rigorous journalism combining with an engaged – and awake – population.

Previously, hard journalism was mostly about exposing lies and scandals that were being kept hidden. Today, a lot of the job of journalism – and activism – involves redefining what is happing right out in the open as scandalous, because it is. For instance, just because everybody thinks their emails are being monitored doesn't mean it must always be so. Just because our borders are increasingly fortressed to refugees in dire need, doesn't mean this has to be our future. And just because living standards have steadily eroded under the banner of 'austerity' doesn't mean that they can't rise once again.

We can still say 'no' – and a great many of us are. From the 'refugees welcome' demonstrations across Europe, to the surges of anti-austerity sentiment in Greece and Spain, to the hundreds of 'kayaktivists' who tried to stop Shell's Arctic drilling rigs from making it to icy waters. Again and again, regular people are drawing a line and saying 'no' to what had very recently been treated as perfectly reasonable by experts and pundits.

One of the most significant roles that the *Guardian* has played in this process has been providing spaces for the subjects of news stories to speak for themselves. That is what the *Guardian* did with its landmark special feature spotlighting 100 immigrants living in Britain. And so readers heard directly from Iraqi journalist Rzhwan Jaff. 'Seeking asylum is viewed as seeking financial support, seeking accommodation and seeking benefit,' he writes. 'But, in fact, it is about seeking protection under international law and the refugee convention of 1951. The conflicts and political crisis in Iraq had forced me to flee Iraq and never look back again. On the other hand, the treatment I have received from the authorities in the UK has made me a hopeless person.'

The good news in all of this is that sometimes, when lines are drawn and everyday traumas are defined as outrages, real victories follow. Take, for instance, Aditya Chakrabortty's powerful reflection on the so-called Camden dinner ladies, the 300 catering workers who won a living wage in London after a fierce, months-long campaign this summer. 'The position of low-paid workers in Britain is first described, then euphemised and finally rationalised,' Chakrabortty writes. 'Meanwhile, the super-salaries paid to the richest 1 per cent are usually passed off as the just reward for top talent.'

Yet the key lesson, he concludes – in what should be the mantra of our time – is 'that what we're told is political and economic common sense can be shown up as nonsense. We've grown used to compromises and accommodations, to accepting whatever's deemed realistic, even if it's useless ... And then 300 women get it together and show that it needn't be so.'

Journalism plays such a critical role in this process of asserting that just because something reprehensible has become commonplace, we do not relinquish our power – indeed our basic responsibility – to declare it unacceptable.

We saw this power many times this year, most vividly with the global sorrow and outrage sparked by the photographs of the corpse of three-year-old Alan Kurdi on a beach in Turkey. The *Guardian* was one of the few British newspapers to publish what many considered the most disturbing image, unaltered. 'Every day kids have drowned,' Kurdi's aunt observed to a journalist. 'But before Alan died, people read it and moved on. That boy, that picture, meant something.'

How such an image is reported and contextualised, of course, matters a great deal. In these pages, Ian Jack ponders the complicated history of how 'pictures, especially of children, have awoken consciences or shaped public attitudes in lasting ways' – or not. Asking difficult questions about the role of 'our own prejudices and desires' in this process, he points to the unique ability of the media to intervene: 'Until recently, those who died in calamities beyond Europe and North America were rarely identified unless they were European or North American. The western media felt easy about using pictures of them as anonymous bodies drowned in a flood or mutilated by war ... The Kurdi family have been named.' That naming – and the fact that members of the family were not only images but also voices and stories – made all the difference.

Discussing the role of news organisations in shaping world events is not always comfortable for journalists. Reporters, after all, are trained to cover the news, not make it. Many don't like to think of themselves as actors in the news at all. And yet, at the same time, journalists routinely praise one another for their acute 'news judgment'. The phrase is a reminder that though much of what makes it on the world's front pages and homepages is there because powerful forces want it to be, news organisations do still have the power to exercise their own judgment, and inevitably do so many times a day.

They have the power to declare something a big story even when it isn't, strictly speaking, new. They can put their full weight behind a story simply because what is happening is wrong (like the killing of unarmed African Americans by police) or because the stakes are unimaginably high (like climate change).

Too often, media outlets abdicate this power, choosing instead to go with the flow. Or, worse, they actively use their enormous power and platform to champion the interests of the already powerful.

The *Guardian* isn't perfect, but it is different. In the face of the most urgent crises we face as a human family, it consistently displays the courage to declare normalised abuses – of people, privacy and planet – to be wholly unacceptable. And in so doing, it helps so many of us to feel less alone, and to find our full voices as well.

That's why we so badly need the *Guardian*. On our bedside, yes. But on our screens and on the stands most of all.

Introduction

MALIK MEER

This summer, Europe experienced the biggest refugee crisis since the second world war, as hundreds of thousands of people attempted to cross borders in search of a better life.

'There were mothers with babies on their backs and fathers with children strapped to their fronts. There were grandmothers from Iraq and grandfathers from Afghanistan. There were Syrians fleeing the remains of Aleppo ...' wrote the *Guardian*'s migration correspondent Patrick Kingsley on the Serbia–Hungary border, included here on p. 281. 'There was a man in a wheelchair. And 22-year-old Mostafa from Baghdad on crutches, one of the very last few to heave his way across the border. And then the gates clanged shut.'

The response to the flow of refugees – the political and cultural implications – can be felt throughout this year's *Bedside Guardian*. David Cameron's use of the word 'swarm' to describe the Calais migrants is rightly met with disgust by Frankie Boyle (p. 255), while Ian Jack explores the impact of the disturbing image of three-year-old Alan Kurdi lying lifeless on a Turkish beach. (It is included in the plate selection.) The PM's visit to a refugee camp in Lebanon is addressed by cartoonist Steve Bell on p. 280, and Martin Chulov's gripping Long Read on the birth of Isis provides some context about the death cult's horrific ambitions, and why so many refugees have been displaced. There's also an extract from 'Immigrants in Their Own Words' (p. 117), a one-off project that was sourced stories via our award-winning GuardianWitness platform.

Yet even with such a range of pieces, an anthology of this kind can't do justice to the twists and turns in the refugee story or the *Guardian*'s rich reporting and digital coverage of it (liveblogs, audio, video, graphics, interactives and more). At the time of writing, we are publishing around 500 articles a day across three continents; *The Bedside Guardian*, the 64th in the series, can only ever serve as a snapshot.

Back in the UK, we experienced a general election where 11 million voters returned David Cameron to Number 10 in his first overall majority. Few predicted the outcome. As Charlie Brooker writes (p. 172), 'Never again need any decision be guided by an opinion poll, or a focus group, or the popularity of a hashtag. Maybe that's a good thing. Or 10 bad ones glued together. I have absolutely no idea and neither do you. Because none of us knows anything.'

Along the way, the election campaign took many surreal turns (Ed Miliband's pledge stone 'has just raised the stupidity bar still higher', sketches John Crace on p. 162), while a desperate Westminster elite did its best to maintain control. 'More lies are told here than on all the world's dating profiles put together,' concludes Marina Hyde from Westminster's post TV debate 'spin-room' (p. 145). In the event, the UKIP threat didn't quite materialise, the SNP triumphed, the Lib Dems were decimated and the Labour party suffered its worst defeat since 1983. After a leadership election the party returned with a 'new politics' under new leader Jeremy Corbyn. Simon Hattenstone's interview with Corbyn, a few hours after he is added to the Labour leadership ballot as the wild card option, makes for a revealing read (p. 200). 'Like the rest of the country, Corbyn doesn't think he has a chance of winning,' wrote Hattenstone. 'But these are funny times in politics.' Three months later, Corbyn won the largest party mandate for any political leader in UK political history.

The *Guardian* had its own change of leadership, too. After 20 years as editor, Alan Rusbridger stepped down in July, passing the baton to Katharine Viner, who became the first female editor in the paper's history. Rusbridger's sign-off pays tribute to the *Guardian*'s greatest asset: '... in the end, we editors just pass through. We all know that you, the readers, are the real carriers of the flame.'

As ever, there were tough editorial decisions to be made. Jonathan Freedland's column on the horror of the *Charlie Hebdo* attack (p. 64) explains why we didn't publish the magazine's cartoons of the prophet Muhammad. 'It is not only violent jihadists who resent representations of the prophet: such pictures trouble many millions of peaceful Muslims too. To print one now would be to take a stand against the former by offending the latter.'

Not everyone was so sensitive as Islamaphobia continued to manifest itself in unlikely ways. 'Little issues such as the name of Muhammad are turned by the far right into vitriolic hate against Muslims,' a criminologist tells Homa Khaleeli in the Mohammed myth (p. 16).

This selection includes other key themes from the year: the rise of Uber, gentrification, Russia's propaganda war and the austerity delusion. One of the year's recurrent themes was the battle for transgender rights. The different responses to Chelsea Manning's plea for the right to define herself (p. 28) and, 11 months later, Caitlyn Jenner's *Vanity Fair* reveal, proved that transgender issues had finally reached the mainstream. As Jess Cartner-Morley outlines (p. 186), the family pop culture loves to hate somehow became 'catalysts for social change'.

There were many exciting new signings across the *Guardian* and this collection includes pieces by Rhik Samadder, Paul Mason and Lindy West. As the social media landscape continued to enthrall and infuriate, West wrote about meeting her online troll (p. 74); it horrified *Guardian* readers around the world and was cited by Twitter CEO Dick Costolo in February as one of the reasons why they were finally tackling cyber-bullying on the platform.

Elsewhere, there were many wins for the *Guardian*. Aside from the success of campaigns such as Keep it in the Ground, The Counted and End FGM, Rob Evans's 10-year battle with the government finally led to the release of Prince Charles's black spider memos.

It's customary for *Bedside* editors to apologise to all the writers whose pieces didn't make the cut and I am sorry I couldn't fit more in. The sheer quality of *Guardian* journalism meant that we were spoilt for choice and final edit was a challenge. At least three major stories broke just after we had finished the selection: Lord Ashcroft's #piggate claims about David Cameron at Oxford university, flowing water discovered on Mars and the expose of Volkswagen's emissions cheating software – a scandal that underlines the importance of the *Guardian*'s focus on environmental issues.

The collection closes with a piece by the former MP Chris Mullin imagining Jeremy Corbyn first 100 days as PM after slaying George Osborne at the 2020 election. In this fantastical imagining of an alternate future under Corbyn's premiership, Rupert Murdoch loses his media monopoly, rent controls are introduced and the public line the streets to hail the Bearded One.

If that sounds fanciful, have you heard the one about the Prime Minister and dead pig's head?

Acknowledgements

I would like to thank Alan Rusbridger for asking me to edit this year's *Bedside Guardian*; Lindsay Davies from Guardian Books for her sound advice and no-nonsense approach to the selection process; the *Guardian*'s head of photography, Roger Tooth; and Richard Nelsson and Maryam Cockar on the research and information team. Thanks also to Suzie Worroll, Tim Lusher, Rob Fearn and everyone on the G2 and features desks. And finally to Sophie Lazar (copyediting), Ilona Jasiewicz (proofreading), Jonathan Baker (design) and Andy at MFE Books (index).

Autumn

History and all its grisly facts are worth more than the illusion of memory

JONATHAN JONES

In 1924 the German artist Otto Dix depicted a skull, lying on the ground, a home to worms. They crawl out of its eye sockets, nasal opening and mouth, and wriggle among patches of hair and a black moustache – or are they growths of grass? – that still cling to the raw bone.

This horror comes from *Der Krieg*, a series of etchings in which Dix recorded his memories of fighting in the first world war. He was a machine gunner at the Somme, among other battles, and won the Iron Cross, second class. But he remembered it all as pure horror, as did other participants who happened to be artists or writers such as George Grosz, Siegfried Sassoon, Ernst Jünger and Robert Graves.

I was thinking of that death's head by Dix when I wrote in an online *Guardian* article earlier this week that I would rather see the moat of the Tower of London filled with 'barbed wire and bones' than the red ceramic poppies currently drawing huge crowds to see what has become the defining popular artwork in this centenary of the Great War's outbreak. I called the sea of poppies now surrounding the Tower 'toothless' as art and a 'Ukip-style memorial' – to quote my words not in their original context but as they have since been republished in angry articles in the *Mail*, *Telegraph* and *The Times*, with the *Mail* in particular denouncing me as a 'sneering leftwing critic' and the *Guardian* for publishing my wicked words. Even the prime minister got drawn in at question time in the Commons. 'Cameron defends "toothless" poppy tribute,' reported Thursday's edition of *The Times*.

But my criticism of this work of art was and is reasonable, honest and founded not in some kind of trendy cynicism but a belief that we need to look harder, and keep looking, at the terrible truths of the war that smashed the modern world off the rails and started a cycle of murderous extremism that ended only in 1945. If it did end.

I strongly believe that an adequate work of art about the war has to show its horror, not sweep the grisly facts under a red carpet of artificial flowers.

Otto Dix told the truth about this war that killed more than eight million men from many nations and left many more disfigured and disabled when he drew that worm-infested skull. Their deaths and injuries were not beautiful. But the installation at the Tower is spuriously beautiful: it allows us to mourn without seeing anything to cause visceral distress. It muffles the terrible facts. It is so tasteful, so decorous.

What a feeble contrast not just with Dix but with the photographs that show this war as it was. On a bookcase when I was a child I remember finding AJP Taylor's *The First World War: An Illustrated History*. On its cover was a photograph of a skeleton in a dugout still wearing a uniform on its fleshless bones. That was the historical reality of this war, which Taylor brilliantly chose to show visually in his classic book.

This war has always been there, for me, in the background of family life. As it happens I quite possibly owe the *Daily Mail* my existence, for it helped get the Jones genes through to 1918. As my great-grandparents in their farmhouse on the edge of Snowdonia faced the threat of their teenage son's call-up in the Great

War, my great-grandmother saw an advert in the *Mail* for volunteers for the new Naval Air Service. So my grandfather worked as a joiner keeping wood-framed flying machines going, and as he said when asked what he did in the war: 'I survived.'

My other grandfather also survived, but with scars on his memory. He was a runner on the western front. He would never speak about what he experienced, except to once tell my dad he had been trapped for days in a pothole in no man's land. Hearing of that I have always believed the photo on Taylor's book, the drawing by Dix. And I don't believe the Tower of London's floral tribute.

These experiences were real, this war was real, and it means absolutely nothing to reduce it all to vague feelings of universal grief. What we owe the youth of that generation is to attend to the details of the history that caught them in its hungry jaws. We need to smell the rotting earth and gunpowder, feel the boots falling apart in muddy water, the pounding in the chest as the guns started up. The installation at the Tower is abstract, and tells nothing about that history. It is instead a representation of grief as such – a second-hand evocation of feelings about the dead.

It does not matter now, a century after it started, how sad we are about those the first world war killed. Our soulfulness won't bring back a single slaughtered soldier. What can make a difference is our historical understanding of the Great War, its causes and consequence. History is worth far more than the illusion of memory, when none of us today actually have a memory of being soldiers in 1914–18.

That brings me to my 'sneering' remark that something about this memorial nurtures the world view of Ukip. Out of the millions who died, this installation is very specific about who it mourns. It does not include the French, who lost a tenth of their young men, or Russia, where the war precipitated revolution, civil war and famine. And of course it does not include a single German. Instead it is accumulating 888,246 ceramic poppies each of which – explains the Tower of London website – 'represents a British military fatality during the war.'

If we can only picture the Great War as a British tragedy we have not learned very much about it. Yet some historians today glibly encourage that blinkered vision. It sells books. Popular history has been invaded by revisionists who tell us that far from being lions led by donkeys in a futile bloodbath, the British soldiers who fought from 1914–18 were fighting, as the propaganda at the time claimed, to defend democracy from militarist authoritarian Germany.

I believe this fashionable view of the first world war to be historically unjustified. I've been interested in its history ever since I spent too many hours as an 18-year-old reading up to win a history entrance scholarship at Cambridge – no, before that, since seeing that photo of an unburied corpse on the cover of Taylor's book. The best current work on the origins of the first world war, Christopher Clark's *The Sleepwalkers*, is a 562-page analysis that does not pander to instant explanations. He demonstrates the absurdity of seeing Germany as the unique culprit and reveals the complex process of diplomatic folly that started the war. So as I asked Lord West on *The World at One*, why not mourn German soldiers at the Tower?

In so explicitly recording only the British dead of world war one, this work of art in its tasteful way confirms the illusion that we are an island of heroes with no debt to anyone else, no fraternity for anyone else.

The war poet Wilfred Owen did not want us to remember him and his contemporaries with the bland sentimentality of this installation. He wished instead we could witness what he witnessed, a young man dying in a gas attack:

> *If you could hear, at every jolt, the blood*
> *Come gargling from the froth-corrupted lungs,*
> *Obscene as cancer ...*
> *My friend, you would not tell with such high zest*
> *To children ardent for some desperate glory,*
> *The old Lie; Dulce et Decorum est*
> *Pro patria mori.*

A true work of art about the first world war would need to be as obscene as cancer. But Owen, who died soon after writing this, is 'represented' by one of those ceramic flowers now, his bitter truth smoothed away by the potter's decorous hand.

19 NOVEMBER

Why I had to turn down Band Aid

FUSE ODG

Saying no to Bob Geldof is one of the hardest decisions I have had to make this year. However, seeing what looked like the corpse of an African woman being carried out of her home on prime-time TV when the video was premiered on *X Factor* crystallised my concerns about this strategy to combat the Ebola crisis. For me it is ultimately flawed.

A week before the recording of Band Aid 30, I received a call from Geldof asking if I would take part. I was honoured to be asked and, connecting with his passion for wanting to tackle the Ebola crisis, said I wanted to offer my support.

But I also had my concerns. I was sceptical because of the lyrics and the videos of the previous charity singles, and I worried that this would play into the constant negative portrayal of the continent of Africa in the west. Geldof and I spoke at length about this and he agreed with me on many levels, assuring me that we could use it as an opportunity to showcase the positives of Africa.

However, on receiving the proposed lyrics on Thursday – two days before the recording was due to take place in London – I was shocked and appalled by their content. The message of the Band Aid 30 song absolutely did not reflect what Africa is truly about and I started to question whether this was something I wanted to be a part of.

I pointed out to Geldof the lyrics I did not agree with, such as the lines 'Where a kiss of love can kill you and there's death in every tear', and 'There is no peace and joy in west Africa this Christmas'. For the past four years I have gone to Ghana at Christmas for the sole purpose of peace and joy. So for me to sing these lyrics would simply be a lie.

In truth, my objection to the project goes beyond the offensive lyrics. I, like many others, am sick of the whole concept of Africa – a resource-rich continent with unbridled potential – always being seen as diseased, infested and poverty-stricken. In fact, seven out of 10 of the world's fastest growing economies are in Africa.

Let me be clear, I'm not disregarding the fact that Ebola is happening and that people need help. Since the start of the outbreak in March it has killed more than 5,000 people. But every human being deserves dignity in their suffering and the images flashed on our screens remove any remnants of this from Ebola sufferers, many in their dying moments, when they should have it the most.

I am not disputing Band Aid's good intentions. But the shock-factor strategy they have used since the 1980s has sparked a whole wave of 'good cause' organisations that have been irresponsible with regard to the images shown to the rest of the world. It's been totally one-sided. That's understandable in part, as they wouldn't raise much money if they showed the affluence, wealth, and happy lifestyles that exist in the continent. But in the process of doing all this 'good work' a huge imbalance has been created.

That image of poverty and famine is extremely powerful psychologically. With decades of such imagery being pumped out, the average westerner is likely to donate £2 a month or buy a charity single that gives them a nice warm fuzzy feeling; but they are much less likely to want to go on holiday to, or invest in, Africa. If you are reading this and haven't been to Africa, ask yourself why.

This is New Africa (Tina) is a movement empowering people to shed a positive light on Africa. I was born in Tooting, south London, and was taken as an infant to Ghana. Returning to London at the age of 11, being African was not something to be proud of because of all the negative connotations it conjured up, and it drove me to be almost ashamed of who I was.

Anyone who has experienced Africa in a positive way is a citizen of the New Africa and needs to play their part in challenging perceptions. I'm sharing my experience through my music – and if I can make chart-topping music that celebrates Africa then surely Band Aid and its extensive network can do the same. I've performed in two of the three countries currently hit by the Ebola crisis, where I have friends and loyal fans, and will be donating the proceeds from my next single to help tackle this issue.

I hope from the bottom of my heart that the disease can be eradicated in Sierra Leone, Liberia and Guinea. But though shock tactics and negative images may raise money in the short term, the long-term damage will take far longer to heal.

21 NOVEMBER

Every day is Bill Murray Day

CATHERINE SHOARD

On the way to Bill Murray's hotel, I keep stepping over bits of his face. An ear here, a chin there. Damp scraps of cardboard Bill Murray masks litter the streets, evidence of the crowd 48 hours before, huddled against the hail, a sea of identical rueful smiles.

It's the day after the day after Bill Murray Day in Toronto – 12 hours of archive screenings and costume competitions and a Q&A at which Murray mistook a woman for a man and no one minded. In the evening, the rain came and he squelched down the red carpet for the premiere of his new movie, St Vincent. As the credits rolled and the audience stood, he took to the stage in plastic crown and beauty queen sash and still-sodden suit.

Thing is: if you're Bill Murray, every day is Bill Murray Day. Every day a Groundhog Day of being treated like a deity. Every morning brings people if not actually wearing your face, then with your features engraved on their hearts. St Vincent's director, Theodore Melfi, tells me of a time at Atlanta airport when a stranger ran up to Murray and told him how much she loved him. He told her he loved her too and kissed her – hard, on the lips. 'It made her life.' Of the waiter in New York who carried around the $50 note Murray once gave him to enrol in an acting class. This is a man whose visitations – crashing a stag do here, rocking the karaoke there – are taken as elusive proof of his divinity. If God was one of us, the logic goes, he'd be Bill Murray.

Official meetings are correspondingly sacrosanct. I'm allotted 10 minutes, stretched to 15 with begging, then 20 through undignified stalling when the publicist comes to fetch me. No more is possible. Off the promo trail, he's absolutely unavailable – no agent, no manager, no point of contact other than an unlisted 1-800 number on which you can leave a voicemail. I ask Melfi if he might like to share it with me. He laughs.

I wait on a deserted floor at the Trump hotel. The hallowed atmosphere intensifies. After a time, a security guard materialises and discusses the carpet. Then he touches his ear. 'Your parcel has arrived,' he says and evaporates. Murray strolls round the corner.

'Well, you look delightful,' he says. 'And you smell nice.' He's wearing blue linen and is very tall. His silver hair is blond at the tips, so when he gives a gummy grin, you think of the baby in the sun on *Teletubbies*. Later, Tilda Swinton says she thinks he has the look of 'a tired child who has laughed so much he aches – but finds it too complicated to fully explain the joke'. That's true. It's like talking to a crumpled bag of sweets.

We're shown to a room and I help him read the Coke bottle label (he only drinks Mexican, on account of the corn syrup). We inspect the facilities. He suggests we take a bath or watch a DVD. Four hardboiled eggs and some fried potatoes are ushered in. He doesn't touch them.

I have quarter of an hour left. How did he find Bill Murray Day? 'OK. Daunting. I was sort of dreading it. But people seemed to think it was as funny as I did. It was just as good as having a birthday and a great cake and fireworks.' He thinks more. 'It was a good day.'

So why do people place such faith in actors? Because what they do seems miraculous? Sure, he says. For him, too. 'It's always a question for me: how are people pulling this off? How can they live with it, how they can be that person up on a screen and then walk down a street or go to a grocery store or drive a car or have a conversation? Like: how does that happen? Where do you get to be superhuman? How can you do it?

'People identify with that. They think: I'd love to be Superman for a while, or be the guy who's being funny and not taking any guff. I wish I could say that to my neighbour or my wife. That's what a hero does.'

In *St Vincent*, Murray is a familiar kind of hero: the lovable gruff, the mensch in grouch clothing. Vincent is a rude boozer who bets on the horses and has got a Russian prostitute (Naomi Watts) pregnant. He's mean to a new neighbour, single mum Melissa McCarthy. But then he starts babysitting her lonesome son and we twig: he's great, under the grump.

The movie plays out like Murray's greatest hits. He sings slurrily and dances funny, cracks wise and rolls his eyes, a dignified clown, brimful of feeling. Melfi originally courted Jack Nicholson, but when he passed, Murray said he was interested, if he could tailor the script to his strengths.

And Vincent's emotional journey follows the same arc as Murray's characters in *Groundhog Day* and *Ghostbusters*, *Broken Flowers* and *Lost in Translation*. He gets domesticated. The curmudgeon finds salvation in conventionality. 'Vincent has got to acknowledge,' says Murray, 'that we all have an obligation to more than just ourselves. In this world it plays out as our fellow man. And ultimately something higher. But the tasks we're given here are our families.'

Yet Murray's root appeal is not based on this third-act incarnation. Movies may need to end that way, but off-screen, the closer to average Murray gets, the less we want to be like him. It's the frank and freewheeling real-life guy we worship.

So why does he connect quite so deeply? Cameron Crowe, who's just finished shooting a movie with him, thinks Murray's detachment from the star system alters his affinity with an audience. Like the new pope, he walks among us. 'He's very skilled at breaking through the barriers that make many celebrities so uncomfortable around their fans. With Bill it's an equal playing field. He's not floating above them in some hallowed showbiz world. Being a fan of Bill Murray never gets boring because he's not bored, he's more mercurial and yet somehow more available than ever. In a world where most careers are xeroxes of each other, his is uniquely his own.'

For Melfi and Swinton, Murray's joie de vivre is key. Swinton recalls him larking about with her children on the set of *Broken Flowers*, partying the night away with the 12-year-old cast of *Moonrise Kingdom* in Cannes. He has, she says, 'a kind of hopeful aspect that suggests a constant readiness to play. The sense that no foolishness you could ever admit would faze him. The impression of knowing where the best fun can be found at all times.'

'From zero to 12,' says Melfi, 'we were all doing what we wanted to. As we get older we start getting reservations. We live by society's code of rules. Bill doesn't. He lives his life with a complete joy and freedom.'

It's only Harvey Weinstein who suggests this could come with a kick. Speaking to *Variety* about being a 'born-again Murray-ite', he said: 'It's a religion, where you can act as badly as you want to people, and they still love you. I used to feel guilty about behaving badly, and I met Bill, and it feels so much better.'

Murray has licence, almost immunity. He's Teflon in the face of anything even vaguely unsavoury (it's interesting that in his films he's often a lothario, but passive, not predatory; more often seduced than seducing). 'He has a certain rare animal – snow leopard – quality,' says Swinton. 'Kinda dangerous as well as exotic.'

Murray was born in the mid-20th century, the middle child of nine, living in a three-bedroom house in Chicago. Before Second City, before *Saturday Night Live*, his improv skills were honed round the dining table. Younger brother Joel has said that the aim was to make their father – a slow eater – laugh with his mouth full.

(Murray himself has six sons, by a couple of ex-wives, and his conversation sometimes gets snagged on custody.)

His parents were Irish Catholics; one of his sisters is a nun. This conspicuous religion adds to his broad-church appeal (there's a citation from the *Christian Science Monitor* on his golfing memoirs). You don't need to ask if his faith is important to him. He talks about how 19th-century candidates risk not getting canonised because the church is keen to push ahead with the likes of John Paul II and Mother Teresa. 'I think they're just trying to get current and hot,' he smiles.

One new saint he does approve of is Pope John XXIII (who died in 1963). 'I'll buy that one, he's my guy; an extraordinary joyous Florentine who changed the order. I'm not sure all those changes were right. I tend to disagree with what they call the new mass. I think we lost something by losing the Latin. Now if you go to a Catholic mass even just in Harlem it can be in Spanish, it can be in Ethiopian, it can be in any number of languages.'

Isn't it good for people to understand it? 'I guess,' he says, shaking his head. 'But there's a vibration to those words. And I really miss the music – the power of it, y'know? Yikes! Sacred music has an affect on your brain.' Instead, he says, we get 'folk songs ... top 40 stuff ... oh, brother...'

Murray is loved for being carefree. But face to face he can seem not just serious, but sober, even sensible. People may tweet when he turns up to serve tequila, but I suspect he also spends quite a lot of time quietly reading the paper. Melfi calls him a 'deep thinker' who's gifted him a lot of books about parenting. And today what really fires him up turns out to be seatbelt safety. In particular the 1965 legislation making them compulsory in new cars. For this, he thinks Ralph Nader is 'the greatest living American'.

'People thought: "Why is this son of a gun making me wear a seatbelt?" Well, in 1965 I think the number was 55,000 deaths on the highway a year. So he's saved just about a couple of million people by now. It's crazy! And that's just one thing he did!

'I mean, they made a movie about the German who smuggled the Jews out. He saved hundreds. Great man. Deserved a movie. Spectacular. Great film and a great human being. But this guy, Ralph – there's no movies about Ralph.'

His eyes catch light and he leans forward. He could sing Nader's praises for ever, and starts to try.

'Businesses bitch about this guy and people hate him because he's trying to make change. He hasn't become like super-crazy-wealthy or anything and it's not about his celebrity. He's really interested in improving the quality of life for the whole world.'

Was he sorry Nader never made president? No, he was depressed that people blamed him for diverting Democrat votes in 2000, leading to Bush's victory. 'You know: that's Al Gore's fault! We didn't all come here to make the world easier for Al Gore. He ran a lousy campaign. He was the vice-president during the greatest economic boom in the history of the country.'

He shakes his head sadly. 'Political parties work to cripple their opponents. They spend all their time in office trying to paralyse the work of the others. They try to stifle. It's cruel, cruel.'

The PR is back and my time is up. So: how might things change in the future, I say, gathering my bag slowly.

'Well, eventually something horrible will happen, something dynamic and powerful. It's going to have to be cataclysmic for people to wake up and say: "OK, is anyone gonna do this?"'

I have to stand now, but don't want to walk away in case he stops speaking. But he rises too, and I've misjudged the distance between our seats, so we're inappropriately close and I'm eyeballing his nipples. It's intense, but I keep quiet and keep rooted and he keeps talking.

'I think something's gonna have to change. Usually it's something like war or 9/11 that makes people come together.' The shooting of Gabrielle Giffords might have been a rallying point, he thought. 'Because that's just a nutter going after someone. And that kind of anger builds and creates horrible events like that.'

He smiles as I inch away. 'You know, I wish you could hold all of Congress prisoner and they'd get Stockholm syndrome and have to go along with their captors. And their captors would be people who were real true American citizens.'

And now I can leave. Later, Melfi tells me Murray is 'on a mission from God to make the world a better place'. And here we have his commandments. I can't wait: a sea of citizens, storming Washington, all wearing Bill Murray masks.

1 DECEMBER

Muhammad: the truth about Britain's most misunderstood name

HOMA KHALEELI

The Muhammad myth is a popular one. For at least four years there have been numerous reports declaring that Mohammed is the most popular boy's name in the country. Or maybe Mohamed. Or should that be Muhammad? Look more closely, though, and there is more to the rise of Muhammad than meets the eye. From Mo Farah to Mohamed Al Fayed and Muhammad Ali, there is no shortage of high-profile people named after the prophet of Islam.

In Muslim families, the name is bestowed with abandon by new parents. Even Muslim men who don't use the name sometimes have it tucked away.

My grandfather and uncle are both Muhammads, which is relatively restrained. One of my friends has a father, father-in-law and brother all called Mohammed – and she has now given it to her son as a middle name. In other cultures, it might hint at an unforgivable lack of creativity, but my friend says she would not consider allowing it to skip a generation.

'It's partly Bengali tradition,' she says, adding that it was also a conscious decision to ensure that her son engaged with his religious heritage. 'I wanted a name that would make my son think about who our prophet was, and what it really means to be a Muslim, rather than any negative media representation of Islam, or the twisted actions of those who claim to do things in the prophet's name.'

Dr Seán McLoughlin, senior lecturer in contemporary Muslim cultures, politics and societies at the University of Leeds, agrees that many Muslims from Pakistan, Bangladesh or India regard it as a blessing to give a baby the name of the prophet. 'There is an especially strong reverence and religious attachment to the prophet in the subcontinent,' he says. 'In some ways, there is more of a devotional attitude than in the culture we have now in the Middle East, for instance.'

He explains that the name is symbolically included as a first name, but it is not used in the way a Christian name would be – in Pakistan, for instance, a second name is often used as a 'given' name. The different backgrounds of Muslims in the UK – from Malaysia to Somalia – partly explain the variation in spelling. The transliteration of the name from South Asian languages is more likely to yield 'Mohammed', whereas 'Muhammad' is a closer transliteration of formal Arabic, says McLoughlin.

But even when the different spellings are collated, Muhammad is not yet Britain's most popular name. The latest research putting Mohammed at the top of the baby-name lists is based on responses from users of the website BabyCentre. According to the most recent figures from the Office of National Statistics, though, Muhammad was only the 16th most popular boy's name in England and Wales, and the 52nd most popular in Scotland last year. In previous years, newspapers have arrived at the conclusion that Mohammed is the most popular name by adding together figures for all the different spellings. But it has been pointed out that if we did the same for other popular names, such as Oliver and Ollie or Henry and Harry, the Mos would not get a look in.

So why does the story keep returning? Partly, perhaps, because it plays on fears of both immigration and cultural change. While Muslims make up 4.4 per cent of the UK population, a more significant factor is that, while the rest of the population is increasingly choosing from a wider pool of names (think Tyrion and Piper, apparently inspired by *Game of Thrones* and *Orange is the New Black*), Muslims are sticking with Muhammad.

And against the background of rising Islamophobia, it's hard not to think that these headlines tell us more about the unease with which Muslims are viewed. Imran Awan, a criminologist at Birmingham City University who has been researching Islamophobia, believes that there is a tendency to sensationalise reporting around Muslim issues, with topics such as naming or halal meat acting as flashpoints. 'Some Islamophobia is perpetuated by fear and a sense that Muslims are taking over and polarising society. Little issues such as the name of Muhammad are turned by the far right into vitriolic hate against Muslims.'

But for men called Mo, it will take more than insults to make them give up their name. Mohamed Al Fayed tells me: 'The Fulham football fans used to call me Mo. I liked that. Serious effort went into making up songs about me. But the big hit at Craven Cottage went: "Al Fayed, oh, ho, ho, ho ... he wants to be a Brit, and QPR are ..." Well, you write your own lines. These days, the best sound I ever hear is when my grandchildren burst into the room, calling out for "Mo-mo". So, I am Mo-mo to them, and Mohamed to the world, and delighted to be so.'

7 DECEMBER

The Syed family on their pain and the 'five million detectives trying to work out if Adnan is a psychopath'

JON RONSON

An elderly man crouches on a rug in a house in west Baltimore. He's alone, and wearing shalwar kameez, so from the back I assume he's praying. In fact he's eating his dinner. When he sees me come through the front door, he quickly hurries to his bedroom. He's Syed Rahman, Adnan Syed's father.

'He spends the whole time in his room,' his wife, Shamim, tells me a few minutes later.

'What does he do in there?' I ask her.

'He reads books,' she says. 'Islamic books.'

'Has he been diagnosed with depression?'

'He doesn't believe in depression,' Shamim says. 'That's the problem.'

'He doesn't believe in antidepressants,' adds Yusuf, their son.

'And this is all because of Adnan?'

'Yes,' they say.

As millions of people now know – although it was barely reported at the time – a murder occurred near here, in January 1999. The crime scene was less than a mile away, in the parking lot of the local Best Buy, if you believe the prosecution's case. Which was this: after school on 13 January 1999, Adnan, then 17, strangled his former girlfriend Hae Min Lee in her car. Then he called his friend Jay and said: 'That bitch is dead. Come and get me. I'm at Best Buy.' When Jay arrived, Adnan opened the trunk, showed him Hae's body, and said: 'I can't believe I killed her where I used to fuck her at.' The two boys buried Hae in a 6in-deep grave in woods three miles away. She was found three weeks later. A few weeks after that, Jay confessed to the police. He led them to Hae's car. Adnan was arrested, convicted of first-degree murder, and has been in jail ever since.

And that would have been that, except that for the past 10 weeks, the radio producer Sarah Koenig has been investigating the case in her ongoing podcast *Serial*. Episode one arrived without much fanfare – just some promotion by its parent show, *This American Life* – but what happened next was dizzying. It immediately became the world's most popular podcast – a sensation. It achieved 5 million downloads on iTunes – faster than any podcast in history. (BBC Radio 4 Extra has just picked it up for broadcast, too.) But Adnan's father isn't listening.

'We don't want him to,' says Yusuf. 'We don't want him to know it exists. He knows it exists but – it's a very fragile state.'

'We can't even discuss the topic,' says Shamim. 'Sometimes we see him going through the photo album and he starts crying.'

'Do you listen?' I ask Shamim.

'After everybody goes to sleep,' she says. 'Eleven, twelve o'clock, I lay down here on this sofa and I listen.' She says she sometimes plays just one part over and over. 'It's the bit at the beginning where the prison operator says, "This is a Global-Tel link prepaid call from ..." and Adnan says, "Adnan Syed".

'So sweet,' Shamim says. 'I listen to that again and again and again.'

Yusuf listens alone too, 'in my room, by myself, so all the information can sink in better. After the episode's done, I think about it all day. What does this mean? What does that mean? Everything Sarah's saying is new to me. All I knew growing up was that my brother was arrested for a murder, but we believed Jay was responsible [for Adnan's wrongful conviction, he means, or maybe even for the murder itself – he doesn't know]. So when I hear the podcast it's all new information. Sarah is so thorough and clean. She's doing a better job investigating than the police did. It makes me so frustrated and furious that there was so little evidence. Really? That's all you had? To take away my brother's life? That's all you had?'

Shamim takes me back to the beginning. It was an arranged marriage that brought her to Baltimore from Pakistan. Syed was already here, working as an engineer. 'We wanted to raise our children in America for a better life,' she says. 'Hah. We got a worse life.' They had three sons: Tanveer, then Adnan, and then, eight years later, Yusuf. Adnan was perfect, Shamim says. He was a straight-A student. The teachers would compliment her: '"Whatever you're practising in the house is working on him." He was very obedient. We never had a problem with him. He only messed up for the last year.'

By messed up she means weed and alcohol and sex and hanging out with sketchy people.

Yusuf's relationship with Adnan was a typically antagonistic older brother/younger brother one, Yusuf says, but they were just beginning to get close when Adnan was taken away.

'What do you remember about him, pre-incarceration?' I ask.

'He'd get Chinese food from the mall and bring me back what was left over,' he says. 'He brought me a Batman action figure when I was young. He'd play video games with me.'

'Homework,' prompts Shamim.

'If I had a report due the next day and it was really late, he'd help me with my homework,' Yusuf says.

I glance down at my list of questions. Usually I never have a list of questions, but this story is different. *Serial* fans are fevered – it's like the Beatlemania of the nebbishy public radio longform nonfiction world – and my editors at the *Guardian* sent me a list of 38 questions I just had to ask the Syeds. Question 17 is: 'Can they talk about the homecoming incident?'

'Can you talk about the homecoming incident?' I ask Shamim.

The homecoming incident: not long before Hae's murder, Shamim discovered that Adnan was taking Hae to the school's homecoming dance. So she showed up and chastised him in front of everyone. The prosecutor made a big deal of this at the trial, telling the jury: 'What is it that this defendant saw on 13 January when he looked down at Hae Lee? He saw his parents standing at the window of the homecoming dance. He saw his mother raise her voice at Hae Lee in front of his classmates. "Look what you're doing to our family."'

Shamim admits she was a strict mother. She'd even listen in on the extension line when Adnan talked to Hae.

'What did you overhear?' I ask her.

'Oh, he'd say some kind of poem,' she replies. '"Roses are blue." I'd say: "Who are you talking to?" He'd say: "Mom, can you put the phone down please?" I'd say: "It's not right, Adnan. It's not right."'

'You don't regret ... ?' I begin.

'Oh no,' she interrupts. 'No way.'

'If anything we regret that our dad was too lenient,' Yusuf says.

'He was lenient,' says Shamim. 'He was the opposite of me. He'd say: "Boys will be boys."'

'Maybe if he'd put his foot down too ...' says Yusuf.

Then Yusuf clarifies: Shamim wasn't 'a crazy strict mother'. She'd take them to baseball games. Plus they were allowed to talk to girls. 'It was just the alcohol and the drugs and the sex,' he says. 'It was like her intuition – that it would lead to bad stuff.'

The police arrested Adnan at 5am on 28 February 1999. It was chaos. Yusuf was crying. He had no idea what was going on. His only clue that something was up, he says, was that Adnan had seemed sad during the previous weeks. They'd had dinner in a restaurant – just the two of them, unusually – and Adnan had barely said a word. Yusuf was blabbing on to him about Dragon Ball Z cartoons, thrilled that his older brother was spending time with him, and Adnan just sat there looking sad. (This is an important detail in Yusuf's story because if you believe Jay's version, Adnan was psychopathic and wouldn't have been in the least bit sad that Hae was dead.)

Then came the conviction, and the family fell apart. Tanveer vanished to Philadelphia, becoming totally estranged from the family. 'Imagine having a family one day, and the next day you wake up and it's completely broken,' Yusuf says. 'It's all gone.'

At this, Shamim suddenly stands up and leaves the room. She comes back a few moments later holding a large board – a kind of mood board. Yusuf looks mortified.

'He doesn't want me to show you,' Shamim says.

'I was depressed,' Yusuf says.

At the top of the mood board, Yusuf has written on a card: 'Conjecture/hypothesis. My family is never going to be the same because my brother is incarcerated and my older brother left the family. My parents are now depressed. I have a broken family. This is not how it is supposed to be.'

Underneath is a second card: 'Belief. This life is filled with too much hurt and the pain is never-ending. There is also no way to stop the pain. I am probably better off dead.'

And then a third: 'Object. When I would see other people's families it would remind me what I do not have. A family.'

And that's it.

'That's very bleak,' I say. 'I thought these boards are supposed to be therapeutic, like with some kind of optimistic final card.'

They both look at the board.

'Oh,' Shamim says. 'The last card has fallen off.'

She goes back out and returns with it. It reads: 'Understanding. Life is not always going to be fair and that no matter what happens God is always there.'

And then came the *Serial* podcast. And suddenly people have started running up to the family with tears in their eyes. Many listeners suspect that Adnan is innocent – or are at least convinced he didn't get a fair trial. There were no eyewitnesses, no physical evidence linking Adnan to the crime. Adnan even had a possible alibi – a girl who came forward to say she saw him at the school library at the time of the murder. But Adnan's defence attorney, who died in 2004, never followed up on it. It was basically Jay's testimony that sunk Adnan.

People listening to the podcast are trying to crack the case themselves. They're forming online discussion groups on Reddit with threads like: 'A Few Observations/Conclusions After Reading Jay's Interviews Several Times' and 'Something that has bothered me – "6-inch grave"' and 'Are there any hints of dissociative identity disorder in Adnan?' I've worked with Sarah Koenig and Julie Snyder, two of *Serial*'s producers, many times on my *This American Life* stories and I can tell you: this kind of thing never happens.

'So your friends are listening?' I ask.

'Everybody!' says Shamim. 'Everybody is waiting so anxiously. What's going to happen next?'

'And you don't know what's coming up in the podcast?' I ask.

'I wish we did,' says Shamim.

'I just hope there's a good ending, that's all,' says Yusuf.

(What does come up next, three days later, is an episode that's in part about the Islamophobia bubbling around the courthouse – like how bail was denied in case Baltimore's Muslim community pooled their resources to help Adnan abscond to Pakistan. When I asked Yusuf about life at their local mosque, he told me he stopped going for years because people would just crowd around him to ask: 'Do you think Adnan did it?' Which was just like at school and everywhere else.)

Yusuf saw Adnan last week. He isn't allowed to listen to the podcast – the maximum-security prison rules don't allow it – but they talked about it, of course.

'Does he understand what a big deal it is?' I ask.

'No,' he replies. 'Sometimes he's, "Oh, man, I can't wait for it to be over."'

'Why?'

'He thinks we might get upset by it. But he doesn't realise the effect it's having on the outside.'

People send Adnan transcripts, Yusuf says, but words on a page don't do it justice. You need to hear the emotions in the voices. So Adnan is unaware of the show's quality. I ask him if any listeners have tried to donate money to Adnan's prison commissary account. He says if they have he's sure Adnan wouldn't accept it, because he wouldn't want to be in the debt of crazy strangers.

Yusuf spends a lot of time online, lurking on Reddit, although he knows 'it's just toxic'.

'Toxic because five million detectives are all studying Adnan's voice for clues as to whether he's a psychopath?' I ask.

(I suspect – from this week's cliffhanger, that next week's episode will examine this possibility. As someone who's written a book about psychopaths, I've had about a million people tweet me to ask if I think Adnan is one. I think it's totally irresponsible to diagnose someone from afar, whether you're a clinician or not, and I'm not. But for what it's worth, nothing in Adnan's conversations with Sarah rings any bells from the time I attended a course that teaches people how to identify psychopaths in part through the nuances of their language.)

'Oh I don't mind that!' says Yusuf. 'People flip-flop back and forth – that's understandable. But there's this group of people on Reddit who are 100 per cent "Adnan did it". And, OK, one of the moderators from Reddit told us Jay is on Reddit.'

'Do you know which name he uses?'

'No.'

'Stop shaking,' says Shamim.

We all look down at Yusuf's leg. It's vibrating wildly – just like my leg does in stressful situations. It's turning the sofa into a massage chair.

'Oh, sorry,' says Yusuf.

I, by the way, have no way of corroborating whether or not Jay is posting pro-Jay sentiments under an assumed name on Reddit. It's been confirmed that Hae's brother posts on Reddit, though, calling Sarah 'an awesome narrator/writer/investigator' but adding: 'TO ME IT'S REAL LIFE. To you listeners, it's another murder mystery, crime drama, another episode of *CSI*.'

Yusuf shows me something he found online that's made him especially happy. It's a message the judge in the second trial posted on her Facebook wall in response to a *Serial* fan telling her she was now famous. 'I listened to the podcast,' the judge wrote, 'and saw how this very intelligent young man manipulated the writer. The evidence was overwhelming. I can see how

16 years later he has regret that he wasted his life by planning and carrying out the murder of his girlfriend. Very sad indeed.'

Yusuf is delighted. He interprets this as the judge being rattled and on the back foot.

It's obvious that Shamim and Yusuf are doing a bit of a PR number on me at times during my evening with them. But that's totally understandable. Their lives have been unimaginably, soul-shreddingly awful these past 15 years, regardless of Adnan's guilt or innocence. And so it's nice to hear that they finally have some good news.

'I haven't told Sarah this,' Yusuf says, 'but we feel *Serial* has brought us all back together. My older brother Tanveer – who was estranged for 15 years – he came home. When he heard my brother's voice, it brought back all the memories. He's visited us three or four times already.'

'And, oh,' Shamim says, 'if you don't mind, I have to share something. It's so funny.' She goes to the kitchen and takes a book out of the drawer. It's a little book Adnan drew when he was nine. It's very assiduously done. One psychopathic symptom is 'proneness to boredom'. But the nine-year-old Adnan obviously spent ages drawing this book.

It's the story of Larry the Lion, who was playing in the woods with his friends when some hunters grabbed him and took him to the zoo. Adnan drew the lion in a cage, behind bars, looking sad. In the end, though, Larry escapes and returns to the woods, 'home to stay for ever'.

Unlike the other pictures, this last one – of Larry back in the woods – hasn't been coloured in.

'Adnan can colour it in when he comes home,' Shamim says.

8 DECEMBER

I am a transgender woman and the government is denying my civil rights

CHELSEA E MANNING

'The arc of the moral universe is long, but it bends towards justice,' reads the oft-quoted line from Martin Luther King.

I am a young trans woman. And I can attest to the 'long' part, but I hope the bend toward justice will soon become more pronounced.

There's a lot of unfinished business when it comes to protecting civil rights for many people. That fight is visible in every story about activists pushing for comprehensive US immigration reform. It's obvious when protesters take to the streets after white police officers kill unarmed people of colour and face few, if any, consequences, as in the recent cases of Michael Brown's death in Ferguson and Eric Garner's death in New York.

The fight for justice for the transgender community is largely invisible to our fellow citizens, despite the rampant systematic discrimination of trans people – those whose gender identity differs from the sex they were assigned at birth.

Unfortunately, it seems to me that when it comes to issues affecting the trans community, most people who are cisgender – a word describing those people whose gender identity is in alignment with the sex they were assigned at birth – focus too much on the administrative, legal and medical aspects of trans identity. Such a focus on these institutional definitions of gender is constricting, and too often it leads to difficult obstacles for most trans people.

Take something as basic as obtaining photo identification. Many people need photo ID for their workplace. You need one to drive, you often need one to vote – especially with many US states passing disenfranchising 'voter ID' laws.

For many in the trans community, just applying for basic identification documents is a hostile experience. You're told you don't belong because you don't fit into one of the tiny boxes offered by the system. And for those of us in the military, this civil rights violation of trans people's basic identity is downright life-threatening.

In the United States, the UK and most of Europe, there are only two options available for gender designation on government-issued identification documents: male and female. As a result, trans people are assumed to have a gender that aligns with the sex they were assigned at birth – that is, male for trans women and female for trans men – and those not conforming to either of those choices are assumed not to exist. So trans people are forced to either use a document that does not reflect their identity or to spend the time, effort and money necessary to alter such records. Both situations are frustrating, embarrassing and can expose us to humiliation, ridicule and even violence.

Despite bureaucratic assumptions, we exist.

The challenges that trans people are forced to navigate – even in accessing identification, but in so much more – are the result of institutional bias that favors cisgender people and assumes that trans people are deviant. When your own government's policies send a message that you don't exist – or that you shouldn't – it's devastating. Despite ample evidence that trans people have existed in most cultures throughout history, and the medical consensus that trans people can live healthy, productive lives, many governments continue to impose barriers on trans people that can make it almost impossible to survive.

I filed a petition to change my name in January of this year. Even with some assistance from counsel, the petition took nearly four months to draft and file before I ever made it to a hearing before the court. The hearing and filings were public, and I had to pay fees for filing and posting a legal notice in a local newspaper costing me nearly $500. And, despite making it clear that I identify as female, and having two military psychiatrists recommend support for my transition, legally changing my name has no effect on the 'legal' gender status that the government imposes upon me.

Photo identification isn't the only thing at stake for trans people. According to the National Center for Transgender Equality, one in five trans people in the US have been denied housing because of their gender identity. One in 10 have been evicted because of it.

We're banned from serving our country in the armed services unless we serve as trans people in secret, as I did.

Many trans people – especially low-income trans people of colour – are also less likely to have access to legal counsel or healthcare because of discrimination. In situations like these, where civil rights are flaunted, the problem is not just inclusion or equal opportunities in institutions like government identification systems or voting – because such systems are inherently, if indirectly, biased to favour high income, straight, white, cisgender people. How can trans people change a system to which we don't even have access?

A doctor, a judge or a piece of paper shouldn't have the power to tell someone who he or she is. We should all have the absolute and inalienable right to define ourselves, in our own terms and in our own languages, and to be able to express our identity and perspectives without fear of consequences or retribution. We should all be able to live as human beings – and to be recognised as such by the societies we live in.

We shouldn't have to keep defending our right to exist.

Isis: the inside story

MARTIN CHULOV

In the summer of 2004, a young jihadist in shackles and chains was walked by his captors slowly into the Camp Bucca prison in southern Iraq. He was nervous as two American soldiers led him through three brightly-lit buildings and then a maze of wire corridors, into an open yard, where men with middle-distance stares, wearing brightly-coloured prison uniforms, stood back warily, watching him.

'I knew some of them straight away,' he told me last month. 'I had feared Bucca all the way down on the plane. But when I got there, it was much better than I thought. In every way.'

The jihadist, who uses the *nom de guerre* Abu Ahmed, entered Camp Bucca as a young man a decade ago, and is now a senior official within Islamic State (Isis) – having risen through its ranks with many of the men who served time alongside him in prison. Like him, the other detainees had been snatched by US soldiers from Iraq's towns and cities and flown to a place that had already become infamous: a foreboding desert fortress that would shape the legacy of the US presence in Iraq.

The other prisoners did not take long to warm to him, Abu Ahmed recalled. They had also been terrified of Bucca, but quickly realised that far from their worst fears, the US-run prison provided an extraordinary opportunity. 'We could never have all got together like this in Baghdad, or anywhere else,' he told me. 'It would have been impossibly dangerous. Here, we were not only safe, but we were only a few hundred metres away from the entire al-Qaida leadership.'

It was at Camp Bucca that Abu Ahmed first met Abu Bakr al-Baghdadi, the emir of Isis who is now frequently described as the world's most dangerous terrorist leader. From the beginning, Abu Ahmed said, others in the camp seemed to defer to him. 'Even then, he was Abu Bakr. But none of us knew he would ever end up as leader.'

Abu Ahmed was an essential member of the earliest incarnation of the group. He had been galvanised into militancy as a young man by an American occupation that he and many like him believed was trying to impose a power shift in Iraq, favouring the country's larger Shia population at the expense of the dominant Sunnis. His early role in what would become Isis led naturally to the senior position he now occupies within a revitalised insurgency that has spilled across the border into Syria. Most of his colleagues regard the crumbling order in the region as a fulfilment of their ambitions in Iraq – which had remained unfinished business, until the war in Syria gave them a new arena.

He agreed to speak publicly after more than two years of discussions, over the course of which he revealed his own past as one of Iraq's most formidable and connected militants – and shared his deepening worry about Isis and its vision for the region. With Iraq and Syria ablaze, and the Middle East apparently condemned to another generation of upheaval and bloodshed at the hands of his fellow ideologues, Abu Ahmed is having second thoughts. The brutality of Isis is increasingly at odds with his own views, which have mellowed with age as he has come to believe that the teachings of the Qur'an can be interpreted and not read literally.

His misgivings about what the Islamic State has become led him to speak to the *Guardian* in a series of expansive conversations, which offer unique insight into its enigmatic leader and the nascent days of the terror group – stretching from 2004, when he met Abu Bakr al-Baghdadi in Camp Bucca, to 2011, when the Iraqi insurgency crossed the border into Syria.

At the beginning, back in Bucca, the prisoner who would become the most wanted man in the world had already set himself apart from the other inmates, who saw him as aloof and opaque. But, Abu Ahmed recalled, the jailers had a very different impression of Baghdadi – they saw him as a conciliatory and calming influence in an environment short on certainty, and turned to him to help resolve conflicts among the inmates. 'That was part of his act,' Abu Ahmed told me. 'I got a feeling from him that he was hiding something inside, a darkness that he did not want to show other people. He was the opposite of other princes who were far easier to deal with. He was remote, far from us all.'

Baghdadi was born Ibrahim ibn Awwad al-Badri al-Samarrai in 1971, in the Iraqi city of Samarra. He was detained by US forces in Falluja, west of Baghdad, in February 2004, months after he had helped found a militant group, Jeish Ahl al-Sunnah al-Jamaah, which had taken root in the restive Sunni communities around his home city.

'He was caught at his friend's house,' said Dr Hisham al-Hashimi, an analyst who advises the Iraqi government on Isis. 'His friend's name was Nasif Jasim Nasif. Then he was moved to Bucca. The Americans never knew who they had.' Most of Baghdadi's fellow prisoners – some 24,000 men, divided into 24 camps – seem to have been equally unaware. The prison was run along strictly hierarchical lines, down to a Teletubbies-like uniform colour scheme which allowed jailers and captives alike to recognise each detainee's place in the pecking order. 'The colour of the clothes we wore reflected our status,' said Abu Ahmed. 'If I remember things correctly, red was for people who had done things wrong while in prison, white was a prison chief, green was for a long sentence and yellow and orange were normal.'

When Baghdadi, aged 33, arrived at Bucca, the Sunni-led anti-US insurgency was gathering steam across central and western Iraq. An invasion that had been sold as a war of liberation had become a grinding occupation. Iraq's Sunnis, disenfranchised by the overthrow of their patron, Saddam Hussein, were taking the fight to US forces – and starting to turn their guns towards the beneficiaries of Hussein's overthrow, the country's majority Shia population.

The small militant group that Baghdadi headed was one of dozens that sprouted from a broad Sunni revolt – many of which would soon come together under the flag of al-Qaida in Iraq, and then the Islamic State of Iraq. These were the precursors to the juggernaut now known simply as the Islamic State, which has, under Bagdhadi's command, overrun much of the west and centre of the country and eastern Syria, and drawn the US military back to a deeply destabilised region less than three years after it left vowing never to return.

But at the time of his stay at Bucca, Baghdadi's group was little-known, and he was a far less significant figure than the insurgency's notional leader, the merciless Abu Musab al-Zarqawi, who came to represent the sum of all fears for many in Iraq, Europe and the US. Baghdadi, however, had a unique way to distinguish himself from the other aspiring leaders inside Bucca and outside on Iraq's savage streets: a pedigree that allowed him to claim direct lineage to the Prophet Muhammad. He had also obtained a PhD in Islamic studies from the Islamic

University of Baghdad, and would draw on both to legitimise his unprecedented claim to anoint himself caliph of the Islamic world in July 2014, which realised a sense of destiny evident in the prison yard a decade earlier.

'Baghdadi was a quiet person,' said Abu Ahmed. 'He has a charisma. You could feel that he was someone important. But there were others who were more important. I honestly did not think he would get this far.'

Baghdadi also seemed to have a way with his captors. According to Abu Ahmed, and two other men who were jailed at Bucca in 2004, the Americans saw him as a fixer who could solve fractious disputes between competing factions and keep the camp quiet.

'But as time went on, every time there was a problem in the camp, he was at the centre of it,' Abu Ahmed recalled. 'He wanted to be the head of the prison – and when I look back now, he was using a policy of conquer and divide to get what he wanted, which was status. And it worked.' By December 2004, Baghdadi was deemed by his jailers to pose no further risk and his release was authorised.

'He was respected very much by the US army,' Abu Ahmed said. 'If he wanted to visit people in another camp he could, but we couldn't. And all the while, a new strategy, which he was leading, was rising under their noses, and that was to build the Islamic State. If there was no American prison in Iraq, there would be no IS now. Bucca was a factory. It made us all. It built our ideology.'

As Isis has rampaged through the region, it has been led by men who spent time in US detention centres during the American occupation of Iraq – in addition to Bucca, the US also ran Camp Cropper, near Baghdad airport, and, for an ill-fated 18 months early in the war, Abu Ghraib prison on the capital's western outskirts. Many of those released from these prisons – and indeed, several senior American officers who ran detention operations – have admitted that the prisons had an incendiary effect on the insurgency.

'I went to plenty of meetings where guys would come through and tell us how well it was all going,' said Ali Khedery, a special aide to all US ambassadors who served in Iraq from 2003–11, and to three US military commanders. But eventually even top American officers came to believe they had 'actually become radicalising elements. They were counterproductive in many ways. They were being used to plan and organise, to appoint leaders and launch operations.'

Abu Ahmed agreed. 'In prison, all of the princes were meeting regularly. We became very close to those we were jailed with. We knew their capabilities. We knew what they could and couldn't do, how to use them for whatever reason. The most important people in Bucca were those who had been close to Zarqawi. He was recognised in 2004 as being the leader of the jihad.

'We had so much time to sit and plan,' he continued. 'It was the perfect environment. We all agreed to get together when we got out. The way to reconnect was easy. We wrote each other's details on the elastic of our boxer shorts. When we got out, we called. Everyone who was important to me was written on white elastic. I had their phone numbers, their villages. By 2009, many of us were back doing what we did before we were caught. But this time we were doing it better.'

According to Hisham al-Hashimi, the Baghdad-based analyst, the Iraqi government estimates that 17 of the 25 most important Islamic State leaders running the war in Iraq and Syria spent time in US prisons between 2004 and 2011. Some were transferred from American custody to Iraqi prisons, where a series of jailbreaks in the last several years allowed many senior leaders to escape and rejoin the insurgent ranks.

Abu Ghraib was the scene of the biggest – and most damaging – breakout in 2013, with up to 500 inmates, many of them senior jihadists handed over by the departing US military, fleeing in July of that year after the prison was stormed by Islamic State forces, who launched a simultaneous, and equally successful, raid on nearby Taji prison.

Iraq's government closed Abu Ghraib in April 2014 and it now stands empty, 15 miles from Baghdad's western outskirts, near the frontline between Isis and Iraq's security forces, who seem perennially under-prepared as they stare into the heat haze shimmering over the highway that leads towards the badlands of Falluja and Ramadi.

Parts of both cities have become a no-go zone for Iraq's beleaguered troops, who have been battered and humiliated by Isis, a group of marauders unparalleled in Mesopotamia since the time of the Mongols. When I visited the abandoned prison late this summer, a group of disinterested Iraqi forces sat at a checkpoint on the main road to Baghdad, eating watermelon as the distant rumble of shellfire sounded in the distance. The imposing walls of Abu Ghraib were behind them, and their jihadist enemies were staked out further down the road.

The revelation of abuses at Abu Ghraib had a radicalising effect on many Iraqis, who saw the purported civility of American occupation as little improvement on the tyranny of Saddam. While Bucca had few abuse complaints prior to its closure in 2009, it was seen by Iraqis as a potent symbol of an unjust policy, which swept up husbands, fathers, and sons – some of them non-combatants – in regular neighbourhood raids, and sent them away to prison for months or years.

At the time, the US military countered that its detention operations were valid, and that similar practices had been deployed by other forces against insurgencies – such as the British in Northern Ireland, the Israelis in Gaza and the West Bank, and the Syrian and Egyptian regimes.

Even now, five years after the US closed down Bucca, the Pentagon defends the camp as an example of lawful policy for a turbulent time. 'During operations in Iraq from 2003 to 2011, US Forces held thousands of Law of War detainees,' said Lt Col Myles B Caggins III, a US Department of Defense spokesman for detainee policy. 'These type of detentions are common practice during armed conflict. Detaining potentially dangerous people is the legal and humane method of providing security and stability for civilian populations.'

Some time after Baghdadi was released from Bucca, Abu Ahmed was also freed. After being flown to Baghdad airport, he was picked up by men he had met in Bucca. They took him to a home in the west of the capital, where he immediately rejoined the jihad, which had transformed from a fight against an occupying army into a vicious and unrestrained war against Iraqi Shia.

Death squads were by then roaming Baghdad and much of central Iraq, killing members of opposite sects with routine savagery and exiling residents from neighbourhoods they dominated. The capital had quickly become a very different place to the city Abu Ahmed had left a year earlier. But with the help of new arrivals at Bucca, those inside the prison had been able to monitor every new development in the unfolding sectarian war. Abu Ahmed knew the environment he was returning to. And his camp commanders had plans for him.

The first thing he did when he was safe in west Baghdad was to undress, then carefully take a pair of scissors to his underwear. 'I cut the fabric from my boxers and all the numbers were there. We reconnected. And we got to work.' Across Iraq, other ex-inmates were doing the same. 'It really was that simple,' Abu Ahmed said, smiling for the first time in our conversation as he recalled how his captors had been outwitted. 'Boxers helped us win the war.'

Zarqawi wanted a 9/11 moment to escalate the conflict – something that would take the fight to the heart of the enemy, Abu

Ahmed recalled. In Iraq, that meant one of two targets – a seat of Shia power or, even better, a defining religious symbol. In February 2006, and again two months later, Zarqawi's bombers destroyed the Imam al-Askari shrine in Samarra, north of Baghdad. The sectarian war was fully ignited and Zarqawi's ambitions realised.

Asked about the merits of this violent provocation, Abu Ahmed paused for the first time in our many conversations. 'There was a reason for opening this war,' he said. 'It was not because they are Shia, but because the Shia were pushing for it. The American army was facilitating the takeover of Iraq and giving the country to them. They were in cooperation with each other.'

He then reflected on the man who gave the orders. 'Zarqawi was very smart. He was the best strategist that the Islamic State has had. Abu Omar [al-Baghdadi] was ruthless,' Abu Ahmed said, referring to Zarqawi's successor, who was killed in a US-led raid in April 2010. 'And Abu Bakr is the most bloodthirsty of all.'

'After Zarqawi was killed, the people who liked killing even more than him became very important in the organisation. Their understanding of sharia and of humanity was very cheap. They don't understand the Tawheed (the Qur'anic concept of God's oneness) the way it was meant to be understood. The Tawheed should not have been forced by war.'

Despite reservations that were already starting to stir, by 2006, Abu Ahmed had become part of a killing machine that would operate at full speed for much of the following two years. Millions of citizens were displaced, neighbourhoods were cleansed along sectarian lines, and an entire population numbed by unchecked brutality.

That summer, the US finally caught up with Zarqawi, with the help of Jordanian intelligence, killing him in an airstrike north of Baghdad. From late 2006, the organisation was on the back foot – hampered by a tribal revolt that uprooted its leadership from

Anbar and shrank its presence elsewhere in Iraq. But according to Abu Ahmed, the group used the opportunity to evolve, revealing a pragmatism in addition to its hardline ideology. For Isis, the relatively quiet years between 2008 and 2011 represented a lull, not a defeat.

By this time, Abu Bakr al-Baghdadi had risen steadily through the group to become a trusted aide to its leader, Abu Omar al-Baghdadi, and his deputy, the Egyptian jihadist Abu Ayub al-Masri. It was at this point, Abu Ahmed said, that Isis made an approach to the Ba'athist remnants of the old regime – ideological opponents who shared a common enemy in the US and the Shia-led government it backed.

Earlier incarnations of Isis had dabbled with the Ba'athists, who lost everything when Saddam was ousted, under the same premise that 'my enemy's enemy is my friend'. But by early 2008, Abu Ahmed and other sources said, these meetings had become far more frequent – and many of them were taking place in Syria.

Syria's links to the Sunni insurgency in Iraq had been regularly raised by US officials in Baghdad and by the Iraqi government. Both were convinced that the Syrian president, Bashar al-Assad, allowed jihadists to fly into Damascus airport, where military officials would escort them to the border with Iraq. 'All the foreigners I knew got into Iraq that way,' Abu Ahmed told me. 'It was no secret.'

From 2008, when the US began to negotiate the transition of its powers to Iraq's feeble security institutions – and therefore pave the way to its own exit – the Americans increasingly turned to only a few trusted figures in the Iraqi government. One of them was Major General Hussein Ali Kamal, the director of intelligence in the country's Interior Ministry. A secular Kurd who had the trust of the Shia establishment, one of Kamal's many duties was to secure Baghdad against terror attacks.

Like the Americans, General Kamal was convinced that Syria was destabilising Iraq, an assessment based on the interrogations of jihadists who had been captured by his troops. Throughout 2009, in a series of interviews, Kamal laid out his evidence, using maps that plotted the routes used by jihadists to cross the border into western Iraq, and confessions that linked their journeys to specific mid-ranking officers in Syrian military intelligence.

As Isis activity ebbed in Iraq, he had become increasingly obsessed with two meetings that had taken place in Syria early in 2009, which brought together Iraqi jihadists, Syrian officials and Ba'athists from both countries. (Kamal, who was diagnosed with a rare cancer in 2012, died earlier this year, and authorised me to publish details of our conversations. 'Just tell the truth,' he said during our last interview in June 2014.)

When I first met him in 2009, he was poring over transcripts of recordings that had been made at two secret meetings in Zabadani, near Damascus, in the spring of that year. The attendees included senior Iraqi Ba'athists who had taken refuge in Damascus since their patron Saddam was ousted, Syrian military intelligence officers, and senior figures in what was then known as al-Qaida in Iraq. The Syrians had developed links to the jihadists since the earliest days of the anti-US insurgency and had used them to unsettle the Americans and their plans for Iraq.

'By early in 2004/05, Islamic elements, jihadists and disenfranchised Ba'athists were starting to get together,' said Ali Khedery, the former adviser to American ambassadors and senior commanders in Baghdad. 'They were naturally disciplined, well-organised people who knew the lay of the land. And over time, some folks who were Ba'athists became more and more Islamist and the insurgency raged. By 2007, General [David] Petraeus was saying there was crystal clear intelligence of cooperation between Syrian military intelligence and the jihadists. Though the motivations never really aligned 100 per cent.'

In our conversations, Abu Ahmed emphasised the Syrian connection to Iraq's insurgency. 'The mujahideen all came through Syria,' he said. 'I worked with many of them. Those in Bucca had flown to Damascus. A very small number had made it from Turkey, or Iran. But most came to Iraq with the help of the Syrians.'

The supply line was viewed by Iraqi officials as an existential threat to Iraq's government and was the main source of the poisonous relationship between Nouri al-Maliki, then Iraq's prime minister, and Bashar al-Assad. Maliki had become convinced early in the civil war that Assad was trying to undermine his regime as a way to embarrass the Americans, and the evidence he saw in 2009 from the meeting in Damascus took his loathing of the Syrian leader to a whole new level.

'We had a source in the room wearing a wire' at the meeting in Zabadani, General Kamal told me at the time. 'He is the most sensitive source we have ever had. As far as we know, this is the first time there has been a strategic level meeting between all of these groups. It marks a new point in history.'

The Ba'athists present led the meeting. Their aim, according to General Kamal's source, was to launch a series of spectacular attacks in Baghdad and thereby undermine Maliki's Shia-majority government, which had for the first time begun to assert some order in post-civil war Iraq. Until then, al-Qaida in Iraq and the Ba'athists had been fierce ideological enemies, but the rising power of the Shias – and their backers in Iran – brought them together to plan a major strike on the capital.

By July 2009, the Interior Ministry had increased security at all checkpoints across the Tigris river into Baghdad, making a commute at any time of day even more insufferable than normal. And then General Kamal received a message from his source in

Syria. The extra security at the bridges had been spotted by the attack plotters, he said. New targets were being chosen, but he didn't know what they were, or when they would be hit. For the next two weeks, Kamal worked well into the evening in his fortified office in the southern suburb of Arasat, before being sped by armoured convoy across the July 14 Bridge – which had been a target only days earlier – to his home inside the Green Zone.

For the rest of the month, General Kamal spent several hours each scorching night sweating it out on a treadmill, hoping that the exercise would clear his head and get him ahead of the attackers. 'I may be losing weight, but I'm not finding the terrorists,' he told me during our last conversation before the attackers finally struck. 'I know they're planning something big.'

On the morning of 19 August, the first of three flat-bed trucks carrying three large 1000-litre water tanks, each filled with explosives, detonated on an overpass outside the Finance Ministry in south-eastern Baghdad. The blast sent a rumble across the Emerald City, raising desert soil that caked homes brown, and sending thousands of pigeons scattering through the sky. Three minutes later, a second enormous bomb blew up outside the Foreign Ministry on the northern edge of the Green Zone. Shortly after that, a third blast hit a police convoy near the Finance Ministry. More than 101 people were killed and nearly 600 wounded; it was one of the deadliest attacks in the six-year-old Iraqi insurgency.

'I failed,' Kamal told me that day. 'We all failed.' Within hours, he was summoned to meet Maliki and his security chiefs. The prime minister was livid. 'He told me to present what I had to the Syrians,' Kamal later said. 'We arranged with Turkey to act as a mediator and I flew to Ankara to meet with them. I took this file' – he tapped a thick white folder on his desk – 'and they could not argue with what we showed them. The case was completely solid and the Syrians knew it. Ali Mamlouk [the head of Syrian general security] was there. All he did was look at me smiling and say "I will not recognise any official from a country that is under US occupation." It was a waste of time.' Iraq recalled its ambassador to Damascus, and Syria ordered its envoy to Baghdad home in retaliation. Throughout the rest of the year, and into early 2010, relations between Maliki and Assad remained toxic.

In March 2010, Iraqi forces, acting on a US tip, arrested an Islamic State leader named Munaf Abdul Rahim al-Rawi, who was revealed to be one of the group's main commanders in Baghdad, and one of the very few people who had access to the group's then leader, Abu Omar al-Baghdadi. Al-Rawi talked. And in a rare moment of collaboration, Iraq's three main intelligence bodies, including General Kamal's Intelligence Division, conspired to get a listening device and GPS location tracker in a flower box delivered to Abu Omar's hideout.

After it was confirmed that Abu Omar and his deputy, Abu Ayub al-Masri, were present at a house six miles south-west of Tikrit, it was attacked in a US-led raid. Both men detonated suicide vests to avoid being captured. Messages to Osama bin Laden and Ayman al-Zawahiri were found on a computer inside the house. Much like Bin Laden's safe house in Pakistan, where he would be killed a little more than a year later, Abu Omar's hideout had no internet connections or telephone lines – all important messages were carried in and out by only three men. One of them was Abu Bakr al-Baghdadi.

'Abu Bakr was a messenger for Abu Omar,' Abu Ahmed told me. 'He became the closest aide to him. The messages that got to Osama bin Laden were sometimes drafted by him and their journey always started with him. When Abu Omar was killed, Abu Bakr was made leader. That time we all had in Bucca became very important again.'

The deaths of Abu Omar al-Baghdadi and Abu Ayub al-Masri were a serious blow to Isis, but the roles they had vacated were quickly filled by the alumni of Camp Bucca – whose upper echelons had begun preparing for this moment since their time behind the wire of their jail in southern Iraq. 'For us it was an academy,' Abu Ahmed said, 'but for them' – the senior leaders – 'it was a management school. There wasn't a void at all, because so many people had been mentored in prison.

'When [the civil war in] Syria became serious,' he continued, 'it wasn't difficult to transfer all that expertise to a different battle zone. The Iraqis are the most important people on the military and Shura councils in Isis now, and that is because of all of those years preparing for such an event. I underestimated Baghdadi. And America underestimated the role it played in making him what he is.'

Abu Ahmed remains a member of Isis; he is active in the group's operations in both Iraq and Syria. Throughout our discussions, he portrayed himself as a man reluctant to stay with the group, and yet unwilling to risk any attempt to leave.

Life with Isis means power, money, wives and status – all attractive lures for young firebrands with a cause – but it also means killing and dominating for a worldview in which he no longer believes so fervently. He said hundreds of young men like him, who were drawn to a Sunni jihad after the US invasion, do not believe that the latest manifestation of the decade-long war remains true to its origins.

'The biggest mistake I made is to join them,' Abu Ahmed said, but added that leaving the group would mean that he and his family would certainly be killed. Staying and enforcing the group's brutal vision, despite partially disavowing it, does not trouble Abu Ahmed, who sees himself as having few other options.

'It's not that I don't believe in jihad,' he said. 'I do,' he continued, his voice trailing away. 'But what options do I have? If I leave, I am dead.'

The arc of his involvement with what is now the world's most menacing terrorist group mirrors many others who now hold senior positions in the group: first a battle against an invading army, then a score to be settled with an ancient sectarian foe, and now, a war that could be acting out an end-of-days prophecy.

In the world of the Bucca alumni, there is little room for revisionism, or reflection. Abu Ahmed seems to feel himself swept along by events that are now far bigger than him, or anyone else.

'There are others who are not ideologues,' he said, referring to senior Isis members close to Baghdadi. 'People who started out in Bucca, like me. And then it got bigger than any of us. This can't be stopped now. This is out of the control of any man. Not Baghdadi, or anyone else in his circle.'

Additional reporting by Salaam Riazk

21 December

Kevin Spacey, Debbie Harry, Slavoj Žižek: the best answers to your webchat questions

Tim Minchin

Are you happy?

I'm very happy. But I was before, too. It's a slightly different kind of happy because it involves a house or two and a pool ... things to which I never really aspired and certainly didn't expect. However, in the 10 years that I've gone from having barely a pot to piss in to having *une piscine* (that shit's why I get the big bucks) I have also acquired two children which didn't cost me anything. So I suppose the nature of my happiness would have changed anyway.

SINÉAD O'CONNOR
What's your favourite insult? And least favourite compliment?
In answer to your first question: Suck my dick, bitch. To your second: I don't like people saying I look good because I'm skinny. I don't like words like 'good' or 'bad' being associated with female weight.

JOHN LYDON
Are you afraid of death?
Yes. Looking forward to it also. It's every person's ultimate condition. So I'm in no rush!!! I have no proof of the afterlife. And therefore wait and see. I had one near-death experience in my life – I was in a coma for four months. There was no 'Hark the Herald Angels Sing', there was no tunnel with the light at the end of it. There were no happy faces floating on clouds. But there was me in agony, which, in the long run, is currently preferable.

TRACEY EMIN
How do you deal with the ugly souls that persecute and attack you?
I just have to get on with it. Once, when my boyfriend left me and we'd been together for years, it was a Saturday night and I went to sleep on the sofa in tears. And I woke up to hear my name – on the TV there was a programme called *The Hundred Most Hated People in Britain*. I was number fortysomething. It's this kind of thing that can really knock people over the edge, but luckily I dined out on it.

KEVIN SPACEY

Who are your top three all-time favourite Kevins?

My favourite Kevins are the ones I'm constantly mistaken for. The best time was when I was in a piano bar. Some guy was absolutely convinced that I was that musician ... what's his name? The guy in Genesis? Phil Collins! To the point that I even put on a British accent and signed a napkin as him.

ALI SMITH

Can you describe why you have such an affinity for trees in your writing?

When you hold a book you're also holding a tree in one form or another, and that direct connection lets me know how important books are in the world. Pages are called leaves, a spine of a book comes from the spine of the animal whose skin was used in the first books as covers; everything about books refers us back to the physical world. Not that ebook readers aren't useful for those of us whose eyes are getting worse with age. But the reading of a book – a physical book – lets us know how time is passing, and how we are passing time, in something more than percentage numbers.

FLYING LOTUS

How do you see yourself 'artistically' in 20 years?

I imagine myself very overweight and maybe, a beard, with lots of young artists living in my house making albums and shit.

KATHERINE RYAN

Was it your time with Hooters that got you into performing comedy?

It's a long story, but I'm very fond of my time as a Hooters Girl. It's like being a cheerleader or beauty pageant contestant – we were objectified, but didn't understand. Dressing identically to everyone else and serving customers chicken with a smile forced me to develop a very strong voice that I'm grateful for today.

SLAVOJ ŽIŽEK
What do you think we can learn from cats, if anything?
Nothing. In classical Hollywood, vampires and zombies designate class struggle. Vampires are rich, they live among us. Zombies are the poor, living dead, ugly, stupid, attacking from outside. And it's the same with cats and dogs. Cats are lazy, evil, exploitative, dogs are faithful, they work hard, so if I were to be in government, I would tax having a cat, tax it really heavy.

KATHLEEN TURNER
Did you and William Hurt sense at the time that you had made one of the all-time great screen couples in Body Heat?
I'm not sure what makes great chemistry other than liking and respecting the other person. We broke new ground in *Body Heat* when it came to sexuality in film. It was very scary. If you feel used it's not going to work. And you have to be very careful of that as a woman.

WILL SELF
Please can you be my life mentor?
I am your life mentor already – I am the still and silent voice you hear muttering evil things at 3am; I am the hortatory, steroid-pumped personal trainer who drives you from under the duvet at the very crack of dawn; I am the motivational speaker who drives you into a coma during the afternoon meeting; I am the fitness instructor who kicks and punches you into the raft that then disappears into a maelstrom of white water ... Be careful what you wish for ...

DEBBIE HARRY AND CHRIS STEIN

When lazy journos riffed that you were a man – did you take it as an insult or a compliment?

CHRIS STEIN: I think most dynamic female artistes have heard that: Marlene Dietrich, Grace Jones ... This is just misogyny: if a woman is powerful, she might be a man.

DEBBIE HARRY: Gender is just a big fucking mess. It's a big glandular mix-up, it's up for grabs. They're applauding men who can express their feminine side, without saying women can express their masculine side. We both have everything, and we both have moments when we need to use them, and society is totally inhibiting and quite cruel really.

HOWARD JACOBSON

What is it about Jewishness that makes for such great writers?

Jews became the People of the Book when they were first exiled. It's not uncommon for marginalised people to value (or even overvalue) culture. You fight with what weapons you've got. The constant sense of impending doom also does wonders for a sense of humour. And if Jews have the blackest humour of anybody it's because they know how much there is to fear out there.

GILBERT AND GEORGE

How do you work as a partnership? Is one of you the ideas man or do you share the creative process equally?

We call this the great heterosexual question. We are equal in our partnership where most mixed couples are not. We don't cook, clean, shop or wash up. This makes a lot of ladies jealous.

SARA PASCOE

Will you marry me?

Okay, but there are some conditions: I don't like the word wife.

We both have to be husbands. I think heart-husbands is how we'll refer to each other. The ceremony will have no men giving away women, and we'll both have to give speeches. Mine has to be funnier. I will get a whole writing team. You will pay for this as my dowry.

If agreed, sign here _____

WILLIAM GIBSON

When does the future begin?

In the 20th century, the '21st century' was used a great deal – in the 21st century we never mention the 22nd century, and culturally that's very significant. Something has changed hugely in the past 30 years. Americans, for instance, no longer believe in the future as some completely other place. Europeans never believed in that, because in Europe the evidence is all around us that the future is built in the past. The American vision of the future was over the hill, down the highway, we'll build a new world. Americans have gotten the message. I think that *Blade Runner* was very important in that, in its wonderfully European depiction of a future Los Angeles that grew perpetually out of its own ruins. A very un-American vision, radically un-American.

CATHERINE TATE

Do you think 'Nan' will be voting Ukip next year?

No way. She lives in a multicultural society, and always has. And is happy to. She'd be very happy to tell Nigel Farage where to go.

JOHN WATERS

Ever going to marry?

I doubt it. I have no real urge to copy a corny heterosexual tradition, even though I believe marriage can work. My parents had a great one. It's the bachelor party I can't face.

CANDI STATON

When you recorded at Rick Halls' Fame Studios I believe you had over 15 big hits, yet your songs seem very difficult to find.

We had an era when DJs were mostly men ... women's lib had not come to be. We were in a jail, in a sense. We could only sing songs about: 'Men, please don't leave me!' The male DJs would play the big pleading songs, 'You can do anything you want to me, just take me back.' Men love to hear that – if you got too liberated they wouldn't play your record. Gloria Gaynor's 'I Will Survive' broke that mould, and then me with 'Young Hearts Run Free' – suddenly women were buying more and more records.

JOHN COOPER CLARKE

Why do you not favour the sock as part of the suit's ensemble?

Good question. I've always seen them as a kind of underwear. They're foundation garments, something that comes in between a boot and the skin. I don't want to be too hard and fast about this, I know people who really work the sock and good luck to them but me, I've always been a boot wearer. You don't need hosiery on a man, there's something effeminate about it.

AMANDA PALMER

How did you become so brave? Did you ever fake being fearless? What are your fears?

I am scared of:
- being unloved
- being alone
- being misunderstood
- being invisible
... and oh the list goes on.

ZACH BRAFF
Who would win in a fight between an otter and a fox?
Where did you buy your weed? I need some. Hopefully no one else is reading this but you and me. The only thing in my hotel is bath salts, and I've already smoked that.

KIRSTY WARK
Do you think the BBC chose the right Kirsty for the Desert Island Discs *gig?*
Kirsty Young is certainly the right woman for the job. Funnily enough the other night we had a pretty clueless London taxi driver and I am not very good on 'the knowledge', so it was a bit tense in the back of the cab. When I got out, he said: 'Don't worry, I'll still listen to you on *Desert Island Discs*.'

SIMON AMSTELL
Please can you tell us more about why veganism is important to you?
I saw the documentary *Earthlings*, and it felt like in the future we will look at what we do to animals with the same horror that we now look at slavery or the Holocaust. Happy Christmas!

22 DECEMBER

Goodbye, cruel 2014: we promise not to miss you once you've gone

CHARLIE BROOKER

So 2014's almost done, and unless you got married, or had your firstborn, or won a Subaru filled with Maltesers in a radio phone-in, it's unlikely to be a year you'll remember fondly. It was filled with huge, grim events. So is every year, of course, but in 2014 it seemed there were fewer light moments to offset the enveloping dread. And everyone seemed angry, all the time. A whole planet, gritting its teeth. Hundreds protesting. Thousands marching. Millions waiting to attach their internalised rage to a hashtag at a moment's notice. We could all use a lie-down over Christmas.

The year started badly for Britain when the sky decided to waterboard the lot of us. It rained incessantly throughout early January; big grey raindrops the size of cupboards. The government issued snorkels to anyone under 5ft 4in, while areas of Devon were submerged for so long the residents evolved gills and blowholes.

No sooner had the waters receded than Channel 4 chose to cheer everyone up by broadcasting *Benefits Street* – part docusoap, part litmus test for pre-existing prejudice – which managed to further polarise an already polarised debate about welfare largely on account of its button-pushing title and emphasis on petty crime. Since about half of Britain's benefits bill goes on pensions, a more accurate version of *Benefits Street* would consist of sedate footage of OAPs enjoying a slice of Battenburg and an episode of *Lewis*.

Mystery of the year was the vanishing of flight MH370. In the immediate aftermath of its disappearance, various theories were bandied about, starting with terrorism and ending with pilot suicide. The total lack of evidence left TV news with nothing to do but run footage of people in spotter planes staring forlornly at the ocean for signs of wreckage that never appeared. In a world of one-click convenience, where you can discover the name of a man who played a milkman in a long-forgotten Shreddies advert courtesy of a two-second Google, the notion that an entire plane could simply up and leave – potentially for ever – with no regard for narrative resolution seems frighteningly alien. Perhaps that's why later in the year, when another Malaysian airlines plane went down, this time in a definitive time and place, the media felt compelled to trawl through the wreckage live on air, like dogs marking their scent.

Showbiz had its ups and downs. The movie *Gravity*, in which Sandra Bullock risked her life by heading up top to fix a sort of aerial thing, just like Rod Hull, had plaudits pissed all over it at the Oscars. And deservedly so: apparently, the entire film was shot in space for tax reasons, so the journey to set every morning must have been hellish.

Speaking of cold voids, following mounting criticism of apparently state-sanctioned homophobia in Russia, the Sochi Winter Olympics passed off largely without incident, although the opening ceremony was slightly marred when, during a climactic lightshow, an Olympic ring failed to fully dilate (fair enough; it's probably quite hard to source poppers in Russia at the moment).

There were two TV mumbling scandals. First, encouraged by the public's appetite for foreign-language TV dramas, the BBC decided to go one better and screen a programme you couldn't understand even though it was in English. Visually, *Jamaica Inn* appeared to be set on the Quality Street tin during a recession; the problem was the script, because you couldn't hear it – at least not unless you squinted really hard with your ears, and even then you could only make out the consonants.

Then the *Mirror* accused Jeremy Clarkson of muttering the 'N-word' in some unaired *Top Gear* rushes. Just to irritate everyone further, he'd mumbled the word – or rather, he'd mumbled at the point in the 'Eeny Meeny Miney Mo' nursery rhyme where the word might be – so it wasn't unequivocally clear whether he'd actually said it, or just flirted with saying it. He claimed he hadn't, while a firm of 'forensic audio experts' hired by the *Mirror* claimed he had. So it was his N-word against theirs. In the end, no action was taken, except by the hundreds of thousands of parents who had to explain to their children what the 'N-word' was after people kept mentioning it on the telly.

It was a grim year for showbiz. Max Clifford achieved the impossible and made himself 10,000 times less popular than he already wasn't. For a self-professed master of public image to end up being widely regarded as an underendowed paedophile has to rank as the biggest career fail in history. Then Rolf Harris went to prison for crimes against children, sending a whole swathe of British nostalgia collapsing into oblivion, like a section of cliff face crumbling into the sea.

Westminster also found itself mired in scandal when a decades-old dossier containing the names of various high-profile figures suspected of paedophilia went missing. A search turned up nothing. Well, these things happen. It's an easy mistake to make, especially in an organisation of that size. Maybe someone just accidentally shredded it with sweating, shaking hands and one foot up against the door.

At around the same time, Theresa May was having difficulty appointing a chairperson for the abuse inquiry. First Baroness Butler-Sloss, then Fiona Woolf ... at one point it seemed to have a different guest host each week, like it was *Never Mind the Buzz-cocks* or something. Turns out, when the establishment holds an inquiry into alleged abuses by the establishment, it has a hard time considering anyone who isn't linked to the establishment already. Perhaps they should look overseas. It has to be someone everyone likes, with absolutely no links to the British establishment. How about Roger Federer?

The sheer number of historic abuse stories meant that just about the only institution not to have been rocked by some kind of paedophile scandal in 2014 was the *Great British Bake Off*, and even that had constant references to PIE during pastry week.

But things were grimmer still internationally. Isis. Syria. Gaza. Ukraine. Pakistan. There was horror piled upon horror. And even at home, things many had taken for granted, such as the United Kingdom itself, were threatening to split apart. Eventually Scotland voted to remain in the union, but not before scaring the shit out of an increasingly despised Westminster. All politicians are less popular than Stalin-flavoured crisps, with the exception of Nigel Farage, who isn't in the House of Commons, and Russell Brand, who isn't a politician.

Farage spent the year outlining an increasingly petty series of complaints. He complained about having to listen to people speaking foreign languages on trains (he must have been relieved when he got home to his German-speaking wife). Then he complained that immigration was causing traffic jams (presumably because he'd scared all the foreigners off the trains). Finally, he complained about public breastfeeding. Yes, public breastfeeding – that grotesque, unnatural spectacle which is a) everywhere you go and b) simply impossible to avoid, unless you take extreme measures, such as looking the other way. Maybe it's not the breasts he's annoyed by. Maybe it's the babies. After all, they make no attempt to assimilate with our culture, can't speak the language, have no qualifications to speak of, and, worst of all, are stopping him from getting a clear view of a lovely naked tit.

In technology news, Apple launched the iPhone 6, which sports a huge suite of improvements: reduced pocketability, increased ugliness, and enhanced pliability, ie it bends if you sit on it. They also brought out the Apple Watch, which will transform the way people ignore you in conversations forever. You know how people look at their iPhones when they're bored of you? Soon they'll look at their watches instead – just like they did when you were boring back in the good old days, before the iPhone existed.

The Apple watch boasts an impressive full colour display, so you can fully appreciate the latest terrorist atrocity videos and stolen celebrity nudes in the comfort of your own wrist. It also tells the time, just like the iPhone you're constantly staring at does, and will cost about £300. Not a wind up. It's chargeable.

Finally, the year was rounded off with a hacking scandal that left Sony reeling. Embarrassing emails were exposed, the script for the next Bond movie was leaked, and, most terrifying of all, the hackers deliberately released the forthcoming reboot of the musical *Annie* online, for free, where innocent human beings might bump into it. Never mind terrorists with weaponised Ebola – that's truly ruthless.

Winter

Pass notes: Victor Spirescu

LUCY MANGAN

Age: 30.

Appearance: Bemused.

I'm bemused, too. Who is he? He was the first migrant to arrive here after EU visa restrictions on Romanians and Bulgarians were lifted last year.

Oh, yes! The first of the waves that Nigel Farage and others promised, of benefit-claiming East Europeans who would engulf this green and pleasant land. Après him, the deluge! It was feared/politically useful to pretend they would be seeking to suckle at the bounteous teat of Britain's social security system. Though it turned out that their immigration numbers actually fell after the rule change.

Whatevs. There was an advert in the Daily Telegraph *about them all being criminals.* Placed by Nigel Farage.

Yes, so I knew it was true. He has a face you can't help but trust. The ad said that 7 per cent of all crime in the EU was carried out by Romanian gangs. 7 per cent! No wonder he said people were right to be concerned if a group of Romanians moved in next door – imagine having only a 93 per cent chance of not being killed by them in the night! Would it help if I told you that it was all crap?

No. Tell me, how much has Spirescu managed to drain from us over the past year? He left his first job, carwashing in Biggleswade, after a day ...

Aha! To float luxuriously on a sea of universal credit and housing benefit, I presume? No, because media attention made it impossible for him to stay. He went to London to work on building sites instead and now makes about 80 pounds a day.

Oh. Well, I bet he's planning to milk the system at some stage. He's planning to go home, actually.

Why? What's wrong with here? Is his wallet too small for his fifties? Are all our diamond shoes too tight? 'I miss my village, my life in Romania. It's all right but I come here to make some money and then I'll go back. I don't want to live for ever here.'

Unbelievable! He comes over here, takes a job that someone else could have had ... but for some reason wasn't taking ...

And then doesn't even have the courtesy to stay! He'd rather go home! To a country full of chickens and vampires! Yes. There's just no pleasing some people, is there?

Do say: 'Home is where the heart is.'

Don't say: 'Your home appears to be where the semi-electable bigots are.'

9 JANUARY

On satire

JOE SACCO

9 JANUARY

Charlie Hebdo: first they came for the cartoonists, then they came for the Jews

JONATHAN FREEDLAND

When terror strikes, we all become mind readers. With no words to accompany the violence, it's left to us to supply the motive. We insert our own guess, ventriloquising the killers who remain enigmatically mute. It happened again this week, following the slaying of 12 people at the offices of the *Charlie Hebdo* magazine with little more than an 'Allahu Akbar' to go on. They hated the cartoons, we say. Free speech was the target, we declare. They wanted to silence satire and gag dissent.

Then on Friday, a siege at a kosher supermarket, four hostages confirmed dead, the murderers apparently linked to those behind Wednesday's carnage. Oh, we say. So perhaps the killers' problem was not with ugly cartoons or vicious depictions of Muhammad after all. Maybe their motive is of a different order, one we find much harder to comprehend. Perhaps the murderers are bent on killing people not only for what they do, but for who they are.

It's hard to live in a senseless world so people, even well-intentioned people, will try to make sense of this latest, desperate twist in Paris. So far there have been mercifully few attempts to make the usual, kneejerk move, insisting that the animating grievance must be western foreign policy. It is hard to draw that conclusion when the targets have been a satirical magazine and a shop selling salt beef and pickles. Some will doubtless talk about

Muslim antagonism to Israel, as if an infant in a kosher deli is somehow responsible for the conduct of a government 2,000 miles away.

Others might note the curious kink in the ultra-Islamist mindset that has anointed Jews as a kind of ultimate symbol of the west. Witness the Iranian newspaper that in 2006 responded to the Danish cartoons affair with a competition for 'the best Holocaust caricatures', as if the most efficient way to hit back at Europe was by attacking ... Jews.

The irony is, of course, bitter and deep: it was not that long ago, within living memory in fact, that most of the nations of Europe either participated in, or did little to halt, the near-successful attempt to rid the continent of Jews once and for all. No matter. To a certain strain of thinking, one embodied in France by the Jew-baiting so-called comedian Dieudonné M'bala M'bala, the best way to attack 'the system' or 'the establishment' is to wound Jews.

So there's little surprise the jihadists who turned Paris into a war zone turned their guns sooner rather than later on Jews. That's what happened in Mumbai in 2008 and again in Toulouse in 2012, when Mohammad Merah killed a rabbi and three children at a Jewish school, pulling an eight-year-old girl by her hair to shoot her in the head.

Or maybe that is to overthink it. Perhaps we should simply see the perpetrators as the latest in a long line of murderous fascists, defined as such by their choice of targets. They hate dissent, they hate satire and, as fascist tradition demands, they loathe Jews.

Whatever else comes out of this bleak week, perhaps now there can at least be some clarity. There can surely be no doubt now as to what we're up against. It is a murderous cult. And, at the risk of mind-reading, it seems bent on fusing itself with Islam, claiming to act in the name, and on the authority, of that faith.

It follows that our responsibility is to thwart that effort. For Muslims, that has meant spelling out that these killers speak only for themselves. Note the speed with which a delegation of 20 imams visited the *Charlie Hebdo* offices, branding the gunmen 'criminals, barbarians, satans' and, crucially, 'not Muslims'.

Of course they should not have to do it. The finger-wagging demand that Muslims condemn acts of terror committed by jihadist cultists is odious: it tacitly assumes that Muslims support such horror unless they explicitly say otherwise. The very demand serves to drive a wedge between Muslims and their fellow citizens. (As it happens, Jews have some experience of this feeling: we too are sometimes told we have to condemn this or that action taken by others – and over which we have no control – if our place in polite society is to be secure.)

So no one else should demand it. But when it comes, as it did so rapidly and spontaneously this week, it speaks with an extra power.

If the challenge, then, is to frustrate the killers' desire to fuse themselves with Islam, then that puts a burden on non-Muslims too. They have to take great care that nothing they do, especially in response to this threat, treats the Muslim majority and the jihadist cult as if they were one group. They are not. Our politicians have to observe that distinction in every decision they take. If a policy appears aimed at Muslims rather than at the handful of jihadist fanatics, then it's the wrong policy.

Those of us in the media have a version of that obligation too. Wednesday's deaths brought a loud chorus insisting that *Charlie Hebdo* was vulnerable because it had been left out on a limb. That was down, they said, to the cowardice of the rest of the press, lacking the guts to do what the French magazine had done. Now, if the declarations of '*Je suis Charlie*' were to mean anything, papers like the *Guardian* ought to make amends and either republish the magazine's offending cartoons or do its own depictions of the prophet – just to prove that it could.

Behind this argument is an assumption that Islam is a unique case. Yet for that to be true, a paper like the *Guardian* would be running images every day that it knew trampled on the sensibilities of, say, women or Jews or people of colour or myriad others – holding back only when it came to Muslims and what matters to them. But that's not how it is. Mostly we do our best, not always successfully, to avoid causing that kind of pain.

And this is the key point. It is not only violent jihadists who resent representations of the prophet: such pictures trouble many millions of peaceful Muslims too. To print one now would be to take a stand against the former by offending the latter.

And that makes no sense. Not when our every move must now be aimed at confounding the killers' wish to make this a holy war, pitting Muslims against everyone else. It is no such thing. Theirs is a dirty little war, a handful of wicked fanatics against the rest of us. And they must lose.

14 JANUARY

Can these 36 questions make you fall in love with anyone?

BIM ADEWUNMI

No two ways about it, the premise is somewhat wacky. You ask a stranger a series of 36 questions in three sets, and then you conclude your encounter with a four-minute session of looking silently into one another's eyes. The process of asking and answering accelerates intimacy – which is, after all, knowledge coalesced, usually over a long period – and makes the two people feel more kindly about one another and, in the fullness of time, foster the emotion that we humans call 'love'. I said yes, because why the hell not?

My stranger for the evening is not technically a stranger: Archie and I have been working in the same office for the past three or so months, separated by a bank of desks and a walkway. We have nodded at one another, and possibly accidentally eavesdropped on each other's conversations. So already we have flouted the most basic element of the study. On the phone, my editor tells me Archie has already agreed to it, and so encouraged, I agree as well. We later realise she played us both. Nefarious.

We begin the evening with photos. At first, we keep our distance as the photographer sets up and do faux-relaxed chat (well, I'm faux-relaxed), but we both know what's coming. We have to stand incredibly close to one another and stare into the other's eyes. The result is awkward. Have you ever done it? Even with a long-term friend or lover? It's just weird. I find myself wondering if my breath is fine (I know it is, because I was chewing fruity gum beforehand; his is fine too, phew) and repeating 'this is FINE' over and over in my head. The staring becomes a looming presence over the course of the evening: not exactly a dark cloud, but always there, nonetheless. It is the thing we keep coming back to – all that staring we are going to do later – a million times more awkward than a goodnight kiss could ever be if this were a traditional date.

Over dinner, we begin. The questions start off fairly innocuously: dream dinner guest (he says George Eliot or David Foster Wallace, both good answers); do you rehearse phone calls (me: yes; him: not really); when did you last sing to yourself (both of us: like, earlier today). They ramp up in significance as they go on:

what in your life do you feel grateful for? What would you change about how you were raised? Then, name three things you and your partner appear to have in common. Written down, it doesn't seem like much, but once required to think about these things – and so quickly – it becomes intense.

The usual route to intimacy is, among other things, winding and often accidental. This thing we are doing, in a largely empty restaurant, is deliberate and accelerated. But as the evening goes on, what was originally discomfiting becomes almost euphoric release. There is no way I would tell someone on a normal first date about my relationship with my mother. But in light of the unusual circumstances, and what we have already shared of ourselves this evening, why not? The questions are probing – your most embarrassing moment, your favourite memory etc – and the great thing about them is how they force reflection. Not looking at the questions beforehand was a good idea, because I think I would have cooked my answers a bit. This is incredibly open; I end up revealing stuff that I have not directly shared with some of my closest friends (we have talked around them, they have fragments and half-told stories). It is also funny and fun, and remarkably relaxed. We both note that, relieved.

Archie is amusing and complimentary, which makes me like him (obviously). And we discover that we have a lot more in common than it appears on paper. A quick truncated list: we both like dogs; we both attended single-sex schools; we both would like to write books one day; we like football (him: Southampton, me: West Ham); we value kindness, we realise how lucky we are to be doing jobs we love, we both grasp the crushing and all-encompassing love our mothers feel for us and understand we are unworthy of it. And so on. The questions give structure to the evening, without awkward pauses. Each answer brings more questions. It's pretty great.

The most difficult questions to answer are the ones where we have to say something we feel about the other person. 'Tell your partner something you like about them already' is a squirm-inducing No 31, and No 26 isn't much better: 'Complete the sentence: "I wish I had someone with whom I could share ..."' I am surprised by how open I am, but then I really shouldn't be, I suppose. Clearly, this is for work, and I imagine we are both squirrelling away quotes for our respective pieces. But I also made the effort to wear contacts – not my spectacles – and applied shaky eyeliner. I put on lipstick, dammit. At the very least, I was open to meeting someone romantically. Acknowledging that gives me a jolt.

Eventually, three hours later, we have to look. Archie sets the timer on his phone, and in a deserted square, with the icy wind whipping about us, we sit on metal chairs and stare across a wet table. I begin to chatter, out of nervous habit. Archie shushes me. Our lips quirk constantly, suppressing awkward smiles. A few people walk past, chatting loudly. Occasionally, the cold makes us gasp. We keep on staring. Archie laughs out loud. 'Nope, lean in to the awkwardness,' I say, like a wanker. Then I laugh. And then, finally, we are silent. The timer rings.

I love technology, and I think it has the potential to be far more intimate than the essayists and columnists would have us believe. But there is something far more arresting in the physical. It is why hysterical film actors bellow 'look into my eyes and tell me!' as tests of sincerity. There is a common human frequency that we all tune into, and a mutual gaze is how we access it. In the end, I am not staring into Archie's eyes so much as into my own state of mind. The clarity is startling. Also, Archie has very kind eyes. So there's that.

21 JANUARY

'Disaster turned to comedy at her touch': saluting Deirdre's raucous spirit

NANCY BANKS-SMITH

For 40 years while reviewing TV I couldn't spell Deirdre. Was the 'i' before the 'e' or neither or either? Did the 'er' come before the 're' or was it widdershins? For 40 flipping years I had to look Deirdre up, and Deirdre cropped up a lot. When 24 million people watch her wedding, you had better get the name of the bride right.

Deirdre means 'sorrowful', which is a funny name for *Coronation Street*. She first appeared in an elderly era of Annies and Enas and Minnies and Elsies and she was something quite different. She wore glasses and she smoked and Ken Barlow and Mike Baldwin fought over her in the street. I was thrilled. I wore glasses and I smoked and, with luck, men would fight over me in the street. Well, never mind. Two out of three. Forty years on, Deirdre was the last person still smoking on TV, puffing away rebelliously in the back yard, knowing it got up Ken's nose.

Annoying Ken was her life's work. He fancied the artistic type who floated about in a negligee and a boat like the Lady of Shalott. Probably reading Proust. Deirdre was altogether more down-to-earth. The last time I saw her on TV, she had made her usual uneatable meal (the look on her family's faces showed just how inedible) and had snuggled down with a magazine and a lowbrow chuckle while Ken walked the dog in the rain.

Disaster turned to comedy at her touch. I can't have dreamed – why would I dream something like that – the night she spent with Dev Alahan, he of the corner shop. I remember the dawning horror on his face as he sobered up and the cat-at-the-cream beam on hers. A smile so wide it seemed hooked over her ears.

Coronation Street is matriarchal, and women came in clumps. Living inharmoniously in No 1 Coronation Street were three generations: Deirdre, her waspish mother Blanche (who had been a corset-maker of the whalebone and laces variety) and her daughter Tracy (who felled an unsatisfactory feller with a well-aimed *objet d'art*). Murder was always on the cards at No 1, loneliness never. Deirdre's premature death has prevented her natural progression to be a gloriously embarrassing grandmother.

A version of Deirdre survives in *The Archers*. Lilian has the same raucous gin-and-it cackle, the lifelong inability to do anything domesticated, the dance-in-the-old-girl-yet spirit. It is something to know that we can still hear, like an echo, that indomitable laugh.

1 FEBRUARY

Benedict Cumberbatch didn't cause me to press my outrage button

HUGH MUIR

Outraged or not outraged? That is the question. Benedict Cumberbatch, bemoaning the lot of minority actors in Britain, said coloured when he should have said black. Point the flamethrower at him? Maybe not.

I'm with David Oyelowo on this. Give Cumberbatch a break.

He didn't suffocate a migrant on a deportation plane. He didn't send anyone to jail because he didn't like the look of them. He used an antiquated term in making a point that most would agree with. Regrettable, but he apologised and seemed to mean it. And there are bigger villains out there.

Still, I am puzzled, for he is 38, not 78. This is not a word commonly used by his generation. From whence did it make its way from his subconscious to his mouth via a fine brain? Was it a word older relatives used? He was in *12 Years a Slave*. Did it creep into his head via a script? Does he know himself?

Still, in these matters, context is all; for almost anyone who is from a visible minority, or a woman, or who has an accent or a disability or a difference, could choose to be outraged about something virtually every day of the week. To react or not to react? That depends on answers to the checklist. How annoyed am I? If I press the outrage button, will that cause me more distress and wear and tear than the target of my ire? Is my case so strong that others will support it, should adjudication subsequently be necessary? Will this correct behaviour? Is the target even worth thinking about in terms of rehabilitation? Is there value in the hand grenade as deterrent? Any or all of these may cause one to press the outrage button; or to walk on by.

Thus I found myself, early in my career, explaining to a middle-aged man at the East Ham Conservative Association that brown skin did not render me more comfortable than fellow east Londoners packed into an overheated room. And smiling the sweetest smile at the old boy in Yorkshire who sought to engage me in the street about coloured folks and tooth enamel. And by contrast, organising public humiliation for the school governor who confided over the phone – never having met me – that his establishment was being ruined by 'darkies'. I called him to the office to discuss it further. He was a better person when he left.

2 FEBRUARY

What happened when I confronted my cruellest troll

LINDY WEST

For the past three years or so, at least one stranger has sought me out pretty much every day to call me a fat bitch (or some pithy variation thereof). I'm a writer and a woman and a feminist, and I write about big, fat, bitchy things that make people uncomfortable. And because I choose to do that as a career, I'm told, a constant barrage of abuse is just part of my job. Shrug. Nothing we can do. I'm asking for it, apparently.

Being harassed on the internet is such a normal, common part of my life that I'm always surprised when other people find it surprising. You're telling me you don't have hundreds of men popping into your cubicle in the accounting department of your mid-sized, regional dry-goods distributor to inform you that – hmm – you're too fat to rape, but perhaps they'll saw you up with an electric knife? No? Just me? People who don't spend much time on the internet are invariably shocked to discover the barbarism – the eager abandonment of the social contract – that so many of us face simply for doing our jobs.

Sometimes the hate trickles in slowly, just one or two messages a day. But other times, when I've written something particularly controversial (ie feminist) – like, say, my critique of men feeling entitled to women's time and attention, or literally anything about rape – the harassment comes in a deluge. It floods my Twitter feed, my Facebook page, my email, so fast that I can't even keep up (not that I want to).

It was in the middle of one of these deluges two summers ago when my dead father contacted me on Twitter.

At the time, I'd been writing a lot about the problem of misogyny (specifically jokes about rape) in the comedy world. My central point – which has been gleefully misconstrued as 'pro-censorship' ever since – was that what we say affects the world we live in, that words are both a reflection of and a catalyst for the way our society operates. When you talk about rape, I said, you get to decide where you aim: are you making fun of rapists? Or their victims? Are you making the world better? Or worse? It's not about censorship, it's not about obligation, it's not about forcibly limiting anyone's speech – it's about choice. Who are you? Choose.

The backlash from comedy fans was immediate and intense: 'That broad doesn't have to worry about rape.' 'She won't ever have to worry about rape.' 'No one would want to rape that fat, disgusting mess.' 'Holes like this make me want to commit rape out of anger.' It went on and on, to the point that it was almost white noise. After a week or so, I was feeling weather-beaten but fortified. Nothing could touch me any more.

But then there was my dad's dear face twinkling out at me from my Twitter feed. Someone – bored, apparently, with the usual angles of harassment – had made a fake Twitter account purporting to be my dead dad, featuring a stolen, beloved photo of him, for no reason other than to hurt me. The name on the account was 'PawWestDonezo', because my father's name was Paul West, and a difficult battle with prostate cancer had rendered him 'donezo' (goofy slang for 'done') just 18 months earlier. 'Embarrassed father of an idiot,' the bio read. 'Other two kids are fine, though.' His location was 'Dirt hole in Seattle'.

My dad was special. The only thing he valued more than wit was kindness. He was a writer and an ad man and a magnificent baritone (he could write you a jingle and record it on the same day) – a lost breed of lounge pianist who skipped dizzyingly from jazz standards to Flanders and Swann to Lord Buckley and back again – and I can genuinely say that I've never met anyone else so universally beloved, nor do I expect to again. I loved him so, so much.

There's a term for this brand of gratuitous online cruelty: we call it internet trolling. Trolling is recreational abuse – usually anonymous – intended to waste the subject's time or get a rise out of them or frustrate or frighten them into silence. Sometimes it's relatively innocuous (like asking contrarian questions just to start an argument) or juvenile (like making fun of my weight or my intelligence), but – particularly when the subject is a young woman – it frequently crosses the line into bona fide, dangerous stalking and harassment.

And even 'innocuous' harassment, when it's coming at you en masse from hundreds or even thousands of users a day, stops feeling innocuous very quickly. It's a silencing tactic. The message is: you are outnumbered. The message is: we'll stop when you're gone. The volume and intensity of harassment is vastly magnified for women of colour and trans women and disabled women and fat women and sex workers and other intersecting identities. Who gets trolled has a direct impact on who gets to talk; in my personal experience, the fiercest trolling has come from traditionally white, male-dominated communities (comedy, video games, atheism) whose members would like to keep it that way.

I feel the pull all the time: I should change careers; I should shut down my social media; maybe I can get a job in print somewhere; it's just too exhausting. I hear the same refrains from my colleagues. Sure, we've all built up significant armour at this point, but, you know, armour is heavy. Internet trolling might seem like an issue that only affects a certain subset of people, but that's only true if you believe that living in a world devoid of diverse voices – public discourse shaped primarily by white, heterosexual, able-bodied men – wouldn't profoundly affect your life.

Sitting at my computer, staring at PawWestDonezo, I had precious few options. All I could do, really, was ignore it: hit 'block' and move on, knowing that that account was still out there, hidden behind a few gossamer lines of code, still putting words in my dad's mouth, still using his image to mock, abuse and silence people. After all, it's not illegal to reach elbow-deep into someone's memories and touch them and twist them and weaponise them (to impress the ghost of Lenny Bruce or whatever). Nor should it be, of course. But that doesn't mean we have to tolerate it without dissent.

Over and over, those of us who work on the internet are told, 'Don't feed the trolls. Don't talk back. It's what they want.' But is that true? Does ignoring trolls actually stop trolling? Can somebody show me concrete numbers on that? Anecdotally, I've ignored far more trolls than I've 'fed', and my inbox hasn't become any quieter. When I speak my mind and receive a howling hurricane of abuse in return, it doesn't feel like a plea for my attention – it feels like a demand for my silence.

And some trolls are explicit about it. 'If you can't handle it, get off the internet.' That's a persistent refrain my colleagues and I hear when we confront our harassers. But why? Why don't YOU get off the internet? Why should I have to rearrange my life – and change careers, essentially – because you wet your pants every time a woman talks?

My friends say, 'Just don't read the comments.' But just the other day, for instance, I got a tweet that said, 'May your bloodied head rest on the edge of an Isis blade.' Colleagues and friends of mine have had their phone numbers and addresses published online (a harassment tactic known as 'doxing') and had trolls show up at their public events or threaten mass shootings. So if we don't keep an eye on what people are saying, how do we know when a line has been crossed and law enforcement should be involved? (Not that the police have any clue how to deal with online harassment anyway – or much interest in trying.)

Social media companies say, 'Just report any abuse and move on. We're handling it.' So I do that. But reporting abuse is a tedious, labour-intensive process that can eat up half my working day. In any case, most of my reports are rejected. And once any troll is blocked (or even if they're suspended), they can just make a new account and start all over again.

I'm aware that Twitter is well within its rights to let its platform be used as a vehicle for sexist and racist harassment. But, as a private company – just like a comedian mulling over a rape joke, or a troll looking for a target for his anger – it could choose not to. As a collective of human beings, it could choose to be better.

So, when it came to the case of PawWestDonezo, I went off script: I stopped obsessing over what *he* wanted and just did what felt best to me that day. I wrote about it publicly, online. I made myself vulnerable. I didn't hide the fact it hurt. The next morning, I woke up to an email:

Hey Lindy, I don't know why or even when I started trolling you. It wasn't because of your stance on rape jokes. I don't find them funny either.

I think my anger towards you stems from your happiness with your own being. It offended me because it served to highlight my unhappiness with my own self.

I have e-mailed you through two other gmail accounts just to send you idiotic insults.

I apologise for that.

I created the PaulWestDunzo@gmail.com account & Twitter account. (I have deleted both.)

I can't say sorry enough.

It was the lowest thing I had ever done. When you included it in your latest *Jezebel* article it finally hit me. There is a living, breathing human being who is reading this shit. I am attacking someone who never harmed me in any way. And for no reason whatsoever.

I'm done being a troll.

Again I apologise.

I made donation in memory to your dad.

I wish you the best.

He had donated $50 to Seattle Cancer Care Alliance, where my dad was treated.

That email still unhinges my jaw every time I read it. A reformed troll? An admission of weakness and self-loathing? An apology? I wrote back once, expressed my disbelief and said thank you – and that was that. I returned to my regular routine of daily hate mail, scrolling through the same options over and over – Ignore? Block? Report? Engage? – but every time I faced that choice, I thought briefly of my remorseful troll.

Last summer, when a segment of video game fans began a massive harassment campaign against female critics and developers (if you want to know more, Google 'GamerGate', then shut your laptop and throw it into the sea), my thoughts wandered back to him more and more. I wondered if I could learn anything from him. And then it struck me: why not find out?

We only had made that one, brief exchange, in the summer of 2013, but I still had his email address. I asked the popular US radio programme *This American Life* to help me reach out to him. They said yes. They emailed him. After a few months of gruelling silence, he finally wrote back. 'I'd be happy to help you out in any way possible,' he said.

And then, there I was in a studio with a phone – and the troll on the other end.

We talked for two and a half hours. He was shockingly self-aware. He told me that he didn't hate me because of rape jokes – the timing was just a coincidence – he hated me because, to put it simply, I don't hate myself. Hearing him explain his choices in his own words, in his own voice, was heartbreaking and fascinating. He said that, at the time, he felt fat, unloved, 'passionless' and purposeless. For some reason, he found it 'easy' to take that out on women online.

I asked why. What made women easy targets? Why was it so satisfying to hurt us? Why didn't he automatically see us as human beings? For all his self-reflection, that's the one thing he never managed to articulate – how anger at one woman translated into hatred of women in general. Why, when men hate themselves, it's women who take the beatings.

But he did explain how he changed. He started taking care of his health, he found a new girlfriend and, most importantly, he went back to school to become a teacher. He told me – in all seriousness – that, as a volunteer at a school, he just gets so many hugs now. 'Seeing how their feelings get hurt by their peers,' he said, 'on purpose or not, it derails them for the rest of the day. They'll have their head on their desk and refuse to talk. As I'm watching this happen, I can't help but think about the feelings that I hurt.' He was so sorry, he said.

I didn't mean to forgive him, but I did.

This story isn't prescriptive. It doesn't mean that anyone is obliged to forgive people who abuse them, or even that I plan on being cordial and compassionate to every teenage boy who tells me I'm too fat to get raped (sorry in advance, boys: I still bite). But, for me, it's changed the timbre of my online interactions – with, for instance, the guy who responded to my radio story by calling my dad a 'faggot'. It's hard to feel hurt or frightened when you're flooded with pity. And that, in turn, has made it easier for me to keep talking in the face of a mob roaring for my silence. Keep screaming, trolls. I see you.

11 FEBRUARY

Keep it dense!

ANDREW HARRISON

At the end of last year, inboxes pinged with news of a person called Shingy, AOL's new 'digital prophet' who travels the world litmus-testing the future, rebooting the CEO's office by taking out all the chairs and adding a special fragrance called London, and handing out a business card with a microchip in it. In an excruciatingly well-observed – and much-forwarded – *New Yorker* piece, writer Andrew Marantz detailed Shingy's comedy haircut, gnomic prescriptions for online success and overcomplicated post-hip-hop handshakes. To American readers he appeared to be only the latest evidence of decadent capitalism's journey to hell in a handcart powered by bullshit. In Britain, though, we reached for the shorthand term we've learned to use for this sort of thing: Nathan Barley.

Yes, Nathan Barley, self-facilitating media node, pioneer vlogger and all-round bumptious idiot. Even if you never saw

Charlie Brooker and Chris Morris's Channel 4 sitcom from 2005, which relayed the adventures of a self-designated digital art terrorist in a fictional (but only slightly exaggerated) Shoreditch called the London borough of Hosegate, you'll be familiar with Nathan and his type. The stupid haircuts, the meaningless catch-phrases ('Totally Mexico! Well futile!'), the massive self-regard, the daft fashion statements and the low-level passive-aggressive insinuation that if you don't get what they're doing then somehow it's your fault ... these are the hallmarks of the modern creative layabout from Dalston to Williamsburg to Kreuzberg to Norrebro.

Nathan was conceived in the early noughties as a snapshot of a small and ludicrous slice of east London. He wasn't supposed to last. But he hasn't just survived, he's metastasised. The start-ups and creative consultancies of every other digital hub from Silicon Roundabout to Silicon Alley resemble nothing so much as Nathan's world of office juice bars, indoor scootering and open-plan thinkpods, plus vast injections of venture capital cash (the haircuts and low-slung denim are certainly the same). *Vice*, which provided at least part of the inspiration for Nathan's odious button-pushing style magazine *Sugar Ape*, is now a multi-million dollar Murdoch-backed business that carries genuinely dangerous warzone reportage while hanging on to its Barleyite roots. A sample headline: 'There's More To The Duke Of Burgundy Than Lesbians Pissing On Each Other'.

With his relentless sadistic pranks against office assistant Pingu – example: plugging Pingu's ears into a lorry battery and then uploading video of his wretched twitch-dancing overdubbed with Motorhead's 'Ace Of Spades' – Nathan established a new normal of online cruelty and self-publicity. From happy slapping to NekNominate to Rude Tube to Vine, anything is permitted now, as long as it fits a 19-year-old idiot's idea of what's funny. Brooker and Morris spotted this before YouTube even existed. And

Nathan Barley was scarcely less prophetic when it came to TV itself. In one episode, Nathan's friend Claire makes a comically po-faced, self-righteous documentary about a choir made up of drug addicts. Nine years later, Channel 4 made *Addicts' Symphony* for real.

Looking for an online guru with an open-ended nanofesto that boils down to 'peace and fucking – believe!'? Sorry, Russell Brand, Nathan beat *The Trews* to the punch by 10 years with the rambling video homilies on his website (back when websites were novel) trashbat.co.ck. Barley aficionados will surely see in Brand some echoes of the show's Preacherman character, the burnt-out style writer Dan Ashcroft who is bullied by style mag *Sugar Ape*'s appalling editor Jonatton Yeah? into adopting a voice-of-a-generation role. Replace the cynical weariness with messianism and you have Russell to a tee. Brand connoisseurs might also enjoy the episode in which Nathan copies a truly asinine haircut made up of paint and bottle tops and random gloop – the Geek Pie as it is known – and then peacocks around Hosegate pointing at it and crowing, 'New fucking paradigm or what?'

From cereal cafes to breakfast raves to adult ball pools, from TV shows like *Sex Box* to newspaper features about the 'meaning' of the Man Bun hairdo to inexplicable online phenomena like Ello, our world has been Barleyed. It is uncanny. Created as a comic figure, Nathan has become an insult and a signifier and maybe even – here's the frightening part – a role model. At 10 years' remove the show seems less a comedy and more a documentary about the future.

'Back when we were shooting it,' says the actor Nicholas Burns, who played Nathan, 'I remember one producer saying, "This show will date terribly. In three or four years it'll look awful." But watching it again, you see how prescient it was. It really is the world we live in now. A friend who lives in Dalston told me they saw someone riding a penny farthing the other day. It's unbelievable really.'

As someone who once saw a fixed-gear cyclist bombing down Stoke Newington High Street in a GENERAL PINOCHET T-shirt, I am inclined to agree.

It is sobering to think that it's fully 10 years since Nathan's TV debut late on Friday 11 February 2005, and more sobering to reflect on how little has changed. We call them hipsters now, and they've got beards, but in every other respect the Barleys are unaltered. 'The anniversary makes me feel fucking ancient,' says the show's co-creator, *Guardian* columnist Charlie Brooker. 'It's actually even longer than 10 years, because Nathan started life on the *TVGoHome* website.'

TVGoHome was Brooker's surreal and scatalogical late 90s collection of fake TV listings, including imaginary shows such as *Inspector Bumhat*, Daily Mail *Island* and the probably-best-not-explained *Mick Hucknall's Pink Pancakes*. 'I had to stop doing *TVGoHome*,' Brooker admits, 'because the real TV programmes were becoming more stupid than any I could make up.' One regular listing concerned a young media man about town called Nathan Barley. It went under the pithy title of *Cunt*.

'When he started out, Nathan wasn't what we'd now call a Shoreditch hipster,' Brooker says. 'I'd never even been to Shoreditch. It was more about moneyed young guys who claimed to be working in television when really they were living off their parents. He was more of a *Made In Chelsea* figure, and he kind of morphed into a Hoxton idiot for the TV show.'

Chris Morris, the creator of *The Day Today* and *Brasseye*, had written listings in secret for *TVGoHome*. Around 2000 he suggested that they try to develop a show around the Nathan character and east London's increasingly absurd club/art scene. 'We talked about the show for years before we made it,' says Brooker. 'Chris was adamant very early on that there should be a tiny acorn of likability to Nathan, something irrepressible. He does terrible things but he has an endearing sort of rabbity enthusiasm to him. In the fake listings he really was a cunt, whereas in the TV show he's a twat – and there is a difference.

'Nick Burns was one of the first people we saw for Nathan, and he was just very funny from the start. He could pull off a preposterous swagger that was both enjoyable but coming from a place of massive insecurity.'

Rather than scripting a series, they created characters with the actors in seemingly endless workshops, then built stories for six episodes around Nathan, the jaded hack Dan Ashcroft – played by Julian Barratt of *The Mighty Boosh* – plus his bad-tempered film director sister Claire (Claire Keelan) and the nightmarish editor Jonatton Yeah?, played by Charlie Condou. The work was so piecemeal and unstructured that even the actors didn't know what was really happening.

'I remember asking Richard Ayoade [who played arch-idiot Ned Smanks], "Have we got this? Are we actually doing it?"' says Condou, who later found more mainstream fame as *Coronation Street*'s Marcus Dent. 'He had no idea and nor did I.'

Of necessity there were research trips to Shoreditch and Hoxton, then far from the gentrified locales they are now but already testing the limits of stupidity. Material seemed to fall into their lap, like the *Vice* party where they burned all the mainstream magazines on a bonfire. One evening Condou met Tracey Emin at a party the Pet Shop Boys had thrown at Sam Taylor-Wood's studio on Redchurch Street. He told Emin how sorry he was to hear about the recent fire that had destroyed all her work. 'She just looked at me and went "meow". I was so taken aback. Did she just meow at me? Did that happen?' The next day he told Brooker and Morris about it. 'We're having that,' they said.

What had begun as Nathan's story slowly evolved into the tale of Dan Ashcroft's building animosity towards this apparently indestructible style goon, who couldn't help succeeding no matter what he did. Even when Nathan makes a total fool of himself with the Geek Pie haircut there's a Japanese TV crew nearby to decide that he's inaugurated the new wave of hair statements and anoint Nathan as a style leader. Some universal law would operate in his favour. 'Chris kept telling me, "Nathan always wins,"' says Burns.

Watching *Nathan Barley* now, the surprise is not just how durable the material is. It's the quality of the cast. The show is full of future stars, sometimes in tiny roles. 'Because of Chris and *The Day Today*, everybody wanted to be in it,' says Burns.

Nathan's assistant-victim Pingu is played by Ben Whishaw, now Q in the Bond series. Stephen Mangan appears for mere seconds as porn star Rod Senseless. And the panicking finance director who tries to stop futurist-poseur Doug Rocket (a very thinly-veiled Dave Stewart from the Eurythmics) from squandering yet more millions on his preposterous arts lab, Place., is played by Benedict Cumberbatch.

Yet *Nathan Barley* was not a success on its first transmission. Ratings began at 1.2 million but dropped to a poor 700,000 for the final episode. The decision to show a comedy about clubbers, druggers, posing scenesters and dreadful DJs on a Friday night – when its core audience was out clubbing, taking drugs, posing on their various scenes and listening to dreadful DJs – was probably not the wisest.

In the *Guardian* the show was denounced as 'five years too late … woefully out of touch' by Neil Boorman of the *Shoreditch Twat*, a fanzine aimed at real-life Barleys who possibly missed the point that *Nathan Barley* wasn't supposed to be a scrupulous reflection of Hoxton groovers but a surreal tweaking of their world. Despite the poor ratings, the people who liked the show really liked it, and talked about it long after it ended.

'We'd been told this show would only be of interest to five people in London,' says Brooker, 'but we thought there were probably Nathans – annoying, show-offy idiots who sometimes/always get away with it – back in the fourth century. He's a type.'

First DVD and then 4oD gave *Nathan Barley* an afterlife. 'Well Jackson', 'keep it dense' and Nathan's other vacuum-brained slogans began to enter the lexicon as ways to show that you fully understood the idiocy of any brave and edgy proposal before you. *Nathan Barley* is now mentioned every single day on Twitter, usually with reference to some new development in tech or fashion. 'And I don't think a day goes by without somebody shouting "Totally Mexico" at me in the street,' says Burns. 'Nathan was the best thing I've ever been involved in. I'd play him again without a second's thought.'

Despite the low ratings there was, at some point, going to be a second series. Brooker, Morris and the cast workshopped scenes in which Nathan's parents staged an intervention at last, cutting off his money and sending him to rehab. *Sugar Ape* magazine would close down and become a website after the editor Jonatton Yeah? realised it was selling no copies whatsoever. 'The basic cast are now adrift,' is how Brooker describes it, 'and Nathan is starting to worry that he's old and maybe slightly irrelevant.'

But Morris had become more interested in developing his Islamic fundamentalist comedy *Four Lions* and Brooker's TV career took off, first with *Screenwipe* and then *Dead Set* and *Black Mirror*. The first series of *Nathan Barley* had begun without any of the core cast realising they had actually started work on a TV show, the second faded away in much the same manner.

Nevertheless, it's tempting to wonder what these characters would be doing now. Nathan would have surely eased into the world of Vines and branded content, Brooker thinks, or perhaps would run some non-specific imagineering department of Google. Burns wonders if Nathan would have had some religious breakdown and gone to get his head together in the country. 'They'd all have children with stupid names by now,' he says. 'What a horrible thought.'

Jonatton Yeah? would doubtless be running some nonsensical creative consultancy. Claire Ashcroft would probably have become a commissioning editor every bit as shallow as the ones she encountered in *Nathan Barley*. As for her journo brother Dan, 'he'd either be dead or finally writing restaurant reviews for *Weekend on Sunday* magazine,' Brooker suspects. 'For the second series we thought about having Dan trying to write a novel and working as a minicab driver. Nathan infuriates him by writing a novel in three weeks. But Pingu, I like to think, would have inadvertently made more money than any of them, from some app or other. The shoe would definitely be on the other foot. That's a comforting thought.'

And there is another comforting thought about Nathan and his world. However vapid and silly he was, in his own way Nathan was almost an idealist. He and his mates represent the twilight of the style mags, the last days before you needed well-heeled connections and independent means to make it into the media. And you never hear anyone at *Sugar Ape* wanting to energise the content space for maximum brand engagement.

'You can laugh at the *Sugar Ape* team, and they are moronic,' says Steve Beale, founding editor of the late style magazine *Sleazenation*. 'But at least they were doing it for the sake of expressing themselves. Back then, the style media was a way into journalism for young talent from outside London. It was feasible then, but that door has totally closed now. Who can just move into Hoxton Square on spec now? Today the media is just a career option for

Head Boy and Head Girl types. Talent without connections and money just can't get a look in.'

Perhaps this is why *Nathan Barley* fans can still watch the show with affection. It is both an alternative vision of now and an image of the way things used to be, when you really could just ride into Shoreditch on a plastic tractor with a tiny bowler hat on your head and start some kind of a career.

But we are all self-facilitating media nodes now, if only because we all hoot our opinions into the void of social media, vainly looking for affirmation. 'Nathan just will not die,' says Burns, 'and that's pretty Nathanic in itself. Whatever happens, someone like him always comes out on top.' The idiots will always win, because maybe – like Shingy – they're actually smarter than you think they are. The future is now, and it's ridiculous. So why fight it? Instead let's raise a glass of Dutch wine to a character who is, in his own appalling way, a kind of hero. Keep it dusty, you bum pilots.

19 FEBRUARY

Skunk talking – guess who said what when high

TOM MELTZER

Channel 4 News presenter Jon Snow has described the experience of getting stoned on skunk (for a forthcoming documentary) as more terrifying than working in a war zone. See if you can tell the difference between his account of the ordeal and lines from Hunter S Thompson's notorious account of getting high in the 1970s, *Fear and Loathing in Las Vegas*.

1. 'Hallucinations are bad enough. But after a while you learn to cope with things like seeing your dead grandmother crawling up your leg with a knife in her teeth.'

2. 'There was no one in my world. I felt I had lost all control and had only the vaguest awareness of who I was and what on earth I was doing.'

3. 'How long can the body and the brain tolerate this doom-struck craziness?'

4. 'I cascaded into a very, very dark place, the darkest mental place I have ever been.'

5. 'It took me four hours to come down. Just toward the end I felt a sense of euphoria and expressed it by drawing a pastoral scene on an old box that was lying around in the lab. I drew trees, a fence, a river, and a couple of people perhaps the very people, trees and water that I had felt so deprived of while stoned.'

6. 'My hallucinations were down to a tolerable level. The room-service waiter had a vaguely reptilian cast to his features, but I was no longer seeing huge pterodactyls lumbering around the corridors in pools of fresh blood.'

7. 'I lay on the slim hi-tech rack that I knew would take me into what already appeared to me to be a tunnel of terror.'

8. 'It makes you behave like the village drunkard in some early Irish novel ... total loss of all basic motor skills: blurred vision, no balance, numb tongue, severance of all connection between the body and the brain.'

9. 'I knew within five minutes or so of taking the first two balloons, that I had taken skunk. What was happening to me outstripped anything I've ever experienced.'

10. 'The only way to prepare for a trip like this, I felt, was to dress up like human peacocks and get crazy, then screech off across the desert and cover the story.'

11. 'I've never been as overwhelmingly frightened as I was right then ... you see me blearily sitting up and hugging young Dr Rebecca for my dear life, as if she was my mother.'
12. 'Turn the goddamn music up! My heart feels like an alligator!'

Answers:
1, 3, 6, 8, 10, 12 – Hunter S Thompson
2, 4, 5, 7, 9, 11 – Jon Snow

21 FEBRUARY

Student volunteering week

MODERN TOSS

24 FEBRUARY

The city that privatised itself to death

IAN MARTIN

I wonder what in 100 years from now it will be, London. The city that privatised itself to death. Abandoned to nature, maybe, the whole place a massive, feral version of that mimsy garden bridge over the Thames currently being planned by the giggling classes. Poor London, the ancient and forgotten metropolis, crumbling slowly into an enchanted urban forest.

Imagine. In 2115, all the lab-conjured animals in Regent's Park Jurassic Zoo are free to roam, reliving their evolution. A diplodocus there, grazing in the jungled Mall. Look, a stegosaurus asleep in the ruins of Buckingham Palace. High above the forest canopy, a lone archaeopteryx soars, where once hundreds of drones glided through YouTubed firework displays.

Perhaps eminent historians will study London in the early 21st century, see how its poorer inhabitants were driven out, observe how its built environment was slowly boiled to death by privatisation. And they will wonder why people tolerated this transfer of collective wealth from taxpayers to shareholders. And they will perhaps turn their attention to Eduardo Paolozzi's fabled mosaics at Tottenham Court Road underground station.

Back in 2015, a debate bubbled briefly after some of these lovely, publicly owned mosaic murals were quietly dismantled as part of the station's thorough £400m Crossrail seeing-to. I say 'debate'; it was really only that polarised quackbait thing we have now: Click If You Think The Mosaics Are Great, We Should Save

What's Left Of Them v Smash Them Up They're Ugly, Anyway Who Cares It's Just Patterns On A Wall.

Arguments about the aesthetics of Paolozzi's mosaics missed the point, it seemed to me, which has less to do with the merit of the art itself and more to do with what, in the long run, it turned out the art was for. Paolozzi's legacy had stood intact for three decades. Not just as 1,000 sq m of charming, optimistic art, but as 1,000 sq m of commercial retardant.

You can't paste an ad on to a wallful of public art. You can't fix one of those irritating micromovies over it, telling a vacuous five-second story about investments or vitamins or hair. The Paolozzi mosaics went up as decorative art, just as privatisation was about to explode like a dirty bomb all over the public realm. What survives at Tottenham Court Road station is a brave, forlorn little seawall set against a stormtide of corporate advertising.

1982 it was, when those mosaics were unveiled. British Petroleum had already been privatised. British Aerospace, too, and a slew of others. The right to buy had been introduced a couple of years earlier. Still to come: BT, ports, buses, British Leyland, British Steel, Rover, gas, electricity, water, the railways. All those non-coloured Monopoly cards? Wait, wait, you can't privatise those, they're public utilities, clue's in the name, oh, too late. It was a free-market frenzy. Everything we owned was being flogged off by pinstriped bastards reeking of lunch.

I say 'we', although the greatest trick Thatcherism ever pulled was this redefinition of 'us and them'. Suddenly, people in your own family were voting Tory. Mrs Thatcher's chief information officer, Rupert Murdoch, was telling us that the firemen and the dustmen were our enemies. That the women of the NUT and Nalgo were the mad, selfish defenders of a doomed elite. The Tory government went after the local authorities, telling us that government itself was our enemy. You were just going: 'Hold on a minute, if you're the government ...' and then they shouted: 'Oh, God, look! The Falklands!', hired more expensive PR guys and carried on privatising. All through the reign of Margaret the Baby-Eater. Through John Major's steady-as-you-go age of dinge. And into the sunlit uplands of Blairvana where, ingeniously, the government launched a full-scale privatisation of the future: the public finance initiative. Of all the Tory policies adopted by the Labour government, none was Torier than PFI. This policy wore a black cape and a top hat. It twirled a moustache and cackled. 'Oh, you'd like a hospital? Allow me to build one for you, no charge. Just rent it back from us for, let's say, 50 years, plus service charges. Exactly, minister, why worry? You'll be out of the cabinet and on our board soon enough. Waiter! We'll see the pudding menu now ...' Instead of snapping this brittle cack in half and binning it, Labour embarked on a massive PFI expansion. Now our children owe billions to PFI shareholders, and it's no consolation at all to think that our grandchildren will, too.

But there was a time when 'we' were winning. The 'we' I always understood to be 'us', that is. The collective us. Before the privatisation of air and space. Let me tell you, little ones, about how popular music and the bright optimism of collective space came together long ago in London's heady, soot-laden, pre-privatised air of 1967. Song of the summer was 'Waterloo Sunset' by the Kinks, with its odd blend of keening melancholy and positivism. Nostalgia for a doomed postwar world, exhilaration for the coming of a new post-industrial one. Terry and Julie, facing the future unafraid. Wherever you went, it floated into earshot on a tide of treble from someone's transistor radio.

And if you were Terry and Julie gazing at a Waterloo sunset in the summer of 67, you'd have seen the Hayward Gallery under construction. The beautiful, brilliant, brutalist Hayward, part of a people's South Bank that had started with the Festival Hall in

1951 and would end triumphantly with the National Theatre in the 1970s. And we did gaze at it, thinking: 'This is us.' This is us, building something amazing, for us. Several eminent architects worked on the scheme, but oversight belonged to the GLC architects department. Imagine that. A time when most architects worked in the public sector, designing a world of public space and collective aspiration, a world of affordable housing with statutory space standards. Crazy days, when a giant yellow Aviva ad on the NT's western wall was unimaginable.

Then, suddenly, architecture, like everything else, was privatised. The 1980s saw deregulation, not only of the financial markets, but also of the professions. The number of local-authority architects plummeted under a regime of cuts; the harsh winter of recession in 1990 finished them off. From now on, space and air would be shaped and primped by the private sector. Architecture was redefined: no longer frozen music, but petrified Thatcherism. The client's brief was to choke as much value out of a site as possible, and the model was Broadgate. That shoulder-padded yuppie citadel, which unlocked so much subsequent property value in east London. It seems so weird that it's old enough now – 30 years – to be listed as a historic building itself, even as it continues to grow, ever more offices cramming in, and a fortune being made from it, somewhere, by tanned people with watchful lawyers.

Very few people now remember what was there before – Broad Street railway station and its environs. The station architecture wasn't particularly distinguished, but that wasn't the loss. It was the space, 32 acres of nationalised space and air, once managed by us as a part of a nationalised industry.

Broadgate looks great in photographs, particularly in night shots. The little central public space, the little public ice rink. Lovely. But this space was and remains a concession, a 'planning gain' to sweeten the deal. Look, nobody's suggesting that Broadgate should have been a 32-acre ornamental garden, as attractive as that sounds. Wait, actually, yeah: public gardens would have been fantastic, come to think of it. However, of course the city needs offices. And Arup's Peter Foggo, highly regarded in the profession, designed much of Broadgate. It looks pretty good, which is why the architectural historians want to save it.

But it has nothing to do with us, does it? It's privatised space and air. Broadgate became a template for capitalism. Broad Street station, British Rail, everything we owned at the time was sold off cheaply to developers, who then sanctimoniously sold us back this narrative of humane regeneration and philanthropy. Hire an eminent architect, stick a public garden in the middle, bosh. Done. We swallowed the lot. Loadsamoney, planner-friendly, enlightened patronage. Suddenly entrepreneurs were 'patrons of the arts'. Of course they were. That's where the money was.

And as more of what used to belong to 'us' was sold off and developed by 'them', the hunger for floorplates and square footage and award-winning design and river views became insatiable. If they ran out of land to build on, no problem. They would now literally monetise thin air. The principle of 'air rights' development in London was nailed by architect Terry Farrell's Embankment Place. A client could commission a great design saturated with Farrell's trademark postmodern wave-it-through-planning magic, acquire the air rights above Charing Cross station and whack a massive office block on the roof. Ingenious. A private incubus squatting on an anaesthetised public space.

Bit by bit, the city has been handed by us to them. It's now acceptable for the privatised space of a shopping centre to be patrolled by private security. There are enforceable dress codes, which is a laugh, considering those ill-fitting security uniforms. No loitering – another hypocrisy, as that's pretty much 100 per cent of a security guard's job. They'll all have Tasers soon. A 2011 London Assembly report – *Public Life in Private Hands: Managing London's Public Space* – said the mayor of London was concerned that 'there is a growing trend towards the private management of publicly accessible space. Where this type of "corporatisation" occurs, especially in the larger commercial developments, Londoners can feel themselves excluded from parts of their own city.'

That's Boris Johnson there, the freewheeling ultra-Tory ox. Like me, like us, he's having an emotional reaction to witnessing the very fabric of the city, and the air around it, and the economy around that, being aggregated into some vast equity milking parlour by the very arseholes who smashed everything to bits the last time. Obviously, the mayor simply wants them to behave in a more gentlemanly fashion, whereas some of us want them roughly arrested, electronically tagged and confined to their extinct volcano lairs, but it's nice to know we're on the same page.

Oh, man, and just look at London's privatised skyline. It would be hilarious if it wasn't so cartoonishly tragic. This one looks like a Nespresso machine. And that one, a cigar, is it? Potato? Full nappy? The utter capitulation of London's planning system in the face of serious money is detectable right there in that infantile, random collection of improbable sex toys poking gormlessly into the privatised air. Public access? Yeah, we'll definitely put a public park at the top (by appointment only). Oh, absolutely, we are ALL about community engagement: members of the public are welcome to visit our viewing gallery in the sky, that'll be 30 quid, madam.

The great modernist architectural mantra is 'form follows function'. I think we can safely call time on that one, don't you? What could possibly be going on in that skyscraper? What would compel it to resemble a Shewee? Are you kidding? Architecture, you're drunk, as usual, on one gin and tonic.

Oh, I know there are those who say it doesn't matter that all this towering sequestered air belongs to them and not to us, that ownership doesn't alter the way the world looks. Really? REALLY? I'd rather be the us who built the South Bank, than the them who built that skein of phlegm, the Shard. That scaly talon, that giant middle finger presented to us all. I loathe its banality. The view from inside is better (no visible Shard), but it feels as if you're inside some giant advert for double glazing. I loathe its monstrous, bullying scale. It's Gulliver big. End-of-level-boss big. Its stupid anything-goes-now size mocks us.

And how I loathe the rhetorical guff, as empty as that 'ultra-prime' floorspace at the top of the building itself. Its architect, Renzo Piano, calls it 'a vertical city'. Really? It's not Milton bloody Keynes, is it? A city must contain members of the public. That's basic. Well, there aren't many members of the public in the Shard, and they're easily identifiable. They're either there for drinks and dinner or they're there for a meeting. They've either got a table reservation or they're wearing a lanyard. Cities don't have guest lists. The Shard is not a city. Where's the school, the hospital, the weird newsagent's that sells tinned pies? Where's the social housing, the dodgy pub, the library? Come on.

Yet the orthodoxy prevails. London must attract investment. It mustn't upset the capricious bankers and fickle wankers of capitalism, the lease-for-lifers, the buy-to-leavers. A low, grey sky of resignation about privatisation has settled over us. But if history and economics teach us anything, it's that we have absolutely no idea what happens next.

On the current track, maybe life does become unbearable in the future, when the last remaining cubic centimetre of public space – a trembling pocket of air perhaps, in a cellar at the Emirates British Library – is finally acquired by a friend of King Charles III. At some point, there'll be no more space left to squeeze and monetise. The city's overlords will own everything. Qatari, Saudi, Russian, Indian, Chinese, some UK hedge funds named after Shakespearian characters – all air will be their air.

In the future, the thin, sad air inside the last maglev night bus to Upminster, infused with metabolised alcohol, will be theirs. The dark, luxury air in the silent bedrooms of empty riverside apartments, their identical curving blocks clustered in threes and fours, grim and silent as gill slits, will be theirs. The once sacred air of St Paul's Cathedral Spa and Pamperarium will be theirs.

Then – who knows? Maybe when London is pixellated into billions of stock-marketable units of sequestered air, boing! The world cracks and changes. Iceland acquires the north pole, discovers tons of diamonds and becomes the richest nation on earth. Ghana puts the first woman on Mars. Scientists announce they can convert rising sea levels into environmentally sustainable 'brinergy'. The global petrochemical industry suffers a fatal prolapse. Its sheiks and warlords, the fawned-upon princes who once did as they wished – buying up most of Streatham in the morning, beheading someone for sorcery in the afternoon – well, they're dust and shadow now. Maybe the global property market follows oil down the plughole. London's last human inhabitants head north, their hovertransits stuffed with electronic belongings and omniplasma, to affordable housing, a temperate climate and a hopeful, collective future.

Or – who knows? Maybe the world economy goes tits up again, only this time we punish the rich instead of the poor. London's part of a future that casts off the yoke of privatisation. Under new management. Ours. Imagine the London skyline repurposed as a collective landscape. A skyline where form no longer follows function, but where change of use might confer beauty.

Suppose those ridiculous blobs all over Waterloo's sunset had different occupants. So a child points to the Shard and asks you what it's for, and instead of trying to explain it's half-full of dicks in haircuts 'doing business', you're able to say it's subsidised housing for key workers. Does it now magically become 'architecturally beautiful'? Yes. YES.

And she points to the Gherkin and says: 'What's that?' and you say: 'It's a university.' What a beautiful world that would be. Maybe we can stop everything heading for a privatised wilderness. Let's renationalise air.

25 FEBRUARY

The Syria-bound schoolgirls aren't jihadi devil-women, they're vulnerable children

NOSHEEN IQBAL

Back in the 90s, when Britpop was a ubiquitous and unfortunate thing, every school had at least one Boyzone fan who emerged overnight as an authority on Blur. Remember how she ditched that lanky pole with greasy curtains for the closest your suburb had to a Damon Albarn lookalike (tufty hair, Adidas Gazelles)? She was average and boring, but somehow pulled the coolest boy in town, having cribbed up on *Shine* compilations and flicked through *NME*. And it was always thus: teenage girls have been changing their personalities, wardrobes and music taste for boys they fancy – teenagers of both sexes, for that matter, have been reinventing themselves – ever since the concept of being a teenager existed. In other words, do you actually remember what it was like to be 15?

This is what springs to mind as I read through many of the comment pieces on the three schoolgirls who seem to have disappeared to Syria. Leave them to rot, scream the headlines. They're colluding with evil! These jihadi devil-women know exactly what they're doing, and will get all they deserve on arrival in Syria! But does anyone actually remember, in hindsight, how stupid they were at that age?

Like the neighbours of serial killers, no one voxpopped from Bethnal Green Academy can believe it: these were three bright young people with families and a future. Why would they do this? How could they do this? 'Academically bright,' came one description from a source in the *Daily Mail*, 'but naive and vulnerable.'

They have been brainwashed by an ideology many times more threatening than a regular cult: Isis is offering religious power to its victims, selling the idea that recruits become a type of turbo-Muslim, and that theirs is a legitimate adventure because it is one sanctioned by God. Isis has Hollywood-ised war, made barbarity so blockbuster, that it looks cartoonishly unreal to a young, malleable mind. Plenty of teenagers love violence – this isn't new. The shock seems to be that girls, as well as boys, appear to have an appetite for it.

Like all predatory internet groomers, Raqqa's warriors wield a sexual power; anyone who has seen their social media feeds will understand that Isis lads brand themselves as rock stars.

Marrying one is a religiously approved way to channel the mad, hormonal energy that powers all teenagers – Muslim girls included.

Grade-A students aren't exempt from grooming. If you make that your starting point in trying to understand why three teenage girls, yet to even sit their GCSEs, would run away from home to join the world's most powerful cult, you are already one step ahead of the bile. Amira Abase, Shamima Begum and

Kadiza Sultana are British schoolgirls, two of them born and raised here.

Being savvy and confident enough to pack a duffel bag and board a flight without their parents or the authorities' knowledge doesn't make them immune from being manipulated. Being sharp and clever in class doesn't make them any less impressionable as children.

This doesn't absolve the three of responsibility – I'm betting each of them is self-aware enough to think that they're independent, acting entirely of their free will and rebelling against their parents in the most perverse way they can: by becoming more pious, more extreme, than their families would ever tolerate.

The reality is that they have barely lived. At their age, extremism and nihilism can easily take root, because real life hasn't really happened to them yet. Isis knows this; that's why it's targeting teenagers so ruthlessly.

Spitting in a full-frothed outrage over both their audacity and their stupidity doesn't make the problem go away, in the same way that trying to understand it doesn't make you an apologist for Isis. Would there be this level of contempt for a victim of sexual grooming? What would the coverage look like if three middle-class schoolgirls upped and left to fight on the frontline of Golden Dawn? It's worth asking, because the argument that we reject these girls and refuse them help is as dumb as the mistake they've clearly made.

It's difficult to remember when a 15-year-old was last taken seriously as an adult in the national press. Why are we affording three brown Muslim girls that privilege now?

2 MARCH

Following the leader

ALEXIS PETRIDIS

Steven Thomas was 37 years old when, as he puts it, 'my world ended'. He had been a Gary Glitter fan since the early 70s: '"Do You Wanna Touch Me" on *Top of the Pops*, 1973, that was it. Bam. Totally hooked.' He had seen him live umpteen times, following him doggedly as Glitter clawed his way back from bankruptcy, from performances at shabby cabaret clubs in the late 70s, to college venues, to the huge venues he started filling in the 90s: Glitter's final show, in 1997, was at Sheffield's 7,500 capacity Motorpoint arena.

Two years later, he was convicted of 54 offences of downloading child pornography and jailed for four months. 'When he got done, when the convictions came along,' says Thomas, 'I threw his autobiography in the bin, put my records in the attic.'

Years later, however, he found himself idly typing Glitter's name into YouTube. 'And it all comes back. I saw there wasn't that many videos on YouTube and I started uploading a couple of Gary Glitter tracks myself.'

Perhaps understandably, not everyone was terribly enamoured of Thomas's renewed interest in, arguably, one of the most reviled figures in British pop history. 'I started getting a bit of shit,' he says. 'A lot of my mates started getting a bit funny about things when they saw Gary Glitter videos on my Facebook page.'

Teasing or threatening? 'There's a fine line, isn't there?' he frowns. But he knew of at least one other Glitter fan who had been beaten up – 'and he's a big lad too' – so he decided to take action: deleting the videos and setting up another page under a pseudonym, where 'all my friends are Glitter fans'. He sighs. 'I believe music chooses you. The type of music, the artist, the song, it chooses you. It's not your fault if you like it or not. And Gary Glitter's music chose me.'

Today, Thomas is part of an apparently burgeoning community of die-hard Glitter fans who congregate around a number of Facebook pages. One, called Gary Glitter's Ganghouse, was set up in 2011 by 33-year-old Richard Smith, who discovered Glitter's music long after the singer's convictions: deeply improbable as it may seem, Gary Glitter is still apparently capable of attracting new fans. 'Before that, one of my favourite artists was Jerry Lee Lewis, and obviously he's a guy that comes with a reputation, he married his cousin and shot his bass player. And that never stopped me from appreciating his music. I knew what Gary Glitter had been convicted of. I don't agree with that at all. Child abuse, child pornography, these are terrible things that people deserve to go to jail for. But that's not a criticism of the music, the performance, the songs, or the production.

'What really inspired me to start the page was that I knew this was music that really excited me, and I realised it was being omitted from history, written out of history. It's not played on the radio, it's not on glam compilation albums or box sets, there wasn't a single picture of Gary in the glam exhibition at the Tate Liverpool. It's treating the public like kids, really. You know, we'll decide on your behalf what you can and can't listen to. My attitude has always been, we'll decide for ourselves, thanks very much.'

The Gary Glitter's Ganghouse Facebook page currently has nearly 7,000 likes. I stumbled across it while writing about one of the glam box sets Smith mentions: Universal's lovingly assembled *Oh Yes We Can Love*. The compilers told me they had omitted "Rock And Roll Part 2" and "I Love You Love" on the not-unreasonable grounds that the furore that including them might provoke would overshadow the whole project. I got in touch with the group because I was intrigued by this odd netherworld of fans who still refer to Glitter as 'The Leader', make their own Glitter calendars and T-shirts and arrange meet-ups to watch videos and discuss the old days, albeit clandestinely. 'I think,' says Smith, 'people are still concerned about going out in public and meeting up and going: "Hi everybody! Here for the Glitter fan convention?"'

I was intrigued by what it was like to see your idol turn into a public hate figure before your eyes; how a continued, defiant love of Glitter's music affected his fans' lives; why anyone would want to expose themselves to the kind of abuse the page inevitably attracted, despite its assurances that it 'celebrates the music ... we do not condone his crimes'.

'I mean, it's not a constant barrage, but obviously I've seen people writing in saying, "Oh, if I ever find out where you live, you're in for it", so I know those threats are out there,' says Smith. 'I'd be lying if I said it didn't concern me. I have friends and family who don't want to see me come to harm by meeting people who would be like: "You listen to Gary Glitter, you must be a fucking paedo." But that's one of the reasons we're putting ourselves out there, to chip away at that stigma.'

To my surprise, fans were only too happy to talk, as long as their names are changed: 'We want people to realise that we're not these subterranean figures in basements with child porn,' says Smith, 'we're ordinary people, with families and marriages and children, who like a bit of glam rock.' The only condition is that we don't meet in public, which is how I've ended up in a Birmingham hotel room on a Saturday morning with six Gary Glitter fans reminiscing about their favourite gigs. All except Smith are middle-aged and followed Glitter before his convictions. Most describe having a moment not unlike when Thomas dumped his albums in the attic:

'For a year or two, I was a bit kind of ... because of my daughter,' says Mary Jackson, who works in social services, 'obviously I've got my daughter, and you know ...' But then they changed their minds. Most of them have come to the conclusion outlined by James Miller, a stocky debt collector from Yorkshire. He initially 'didn't want to believe' the charges against Glitter – 'He was my hero' – but when he pleaded guilty to 54 counts of downloading internet pornography, 'you sort of wonder and scratch your head, and then I thought, well I've made my distinction now, that was Paul Gadd, that was not my Gary Glitter.'

But, occasionally, you get the queasy sense of people in denial of Glitter's crimes. Jane Green is a fortysomething shop assistant who spent a significant proportion of her teenage years hanging around soundchecks and studios where Glitter was recording: 'He was never anything other than a perfect gentleman.' She is the most outspoken of the group. It was she who made the Glitter calendars, she who 'goes out all proud' around London in a Glitter T-shirt, she who last November opened a Twitter account, @leaderisback, with the name Gary Glitter, and ended up in the *Sun* and the *Daily Mail*.

There is a moment when she starts talking, a little vaguely, about how Glitter has had 'a really rough deal' from the legal system. She starts saying something else, about Glitter's conviction in Vietnam, but Miller, perhaps realising how complaining about the rough deal meted out to a convicted paedophile is going to play with the wider world, interrupts: 'You haven't got long enough to talk about all that.'

For all their jokes about how there was a stigma attached to being a Glitter fan even before the singer's downfall, and assurances that most people are 'fine' about their undying devotion, it's clear their continued interest in Glitter has had some kind of negative impact on all their lives. Most have been sent threats via the internet. 'I got one that went: "You work in social services, you must be sick, I'm telling your employer,"' says Jackson. 'I just deleted it.'

Occasionally the threats have spilled over into real life. 'I would often get it off the smallest person in the room, because the smallest person's the one who wants to take a dig at me,' says Miller. 'I've had to walk away and not rise to it.'

Green says she was called into work and told to remove a photo of her homemade Glitter calendar from her Facebook page. 'I've had some people say to me, especially where I live now, in Gloucestershire: "You'd better watch what you say."'

So why do it? Why risk your job or your personal safety by taking a public stance about the music of a convicted paedophile? Why not just keep your memories and your music taste to yourself? The prosaic answer is that they genuinely love Glitter's music and genuinely believe that if only they can convince others to listen to it, its undeniable brilliance will overwhelm any moral objections and then, as Smith puts it: 'His music will be restored to its rightful place in history.' They trot out well-rehearsed arguments about other artists who have committed crimes yet still get played on the radio, about the impact and importance of Glitter's music in the 70s – 'Did you know he was the first artist in the history of the UK charts to debut with 11 consecutive Top 10 hits?' – about how Glitter can't actually be profiting from his music in the way the tabloids suggest because he sold parts of his back catalogue years ago.

But as they talk, another reason becomes obvious, which has less to do with Glitter's music than with them. Whatever they say about being able to separate the man from the music, these are largely people whose memories of their youth have obviously been tarnished: 'It's not just wiping him out of history is it?' says Thomas at one point. 'It's us, they're whitewashing us as well, we don't exist any more. They've nicked 15, 20 years of my history.' 'You can't take a huge chunk of your life away,' nods Jackson.

You get the feeling that they believe if they can somehow persuade the rest of the world, then those memories will regain their lustre. They grab at any scrap of information that suggests it might happen: the number of likes on Facebook, the fact that BBC4's repeats of Top of the Pops didn't excise a couple of Glitter performances from 1977, vaguely apocryphal-sounding stories about a DJ on Radio Solent who played 'Rock and Roll Part 2' on air and hosted a phone-in on whether Glitter's music should be played. To hear Green tell it, the biggest danger facing someone who chooses to walk around London in a Glitter T-shirt is that you might be trampled to death by fellow fans, eager to tell you that they think he should be back on the radio as well.

But it isn't going to happen. After I meet the die-hard fans, Glitter is charged with 10 child sex offences dating from the 70s and 80s: he is convicted of the attempted rape of an eight-year-old girl, four counts of indecent assault and having unlawful sex with a 12-year-old girl. In the wake of the conviction, Green appears in the tabloids again. Her local newspaper got wind of her 2015 Gary Glitter calendar – 'packed with sensational photos of The Leader' as her Facebook page puts it – and the *Daily Mirror* picks up on the story: the operations manager for the National Association for People Abused In Childhood claims that 'for survivors of child sexual abuse these images could put them right back in that same emotional experience, reliving it'.

The Ganghouse Facebook page stops being updated, as does its Twitter feed: one of the last messages dates from before the trial begins, encouraging fans to go to court and show their support. It turns out Smith is no longer running the Facebook page. It's nothing to do with the court case, he says, but squabbling between different factions of die-hard Glitter fans over rarities and memorabilia: amazingly, it appears that people are fighting over who gets to curate a musical legacy that no one but them seems interested in. Miller is now in charge of Gary Glitter's Ganghouse, and has decided to merge it with another Facebook group called Forever The Leader. When I speak to him, he sounds remarkably upbeat for a man whose idol will more than likely spend the rest of his life in prison. Likes on the Ganghouse page are going up again, he says, even though he's not updating it. He claims that after 'an initial few days', the abuse has died down: 'There's not been as big a backlash as expected.' He insists the latest convictions don't change anything: 'Everybody that you met has the same thoughts. It's about the music, the entertainer.'

Nevertheless, he now concedes, Glitter's music is never going to get back on the radio: 'Even if the convictions were overturned, it's not going to happen. There's never, ever going to be acceptance.'

Even so, 'there's still an awful lot of fans out there', some of whom are apparently organising mass download campaigns to try to force Glitter's music back into the charts. Of course people are going to criticise them, but they're 'mindless minorities', people who believe everything they read in the *Sun*, online trolls. 'Whatever good the internet has been,' he says, heavily, 'it's given the voice to some right idiots out there.'

All names have been changed

7 MARCH

Global crisis: why we put the climate on the cover

ALAN RUSBRIDGER

Journalism tends to be a rear-view mirror. We prefer to deal with what has happened, not what lies ahead. We favour what is exceptional and in full view over what is ordinary and hidden.

Famously, as a tribe, we are more interested in the man who bites a dog than the other way round. But even when a dog does plant its teeth in a man, there is at least something new to report, even if it is not very remarkable or important.

There may be other extraordinary and significant things happening – but they may be occurring too slowly or invisibly for the impatient tick-tock of the newsroom or to snatch the attention of a harassed reader.

Even more complex, there may be things that have yet to happen. If it is not yet news – if it is in the realm of prediction and speculation – it is difficult for a news editor to cope with.

For these and other reasons, changes to the Earth's climate rarely make it to the top of the news list. They may be happening too fast for comfort, but they happen too slowly for the newsmakers – and for most readers.

Yet these events that have still to materialise may dwarf anything journalists have had to cover over the past troubled century. There may be untold catastrophes just around the corner. But that is futurology, not news, so it is not going to force itself on any front page any time soon.

Even when the overwhelming majority of scientists wave a big red flag in the air, they tend to be ignored. Is this new warning too similar to the last? Is it all too frightening to contemplate? Is a collective shrug of fatalism the only rational response?

The climate threat features very prominently on the front page of the *Guardian* even though nothing exceptional happened today. It will be there again next week and the week after. You will, I hope, be reading a lot about our climate over the coming weeks.

One reason for this is personal. This summer I am stepping down after 20 years of editing the *Guardian*. Over Christmas I tried to anticipate whether I would have any regrets once I no longer had the leadership of this extraordinary agent of reporting, argument, investigation, questioning and advocacy.

Very few, I thought, except this: that we had not done justice to this huge, overshadowing, overwhelming issue of how climate change will probably, within the lifetime of our children, cause untold havoc and stress to our species.

So, in the time left to me as editor, I thought I would try to harness the *Guardian*'s best resources to describe what is happening and what, if we do nothing, is almost certain to occur.

We will assume that the scientific consensus about man-made climate change and its likely effects is overwhelming. We will leave the sceptics and deniers to waste their time challenging the science. The mainstream argument has moved on to the politics and economics.

The coming debate is about what governments can do to attempt to regulate, or otherwise stave off, the now predictably terrifying consequences of global warming beyond 2˚C by the end of the century, and how we can prevent the states and corporations that own the remaining reserves of coal, gas and oil from being allowed to dig most of it up.

There are three simple numbers which explain this, and if you have even more appetite for the subject, read the July 2012 *Rolling Stone* piece by Bill McKibben, which – building on the work of the Carbon Tracker Initiative – first spelled them out.

2˚C: There is overwhelming agreement that a rise in temperatures of more than 2˚C by the end of the century would lead to disastrous consequences for any kind of recognised global order.

565 gigatons: 'Scientists estimate that humans can pour roughly 565 more gigatons of carbon dioxide into the atmosphere by mid-century and still have some reasonable hope of staying below 2˚C,' is how McKibben puts it.

2,795 gigatons: This is the amount of carbon dioxide that if they were burned would be released from the proven reserves of fossil fuel – ie the fuel we are planning to extract and use.

You do not need much of a grasp of maths to work out the implications. There are trillions of dollars' worth of fossil fuels currently underground which, for our safety, simply cannot be extracted and burned. This was the starting point for the group of journalists who met early in January to start considering how we would cover the issue.

But how? Some will make the case for governmental action. Within nine months, the nations of the world will assemble in Paris. Can they find the right actions and words where they have failed before? It is important that they feel the pressure to achieve real change.

Others will make the case for reducing the fossil fuel exposure of investment portfolios, or full divestment from the most polluting fossil fuel extraction companies. Next week, McKibben will describe how the cause of divestment is for banks and fund managers. It is now on the radar of the financial director rather than the social responsibility department. If most of these reserves are unburnable, they are asking, then what does that say about the true value of carbon-dependent companies?

We will look at who is getting the subsidies and who is lobbying. We will name the worst polluters and find out who funds them. We will urge enlightened trusts, investment specialists, universities, pension funds and businesses to take their money away from companies posing the biggest risk to us. And we will report on how Guardian Media Group itself is getting to grips with the issues.

In addition to words, images and films, we will be podcasting the series, to give some insight and transparency about our reporting. We begin today and on Monday with two extracts from the introduction to Naomi Klein's recent book, *This Changes Everything*. This has been chosen because it combines sweep, science, politics, economics, urgency and humanity. Antony Gormley has contributed two artworks that have not been exhibited before – the first of many artists with whom we hope to collaborate.

Where does this leave you? I hope not feeling impotent and fearful.

Some of you may be marching in London today. As McKibben will argue next week, the fight for change is also full of opportunity and optimism. And we hope that many readers will find inspiration in our series to make their own contribution by applying pressure on their workplace, or pension fund, to move.

Most of all, please read what we write. Real change can only follow from citizens informing themselves and applying pressure. To quote McKibben: 'This fight, as it took me too long to figure out, was never going to be settled on the grounds of justice or reason. We won the argument, but that didn't matter: like most fights it was, and is, about power.'

12 MARCH

Don't weep for Clarkson – his friends will look after him

HADLEY FREEMAN

Jeremy Clarkson, voice of the people/mega-sized tool (delete as appropriate to you, dear reader) has, you might have heard, got himself into a spot of trouble – again! The wee scamp. He's such a rebel, you know. It's really great to have Jeremy fighting in our corner for that under-represented demographic, the self-entitled, middle-aged white man who just wants to beat up on those in a less privileged position than him – from ethnic minorities to a producer who, we are now told, failed to provide Jezza's din-dins on demand.

The blogger Guido Fawkes, a true revolutionary firebrand if there ever was one, has already started a petition to bring back Clarkson, and I personally could not applaud this more. I think we in Britain can all feel a little bit of pride in the fact that, at the time of writing, about half a million people have signed a petition demanding the reinstatement of an insanely wealthy man who is alleged to have physically assaulted a junior colleague.

Sure, the world might have laughed at Christian Bale when he lost his temper to a hilarious extent at a director of photography in 2009. But when a towering mega-talent such as Clarkson gets suspended for throwing a punch at a producer when he doesn't get fed, well, I think we all have to stand back and say, 'Political correctness has just gone too far in this country!'

As many commenters have already pointed out on the *Times* website – a website where they have to pay to leave such words of wisdom, remember – *Top Gear* is literally the only show on television for men. The only one! Honestly, the rest of the TV schedule is just overrun with middle-aged women talking about feminism and vaginas, 24/7. To get rid of Jeremy is just part and parcel of the feminazi thought-police tactics that are strangling this country, and it's unacceptable.

I think what Jeremy's detractors (which probably means you, you pinko *Guardian* readers) are missing when they run him down is that the man is, in fact, a genius. Granted, he does not talk, act or look like one, but let's look at this in detail. I once assumed that, like tripe and the appeal of the Gallagher brothers, Clarkson was something that appealed only to British people. Like most airy assumptions I make about the human race, I soon learned that this one was based purely on my own narcissistic naivety.

But the deeply lucrative global popularity of *Top Gear* is not our subject today. Rather, Clarkson's genius lies in his skill at styling himself as the maverick, the unfairly maligned, say-it-like-it-is outsider, when the only way he could be more inside is if he gave himself a proctology exam. He is the Nigel Farage of TV presenters: just as Farage (public-school educated former banker married to a German) presents himself as the man of the European Union-loathing people, so Clarkson styles himself as the decent geezer who has the terrible misfortune to work for the Thought Police – I mean the BBC – who keep trying to tamp him down.

And yet I really am struggling to think of anyone else who has repeatedly used racial slurs on international TV and still brought home an estimated £3m annual earnings. It is absolutely in character that Clarkson is, judging from his larky Twitter feed, absolutely revelling in his suspension, because it feeds into this pose of his, just as media attacks on Ukip feed into that of Nigel Farage.

I don't know if this insider-as-faux-outsider is a uniquely British trick, but it is one that is remarkably effective here (see also Russell Brand). At least in the US, when you come across a self-styled outsider politician he is, for better or worse, genuinely out there, like the loopy libertarian Ron Paul, with his belief that heroin should be decriminalised – not an old Etonian and Oxbridge graduate like Boris Johnson.

Just as a quick reminder: Jeremy Clarkson is the highest paid presenter at the BBC, not a corporation known for stinting on the salaries of its star presenters (producers expected to provide food for such well-remunerated presenters get, one suspects, slightly smaller pay cheques). When the BBC bought out Clarkson's stake in the production company specifically set up to make more money out of *Top Gear*'s endless commercial opportunities, he was given so much cash he probably could have built a car out of £100 notes. And, you know, it would have driven better than a Japanese car – amirite, Jezza?! The only surprising element to this latest development in the story that I call The Picaresque Adventures of Jeremy is that the BBC finally found the gumption to actually suspend him, its deeply valued cash cow. Still, at least the Clarkson saga has taught us where the BBC draws its line in the sand: racism: OK, physical violence: not OK.

And then there are Jeremy's friends. It must be a source of sadness to Hieronymus Bosch that he died too soon to include in his 15th-century painting *Hell* the true image of damnation: a 2010 Chipping Norton dinner party with darling David and Samantha Cameron, hilairz Rebekah and Charlie Brooks, fabulous Elisabeth Murdoch and Matthew Freud, crazy Alex James and a block of cheese, and Jeremy Clarkson. Just imagine the banter!

David: So I was on the phone yesterday with my good mate Barry Obama –

Jeremy: Rebekah, do you think the *Sun* would have a recording? I'd love to listen to it with Elisabeth's father.

Everyone: Oh Jeremy! Hahaha!

Charlie: More fizz, anybody?

Alex: Has anyone tried my cheese yet? It's made from the milk of French cows –

Jeremy: Yes, and like all things French it's limpwristed and useless. If a German was here it would immediately surrender itself.

Everyone: Oh, Jeremy! Hahaha!

Jeremy: Seriously, that cheese is about as effective as a Citroen. If the Third Reich took over Chipping Norton ... [continues and repeats joke forever].

So, I come here not to bury Jeremy Clarkson – the endeavour would be impossible, for the man is like Piers Morgan in his Teflon tendencies. Rather, I come to celebrate him and his lucrative talent at playing the outsider on the inside. Do not weep for his departure, Britain. With his political nous, not to mention his circle of friends, he'll probably be the new MP for Kensington and Chelsea. Keep it real, Jeremy!

24 MARCH

'I am here to stay...': immigrants in their own words

INTRODUCTION BY HUGH MUIR

Immigration is weaved throughout the fabric of British society but, by tradition and custom, the colours are muted. Immigrants who have made their mark become part of the mainstream story. That is as it should be. But it also allows the uninformed and those of malign intent to pose the rhetorical question: what have immigrants ever done for us?

The forthcoming election threatens to become a referendum on the challenges of recent mass immigration. Amid the clamour, this special issue gives voice to people who have come to live in the UK, chosen from over 100 whose testimonies we have published online in our *Immigrants In Their Own Words* interactive. Today, they control their stories. What they say is instructive.

They tell us about themselves and their journeys from every continent; trajectories beginning in places such as Jamaica, Bulgaria, Iraq, New Zealand, the US, India, Pakistan, Bangladesh and Afghanistan. They tell us why they came and, in so doing, they urge us to think a little about ourselves. Read the front pages of the tabloids and you might believe that immigrants' dominant motivations are to appropriate council houses, siphon benefits and impoverish the NHS. Among our voices are those who came to study, to work in the health service, those who came to teach, those who came to bolster our economy with businesses.

But there are also those for whom the attraction was less a matter of practicalities, more a pilgrimage towards an idea. The woman for whom the lure was a love of Shakespeare. The people who saw in Britain a chance to be themselves. 'Britain offered indefinite leave to remain for same-sex couples, so it was the only place where we could go to stay together,' one respondent told us. Repeatedly, they raise the things we take for granted. 'To appreciate the NHS you need to realise how sickness comes without a warning and takes away all your life's earnings, which is a reality for 80 per cent of this world,' said one respondent, an Indian-born surgeon.

We asked people to upload their photos, videos and comments via our platform for readers' content, GuardianWitness and also a secure form for those who wished to remain anonymous because of the sensitive nature of their experience. We worked with migration organisations to contact non-English speakers and had reporters contact others – such as an Afghani translator who worked for the British army and now seeks asylum.

When public figures and a poisonous media jostle to be tough on immigration, tough on immigrants, there is inevitable cause and effect. 'I have to deal with prevailing Islamophobia, the rise of the BNP and anti-immigration rhetoric,' one respondent tells us. 'The Home Office has, in seven years, denied three of my visa applications, and I have had a constant fight to remain,' says another. They mention Ukip, they mention Nigel Farage. Neither emerges with much credit.

'You never hear on the news about how migrant students are contributing to the economy but rather about how immigrants come here to steal jobs or commit delinquencies,' is one lament.

That may be true 364 days of the year. Thankfully, it isn't today.

'I teach them eastern European songs, they teach me "Ye Banks and Braes o' Bonnie Doon"':
I'm a curious person. I've always wanted to learn new languages and experience different cultures. I spoke German so I was thinking of living in a German-speaking country but my boyfriend migrated to Scotland so I followed him from Poland. I'm really glad that it turned out this way!

It wasn't easy with only a few phrases in English but that was enough to get a factory job. I also worked as a cleaner, and whenever possible I'd be working with my earphones on, listening to countless English-language programmes. I also volunteered in various places to improve my speaking skills and to find out more about life here. Those efforts, together with a language course at college, brought my English to a good standard within just two years. Life has been spoiling me ever since.

Glasgow is my place. I'm surrounded by some wonderful people. We come together, I teach them various eastern European songs, they teach me 'Ye Banks and Braes o' Bonnie Doon' and 'Comin' thro' the Rye'. We dance ceilidh and read poetry in all sorts of languages. And my friend Annie's homemade soup is the best ever! I've found my tribe in Glasgow. The city is so green and it's perfect for cycling. And I can teach Polish here. Who would have thought? I believe people who are generally happy are likely to have a happy life anywhere they go. I was happy in Poland too. But now I belong to Glasgow. And Glasgow belongs to me.

MARZANNA

'I was receiving threats from the Taliban':
Life in Afghanistan was very bad for those people who worked with the international security assistance force (Isaf). After the war, the situation got even worse. As an interpreter I used to go out on missions with the British army. I would work for six to eight months, and then would have a vacation. I would go to the fish shop or get kebabs and go to the park on picnics with my friends and talk, and see my family. I left as I was receiving threats from the Taliban because I was an interpreter for the British and American army. Ever since I got here I believed that the UK government would be proud of me and I was 100 per cent sure that the UK government would protect me and will give me shelter, but I was wrong. I miss my country and I am so sad for the situation of my country. It is getting worse and worse, day by day. I miss my mum.

I served the British army in Afghanistan; I saved their lives and I was at the frontline with them, so today I need help for my safety. The Taliban are targeting the interpreters because the interpreters are key for the Isaf – without us they can't go out for a single mission. I am asking why the UK government turned their back to me and said that my life is not in danger, even though I have given them proof and evidence?

ANONYMOUS

'The UK authorities have made me a hopeless person':
As a journalist in Iraq I did not have a safe environment. I was born in the northern city of Iraq, Kirkuk, in 1980, a year before the war started between Iraq and Iran. I still remember the Gulf war in Iraq in 1991, when, as Kurds, we fled Iraq to Iran for the second time since 1974. Between 1991 and 2003, Iraqis suffered all kinds of poverty, corruption and lack of health service. After the US and British invasion in 2003, a new phase was revealed. The external forces into Iraq have directed Iraqis to another agony, and the press was censored. Human Rights Watch stated that more than 3,000 academics, journalists and doctors were killed between 2003 and 2010. They were targeted by the local authorities and extremist Islamic groups. Neither the Americans nor the British in Iraq could prevent the abuse and killing of civilians.

My journalism activities in Baghdad and Kirkuk had pressured me and I noticed the real danger of my stay in Iraq. But in Britain the Home Office dismissed that, despite all the evidence I submitted. As an asylum seeker, we are victim of two wars: the terrorist war on the people of Iraq and the war of injustice in Britain.

Seeking asylum is viewed as seeking financial support, seeking accommodation and seeking benefit. But in fact, it is about seeking protection under international law and the Geneva Convention of 1951. The conflicts and political crisis in Iraq had forced me to flee Iraq and never look back again, on the other hand, the treatment that I have received from the authorities in the UK has made me a hopeless person.

A rational question for the Home Office: how do they expect a refused asylum seeker to survive without any support? Is that what they call protection?

I cannot be convinced. Living without hope is my daily life.

For the above reasons, Britain is not great for me at any point.

RZHWAN JAFF

'The concept of clean water amazed me':
Living in a war-zone with no sense of security or stability, it was only right for me, along with many other Somali citizens, to seek refuge elsewhere. The UK boasted basic necessities which, back then, seemed immense. The concept of clean water amazed me, but what really built my appreciation for the UK was its stability – it was a place where you were sure that a grenade wouldn't destroy everything the next second. I had to go. Once I arrived in the UK, a sudden sense of relief overcame me. There was a stark contrast between life in Somalia and the minutes I had spent in the UK, where I was sure of my security. Everything was strangely calm; this was something I hadn't experienced since years before the civil war started in Somalia in 1991.

Luckily for me, I spoke moderately fluent English so this eased my transition into British life to some extent. However, a large proportion of Somali refugees I knew spoke limited English so this posed a serious problem. I went with them on their journey to learn English and the British way of life, helping me build on the English I knew but also allowing me to identify with others in this country. The first thing that I realised was that I had a lot in common with British people, and that the Somali community is not as different as I first presumed.

I began to reflect on my life before Britain and the multitude of opportunities that the UK gave refugees, many of them basic necessities that we cannot take for granted. I believe that just as I did, many Somalians realised that it is crucial that we give back. For me, this meant working for a charity to help my local community.

HUSSEIN MOHAMED HASSAN

'The utter sense of isolation ... words can't do it justice':
I came with my parents in 1995. We emigrated because my father had got a prestigious research position at the University

of Cambridge. My father earned far less in the UK as a researcher than he did as a doctor in China. It did eventually help his career to be here, but our quality of life plummeted from what we had been used to in China.

My mother found it very difficult to find work because her English was much poorer than my father's. She suffered depression from being cut off from family and friends in an era when long-distance phone calls were very expensive. She didn't know how to do some of the most basic things that most people in this country seem to think are intuitive. She didn't understand that she had to register us with a GP or a dentist. Her depression was never treated appropriately. She couldn't use a credit card or ATM. She didn't understand how to use the checkout at the supermarket.

We had no emotional support. I would try to describe the utter sense of isolation, but words can't do it justice. When my mum did find work, she used to just leave me alone at home because she couldn't get anyone to babysit. I would just sit at home and cry for hours.

Life did improve gradually. My father was able to re-qualify as a doctor. My mother got a degree in computer science and now has a steady job and a sense of self-worth. I think the biggest improvement was when we moved to a much bigger city than Cambridge, where there were more Chinese people, Chinese shops, a Chinatown. We made friends and put down roots, and now my parents spend a lot of time supporting new immigrants (mostly students).

As much as we tried our best to assimilate, it's very difficult to cross that cultural boundary. For example, my parents never understood the concept of going to the pub after work – they still don't. When politicians deplore a lack of assimilation and blame ethnic minorities for forming ghettos, I always want to point out that British expats are doing the exact same thing in Dubai,

China, Spain etc. Assimilation is very difficult, and the government is not doing anything positive to encourage it. In fact, the free English classes that helped my mother two decades ago have now disappeared.

As for me, I went back to Cambridge for university and I am now working in London as a doctor. I can't say whether my life would have been better had I not emigrated, but I feel that the UK is my home.

ANONYMOUS

26 MARCH

The black spider memos: a victory for the rule of law, a warning to Prince Charles

GUARDIAN LEADER

When a man of cranky interests picks up his fountain pen, the result is, very often, nothing of any consequence. Occasionally, he will be eccentrically right, and may even get others to see this by obstinate repetition; more often he will – whether fairly or not – run into irritation and brush-off replies. When the man in question is heir to the throne, however, the reaction might well be different, and questions of crowning importance arise.

For a decade, the Guardian has pursued Prince Charles's 'black spider memos' to seven Whitehall departments because it's as well to know how the man who will be king interacts with what will, however preposterously, one day be called 'his' government.

Officials, a commissioner, divisional court judges and – ultimately – the attorney general wove a web of secrecy around the correspondence. On Thursday, however, the supreme court stood by the tribunal that had originally ruled that the letters should be released.

The ruling was, as it usually is when things reach the highest court, on a point of law. The decision was that the former attorney general Dominic Grieve was not empowered to issue a certificate blocking the tribunal's ruling, which may sound like a narrow point. But as Lord Neuberger wrote in the judgment, it could hardly be more important. In his scramble to spare the prince's blushes, not a scramble that would have been made for anyone else, Mr Grieve was, as a government minister, seeking to overrule the tribunal's meticulous verdict reached after hearing extensive argument. And in doing that, he trampled on two aspects of the rule of law: first, that the ruling of the courts is binding; second, that it is for the courts to review executive actions, not the other way round.

Mr Grieve is a meticulous and intelligent lawyer, so it is particularly striking that – by dint of his seat in the government – he felt obliged to engage in this ridiculous dance to keep private the prince's meddling in public affairs. We don't know the contents of any of the letters just yet, nor even exactly what we will eventually see, after Downing Street's promised 'preparatory work' with the black marker pen. But on the strength of the effort expended on the right royal cover-up thus far, it seems a fair guess that officials and ministers will have given the prince's letters rather more favourable attention than routine correspondence with a member of the public.

Secrecy always stirs thoughts of intrigue, but let's not get too carried away about what's likely to be in the letters. The prince has, after all, hardly kept his hobby horses bolted up in the stables over the years. Old-fashioned architecture, old-fashioned food, ecology and a somewhat spiritual approach to life and health are the familiar Carolingian themes, and mostly benign enough in isolation, even if in combination they betray regret about the fact of the industrial revolution. The issue, however, really isn't the merit or otherwise of this or that princely opinion, only the propriety – or not – of his efforts to secure a special hearing.

Modernising monarchists, if such oxymoronic creatures exist, might argue that it's unreasonable to ask the prince to pretend, as his mother doggedly has, that there is no room for personal opinion between the ears of the head of state. In more open times the next monarch should, they might say, be entitled to his views, just so long as he understands that it's the government's duty to govern, and his to keep calm and carry on. This argument, however, really can't stand without applying the openness prin-ciple to the dealings of the next monarch himself. A provocative speech for a good cause might be allowed; a missive on the quiet never could.

The true logic of what we like to think is a democratic era, however, surely points in another direction. If it is accepted that the head of state is going to have opinions, and perhaps give them an airing for time to time, then – for a newspaper of principled republicanism, at least – the answer is clear. Not any longer to allow the job to be filled by accident of birth, but instead to select for the post by democratic means. Perhaps that is a discussion for another day. But after Thursday's ruling, the immediate point is simply that mail that comes on his majesty's service must no longer be kept from his majesty's subjects.

Spring

Troll army behind Putin's phoney war

SHAUN WALKER

Just after 9pm each day, a long line of workers files out of 55 Savushkina Street, a modern four-storey office complex with a small sign outside that reads 'Business centre'. Having spent 12 hours in the building, the workers are replaced by another large group, who will work through the night.

The nondescript building has been identified as the headquarters of Russia's 'troll army', where hundreds of paid bloggers work round the clock to flood Russian internet forums, social networks and the comments sections of western publications with remarks praising Vladimir Putin and raging at the depravity and injustice of the west.

The *Guardian* spoke to two former employees of the troll enterprise, one of whom was in a department running fake blogs on the social network LiveJournal, and one who was part of a team that spammed municipal chat forums around Russia with pro-Kremlin posts. Both said they were employed unofficially and paid in cash.

They painted a picture of a humourless and draconian work environment, with fines for being a few minutes late or not reaching the set number of posts each day. Trolls worked in rooms of about 20, each controlled by three editors, who checked posts and imposed fines if the words had been cut and pasted, or were ideologically deviant.

The LiveJournal blogger, who spent two months working at the centre until mid-March, said she was paid 45,000 roubles (£520,

$790) a month, to run a number of accounts on the site. There was no contract – the only document she signed was a non-disclosure form. She was ordered not to tell her friends about the job, nor to add any of them to the social media accounts she ran.

'We had to write "ordinary posts", about making cakes or music tracks we liked, but every now and then throw in a political post about how the Kiev government is fascist, or that sort of thing.'

Scrolling through one of her LiveJournal accounts, the pattern is clear. Posts about 'Europe's 20 most beautiful castles' and 'signs that show you are dating the wrong girl' are interspersed with political posts about Ukraine or suggesting that the Russian opposition leader Alexei Navalny is corrupt.

Instructions for the political posts would come in 'technical tasks' that the trolls received each morning, while the non-political had to be thought up.

'The scariest thing is when you talk to your friends and they are repeating the same things you saw in the technical tasks, and you realise that all this is having an effect,' the former employee said.

Marat, 40, worked in a different department, where employees went methodically through chat forums in various cities, leaving posts. 'First thing in the morning, we'd come in, turn on a proxy server to hide our location, and then read the technical tasks we had been sent,' he said.

The trolls worked in teams of three. The first would leave a complaint about some problem or other, or simply post a link, then the other two would wade in, using links to articles on Kremlin-friendly websites and 'comedy' photographs lampooning western or Ukrainian leaders with abusive captions.

Marat showed six of his technical task sheets to the *Guardian*. Each has a news line, some information about it, and a 'conclusion' that the commenters should reach. One is on Putin offering his condolences to President Hollande after the *Charlie Hebdo* shootings.

'Vladimir Putin contacted the French leader immediately, despite the bad relations between Russia and the west,' reads the section explaining the conclusion the troll posts should reach. 'The Russian leader has always stood against aggression and terrorism in general. Thanks to the president's initiatives, the number of terrorist acts inside Russia has decreased dramatically.'

The desired conclusion of one reads: 'The majority of experts agree that the US is deliberately trying to weaken Russia, and Ukraine is being used only as a way to achieve this goal. If the Ukrainian people had not panicked and backed a coup, the west would have found another way to pressure Russia. But we will fight for our sovereignty on the international stage.'

To add colour to their posts, websites have been set up to aid the troll army. One features thousands of pasteable images, mainly of European leaders in humiliating photoshopped incidents or with captions pointing out their stupidity, or showing Putin making hilarious wisecracks and winning the day.

Many of them have obvious racist or homophobic overtones. Barack Obama eating a banana or depicted as a monkey, or the Ukrainian president, Petro Poroshenko, in drag, declaring: 'We are preparing for European integration.' The trolls have to post the photographs together with information they can pull from a website marketed as a 'patriotic Russian Wikipedia'.

The entries for the Maidan revolution in Kiev explain that all the protesters were fed special tea laced with drugs, which is what caused the revolution.

'I would go home at the end of the day and see all the same items on the television news. It was obvious that the decisions were coming from somewhere,' said Marat.

After two months of working in the troll agency, Marat began to feel he was losing his sanity, and decided he had to leave. From the snatched conversations over coffee, he noted that the office was split roughly 50/50 between those who believed in what they were doing, and those who thought it was stupid but wanted the money. Occasionally, he would notice people changing.

'If every day you are feeding on hate, it eats away at your soul. You have to be strong to stay clean when you spend your day submerged in dirt,' he said.

The most prestigious job in the agency is to be an English-language troll, for which the pay is 65,000 roubles (£640, $1000). As he spoke decent English, Marat was sent for a test in the English language department, where he had to write a one-page text in English about his political views. Not wanting to overdo it, he wrote that he was apolitical, and thought all politics were cynical. It was not good enough to pass.

Before he was told he had failed, however, others in the room who passed were set to work composing comments on two English-language articles about Ukraine – one by the *New York Times*, the other by CNN.

Lawyers in St Petersburg said it was extremely rare for such a big enterprise to be working on the 'black economy'. Leaked documents have linked the company running the troll factory to structures close to the Kremlin, but there has been no hard evidence.

It is unclear whether the St Petersburg troll hub is the only one, but what does seem clear is that the enterprise has grown enormously since it was discovered two years ago.

'When I got the job there in 2013 it was a small building, I was working in the basement, and they didn't have enough space,' said Andrei Soshnikov, a St Petersburg journalist who infiltrated the company two years ago.

He linked the move to a much bigger office to the Ukraine crisis, and said that, while the trolling can seem farcical, it would be naive to write it off as ineffectual.

'People of my generation who grew up with the internet can perhaps spot the troll comments easily. But for the older generation, they look at all these forums and networks, and it turns out that everyone else out there is even more radical than they are.'

4 APRIL

Political Blind Date

INTERVIEW BY ABIGAIL RADNOR

Natalie Bennett, leader of the Green party, meets Jacob Rees-Mogg, Conservative MP for North East Somerset

NATALIE ON JACOB

First impressions? He is a very urbane, pleasant individual on a personal level. I'm sure he means well.

What did you talk about? Political reform, agriculture and, on my insistence, about poverty and the way this government has treated disabled people. We then did a little bit of personal stories exchange. I was interested in his childhood, and I guess he was a little interested in mine, since they are very different.

What did you agree on? We agreed there is much wrong with our current economic system, although we might disagree entirely on the solutions. We agree on supporting farmers, but very much disagree on the nature of the farming that we need to support.

What did you disagree on? We fundamentally disagreed on the impact of this government on poor people, particularly the lives of disabled people. I think that perhaps his constituency isn't representative of the whole country.

Any awkward moments? No, he is obviously a man who is very socially comfortable and who has been brought up to navigate through them.

Would you introduce him to your colleagues? It would certainly introduce a lot of my work colleagues to a different kind of life, one we don't have many encounters with.

And what about your friends? Most of them would find him entertaining, but possibly also quite frustrating. I suspect the arguments would get quite heated.

Why should people vote for him? I am not sure I can think of a positive answer to that question.

Why shouldn't they vote for him? Well, if you're thinking of your local MP as a representative of you, who understands your problems, I don't think there is anything in his life experience or philosophy that answers the problems of 99 per cent of the British population.

Describe his politics in three words: I am going to go with one phrase rather than three words: for the 1 per cent, for the finance sector, not attached to reality.

What do you think he made of you? Because he is a very polite man, it is hard to tell.

Would you form a coalition? No.

If you could change one thing about the date, what would it be? It would have been good to meet somewhere a bit more real, such as in a working man's cafe. A £1 cup of stewed tea might have been a new experience for him.

Marks out of 10? 5. He is what he is and he's honest about that.

Would you meet again? I very much hope we meet again in the Commons when I am MP for Holborn and St Pancras. I would expect there would be some issues – perhaps some forms of supportive agriculture – we could vote the same way on. You can find points of agreement with nearly everybody on some issue. I am not sure that we identified a particular bill, and I very much disagree with his filibustering on sustainable agriculture. But I am sure there would be something.

JACOB ON NATALIE

First impressions? Natalie is a highly intelligent person. Very capable. I knew of her as an effective campaigner, and she absolutely lived up to expectations. Her views diverge with mine somewhat.

What did you talk about? We started off with localism and moved on to agriculture and energy. There is a difference in priorities.

What did you agree on? Localism: we want to get powers as far down the chain as possible, and we agreed on the importance of agriculture, although we would go about it in very different ways.

What did you disagree on? The priority we give to people's standard of living against the environment. My priority is individuals in my constituency who want to be able to heat their homes and feed themselves as cheaply as possible. Natalie would prefer to put the environment and carbon emissions at a higher priority than that. The Green party admits that standards of living would not rise and the economy would not grow if their policies were followed, so it's not as if they're trying to pretend. The thing I like about the Green party is that it is very honest about what it would do, and that makes for a good political argument.

Any awkward moments? No, it was a friendly conversation between two people who knew they weren't going to agree and therefore it was more of a pleasant surprise when we did, rather than a shock when we didn't.

Why should people vote for her? The electorate should vote for her if they believe that we are on the cusp of an environmental catastrophe that will be solved only by a significant reduction in our standard of living.

Why shouldn't they vote for her? Because the economic policy of the Green party would be ruinous for the nation. We would face a serious governmental financial crisis within a pretty short order.

Would you introduce her to your colleagues? Happily. It's great discussing things with people who do agree with you, and that's a very nice way of spending an evening, but actually, it's important to discuss things with people who not only strongly believe in opposing ideas, but also have the arguments lined up for what they believe in – and then to see if, by the end of it, you think they are right. Politicians get into a lot of trouble for U-turns, but actually a U-turn is a sign of a subtle mind, and we ought to be more open to people changing their minds. Having said that, nothing in the discussion has changed my mind.

Would you introduce her to your friends? I'd be delighted to. Not only is she intelligent, but she is also charming, friendly and not instinctively hostile to a Tory, which is very reassuring.

Describe her politics in three words: Old-style socialism.

What do you think she made of you? No idea. To see oneself as others see one is a great gift, but not one I necessarily have.

Would you form a coalition? I think it would be impossible for Conservatives to form a coalition with the Greens. Their economic policy is so far away from ours. The Greens are the natural allies of the Labour party, in the way that Ukip are the natural allies of the Conservatives: the Greens are essentially part of the broadly left vote and Ukip part of the broadly Conservative vote.

The coalition with the Lib Dems was possible because the Lib Dems have two strains: the classic liberal strain, which is essentially Peelite and quite conservative, and the Social Democrat strain, which is closer to Labour so they could emphasise one bit of their personality to do a deal with either side. The Greens don't have a strand that is any way small-c conservative.

If you could change one thing about the date, what would it be? I might have had another coffee.

Marks out of 10? 10. She would be a formidable political opponent, and we need to make sure we've got our arguments at the ready, not to be overrun by greenery.

Would you meet again? I would be delighted to. Before I got into parliament, I had a vision of people from having seen them on television – I expected that meeting them would be more difficult. I thought they would not necessarily want to engage with a Conservative, but I've found that there is a great deal of friendly interchange between people from different parties.

7 APRIL

A Marxist *Game of Thrones*

PAUL MASON

The elite are in trouble, their sources of wealth exhausted, their civilisation assailed by crazed fanatics from without – while, within, the masses are in open revolt. No, it's not the eurozone – it is Westeros, the mythical venue for *Game of Thrones*.

It was JRR Tolkien, the father of fantasy fiction, who summed up the attraction of a genre that has become, in the past 60 years, a staple of modern culture: 'a Secondary World into which both the designer and spectator can enter, to the satisfaction of their senses while they are inside'.

But why do so many of these secondary worlds resemble feudalism in crisis? From Tolkien and CS Lewis, through to interstellar-world builders like Frank Herbert in *Dune*, and now *Game of Thrones* itself, the most successful fantasy worlds invoke not just the trappings of feudalism – kings, torture and trial by combat – but the actual crisis of feudalism.

In modern fantasy fiction there is always a crisis of the system: of the economic order and the auras of power – the magic – that emanate from it. There is, in literary theory, even a technical term for this critical point: 'thinning'. In their *Encyclopaedia of Fantasy*, John Clute and John Grant define thinning as 'the constant threat of decline', accompanied by a pervasive mourning and sense of wrongness in the world.

As Westeros girds its gym-toned and wax-depilated loins for season five, the thinning process is well under way. There is the encroachment of the spirit world from the icy north; there is a slave revolt happening across the sea.

But there is also more clearly systemic doom hanging over the economy of Westeros. The ruling Lannister family obtained its wealth from owning most of the gold mines. The currency of Westeros is tri-metallic: there are gold, silver and copper coins deriving their value from the metal contained in them – not from a central bank and its 'promise to pay', as in real life.

The problem is, in season four, the Lannisters' big cheese, Tywin, dropped a bombshell: the gold mines have not produced for three years. On top of that, the Lannisters owe loads of money to something called the Iron Bank. 'All of us live in its shadow,' says Tywin, 'but none of us know it. You can't run from them, you can't cheat them and you can't sway them with excuses. If you owe them money, and you don't want to crumble, you pay it back.'

If this sounds a lot like Greece and the European Central Bank, that's only because their current standoff replicates the essential power shift that happened towards the end of feudalism: debts accumulated under a corrupt patronage system, whose sources of wealth dried up, destroyed the system in the end.

If you apply historical materialism to Westeros, the plot of season five and six becomes possible to predict. What happened with feudalism, when kings found themselves in hock to bankers, is that – at first – they tried to sort it out with naked power. The real-life Edward III had his Italian bankers locked up in the Tower of London until they waived his debts.

But eventually the power of commerce began to squash the power of kings. Feudalism gave way to a capitalism based on merchants, bankers, colonial plunder and the slave trade. Paper money emerged, as did a complex banking system for assuaging problems like your gold mine running dry.

But for this to happen you need the rule of law. You need the power of kings to become subject to constitutional right, and a moral code imposed on business, trade and family life. But that won't happen in Westeros, where the elite lifestyle is synonymous with rape, pillage, arbitrary killing, torture and recreational sex.

So what Westeros needs is not an invasion of werewolves from the frozen north, but the arrival of a new kind of human being: they should be dressed in black, with white lace collars, stern faces and an aversion to sex and drink. In a word, Westeros needs capitalists – such as those who frown puritanically at us from Dutch portraits in the 17th century. And they should, as in the Dutch Republic and the English civil war, launch a revolution.

But that can't happen in the secondary world of fantasy fiction. The thinning process can never be allowed to end; it must be perpetual for the conceit of the drama to work.

There is a reason so much fantasy fiction adopts the conceit of a feudalism that is always in crisis but never overthrown. It forms the ideal landscape in which to dramatise the secret desires of people who live under modern capitalism.

Tolkien's generation – scarred by industrial-scale warfare – craved the values of heroism and mercy associated with the face-to-face combat of yesteryear. For William Morris, whose utopian socialist novel *News From Nowhere* is set in a quasi-medieval Hammersmith, the craving was for skill, craft, beautiful individual objects – an escape from the brutalism of industrial mass production.

Future social historians, as they look back on the popularity of *Game of Thrones*, will not have much trouble deciphering the inner desires of the generation addicted to it. They are: 'all of the above', plus multipartner sex.

Trapped in a system based on economic rationality, we all want the power to be something bigger than our credit card limit, or our job function. Nobody sits at home watching these dramas imagining they are a mere slave, peasant or serving girl: we are invited to fantasise that we are one of the characters with agency – Daenerys Targaryen, a beautiful woman with tame dragons, or the unkillable stubbly hunk that is Jon Snow.

It is for social psychology to explain the enduring popularity of fantasy, and its evolution towards soft-porn gore. All political economy can do is point out the contradictions and where they lead.

So sometime in season five or six, I predict the Lannisters are going to fall, as the feudalists did, unless they discover some previously unknown territory, full of gold and easily killable people, just as the Spanish monarchy did during the real-world crisis of feudalism.

It has always been a mystery as to whether there is a land to the west, across the sea from Westeros. My suspicion is: there has to be, and someone will soon be despatched to find it.

7 APRIL

Back on the Isle of Wight, Tory Britain rehearses its collapse

POLLY TOYNBEE

Distant childhood memories blur into an idea of a backwater frozen in the 50s – white sliced bread, spam, a doll's ration book, my father playing cricket on Shorwell village green, walking to the tiny two-class village school, a tiddly winks contest, Virol, Fru-Grains, cod liver oil and blue-top orange juice from the clinic. Why my father brought my mother here in the war, I don't know, but I was born in the bitter December of 1946, when snow reached the windows until March. The Attlee government struggled with an energy crisis, while my mother struggled with a new baby and a rationed one-bar electric fire.

This time I come away no wiser as to why they came here, but not entirely surprised my mother divorced my father and fled. Escaping is what many of the young do here. The long-serving editor of the island's *County Press* says he urged his children to go. But, he says, people get stuck. I met a good few – professionals too – who hadn't left the island in months. I never came back, except to see Bob Dylan in 1969. How do the young feel? I noted a youth club called Wight Trash. And to London eyes, the place does feel bleached at 98 per cent white, plus 1 per cent Filipino nurses and care home staff. It's not rich – posh Royal Yacht Squadron Cowes is a fragment of island life, with the food bank HQ nearby and Ofsted denouncing island schools as among the nation's worst.

My expectation as an outsider – 'overner', as they call us here – was of a sleepy memory lane on solid Tory turf. But no, the island is a hotbed of turmoil. The *County Press* has bristled with civil war in Toryville – his biggest story, says editor Alan Marriott. Andrew Turner, MP since 2001, was almost ousted in a January coup, surviving deselection by just one vote. The putsch came from some Tory councillors. Why? Certainly not politics: Turner is well tuned to local sentiment – adamantly anti-EU, anti-immigration, anti-wind turbine. When, eventually, I squeezed a cautiously chaperoned interview out of him, he said his politics were 'not that different' from the Ukip candidate's. 'I voted no in the 1975 referendum', and he was a rumoured Ukip-defector. What does he think of Cameron? 'I'm reasonably happy with him' is his grudging best.

The trouble began at a Valentine's ball, when Turner's partner of many years had a noisy row with a Tory councillor's partner and things escalated. Turner's Tory opponents challenged his expenses: he had flipped a large Georgian pile in Newport with a London flat and claimed £103,000. But they'd left it too late, said the parliamentary standards commissioner, as all the bills had been shredded in 2010. She warned they should not 'make use of the work of my office as a way of trying to resolve internal difficulties'.

Turner's partner was suspected by Tory councillors of defecting to the independents who took control of the council, as she was photographed hob-nobbing with them and their champion Martin Bell. The hostile Tories described her as a Svengali-type who ran everything Turner did. Then the *County Press* reported that she had run off with Turner's transport adviser. Turner's enemies said that after suffering a stroke in 2006 he was no longer fit to be an MP. It got very nasty. Never say island life is dull.

Turner is positively serene compared with his Ukip challenger, Iain Mackie, who brims with aggression, combat-ready after his party won 41 per cent in the EU elections. 'I'm passionate!' he kept saying, as he hammered on about Turner's expenses. But the odds are strongly on a Tory victory. 'Anything in a blue rosette wins here,' said one islander waiting at the ferry port.

But that's not the whole island story. My birth certificate was issued in Ventnor, a gem of a mini-Victorian resort where Labour candidate Stewart Blackmore is a town councillor. Despite 38 years here, he still speaks strong Aberdonian, as he introduces me to some un-Tory Ventnor people. The hyperactive 77-year-old town clerk, tall and craggy, spent his pre-island life in Rochdale community work, skilful at raising funds and grants: half Ventnor's four wards are among the UK's most deprived. One councillor is a former Leeds university politics lecturer and their leader is a live-wire activist. They beam at the Tories calling this 'the independent socialist republic of Ventnor'. Cuts have hit hard, as everywhere. 'I've had people in tears over the bedroom tax,' Blackmore says. If Ukip, the independent council leader and the Tory vote splits three ways, he might break through to second place.

Good reasons not to dismiss the Isle of Wight as a forgotten backwater include Vestas, the Danish wind turbine company. It recently reopened to make gigantic offshore sails, a third bigger than the London Eye, each powering 7,500 homes, bringing 200 island jobs. Its enthusiastic manager is island born and bred – and not a Tory, partly because Wight has refused all windmills. Tory Bournemouth even resists one 12 miles offshore, which would use Vestas sails.

Another island first: far from Westminster, it has developed its own innovative NHS and social care system. In St Mary's hospital I saw the integrated care hub that takes both 999 and 111 calls, no outsourcing. The room shares desks for district nurses, social workers, care staff, mental health staff, physios and others fielding the crisis calls. Ambulance time is saved, with hospital admissions cut, a former ambulance driver managing A&E, hospital beds and community, with no silos. But the Lansley

Act forcing services out to tender threatens this unity. You don't find many Tories in these services or in the pooled advice services under one roof – CAB, law centre, Age UK – fielding crises in benefits and debts.

In the house where I was born, I found a former director of Red Funnel ferries, with a 1941 Tiger Moth in his back garden. He's a firm Tory but out of kilter with the party, an old world Macmillan type, appalled by rampant executive pay, horrified by property prices beyond young people's reach, wanting an economic shift away from finance to making and inventing things again. However cocky and seamless the Tory campaign looks from Westminster, you just need to lift a stone or two in the heartlands to find all kinds of fissures just beneath the surface.

17 APRIL

Everyone's a winner in the relentless world of spin

MARINA HYDE

To the post-debate spin room, readers – a space so emotionally soiling that its movie title would be *Mr Smith Goes to Washimself*. The important thing to remember about the spin room is that if one of the leaders took a kitten out of their pocket and shot it live on stage, there would be someone from their party on hand afterwards to cast the incident positively.

'Ooh I think you're wrong, Emily, I think he showed real guts out there. His own, as well as the kitten's. Being prime minister is about doing some very difficult things and doing them decisively.'

It is the Westminster museum of artless bullshit, containing well over 300 talking exhibits.

More lies are told here than on all the world's dating profiles put together. Hacks, politicians and spin doctors are condemned to scurry about, indulging in wanton political frottage, while the TV networks flaunt their ever-expanding array of debate-related gizmos: live worms, insta-polls, giant malfunctioning touch-screens, mobile Karen Silkwood shower units.

As far as spin room formalities go, you know the drill: once the telly debate has finished – in fact, well before it has finished – party operatives are released into it to explain to TV and print journalists why that shambles is exactly what a rainbow coalition would look like, or why Nigel was absolutely right to attack the studio audience because it just shows how relaxed he is out there.

People who genuinely want to be foreign secretary – people who already are the actual chief secretary to the actual Treasury – wander round trying to parrot the same centrally scripted 'observation' to as many anchors and reporters as they can.

Naturally, the spinners-in-chief clamber out of their coffins for a feed: your Craig Olivers, your Tom Baldwins. Think of them as the League of Extraordinarily Awful Gentlemen, their mission being to save the electorate from the peril of forming its own opinions.

'It's already clear the biggest loser tonight was David Cameron,' Douglas Alexander was saying repeatedly. 'There was a real alternative prime minister on stage and that was Ed Miliband.'

Fairly sure he said those precise words at the last debate two weeks back, so Labour might want to check there isn't a problem with the software.

Taking a slightly different tack on Cameron's absence was Jeremy Hunt. 'He wasn't invited,' he claimed. 'The format the broadcasters wanted was for the challengers.'

He turned to repeat himself to the next camera crew, only for the smile to fall off his face at the discovery that they were from Vice News. 'Vice News ... I'm sorry ... I'm going to ...' Pretend you're getting a phone call? Ah no – you're going to let them chase you as you make a panicked trot away in search of someone you perceive as more worthy of your soundbite.

'Our lot at home would have been getting more and more worked up during that,' a Ukip huddle were agreeing.

You could see a TV producer wondering whether pickings were slim enough to get one of them on, or whether she could get away with waiting for Douglas Alexander without being bawled out by her studio anchor, like that bit in *The Day Today* where Chris Morris shouts at his hapless correspondent: 'Peter! You've LOST THE NEWS!'

Despite having no skin in the game, the Tories were allowed spin in the game, with the broadcasters cravenly having agreed to let their people into the room to trash the leaders who did show up.

I'd like to tell you that everyone ignored the likes of William Hague on principle, but you might have seen the telly footage of hacks crowding round him like he was giving out free girlfriends. 'Coalition of chaos', was the Conservatives' pre-programmed observation, and they weren't going to let up on it.

Notable absentees? I didn't spot either David Axelrod or Jim Messina, the former Obama campaign bigwigs who have been hired by Labour and the Tories respectively for seriously big bucks – or rather, seriously big pounds. They would both always have been locked-on fixtures for Spin Alley during US elections, but presumably regard it as way too infra dig to get involved in this excruciating tribute act.

Frankly, the spin room is a location desperately in need of a sinkhole. Failing that, it is crying out for live infiltration by some telly satirist.

There is a precedent for that, which I'm afraid I had cause to mention last time I was forced to spend an evening in one of these spaces.

After one US election debate, host Conan O'Brien's TV show somehow contrived to get its sensationally impertinent puppet, Triumph the Insult Comic Dog, into Spin Alley. I urge you to watch the majestic clip that results, in which Triumph asks spinners like Karl Rove things like: 'So tell me, how painful was it when the doctor removed your sense of shame?' And apologises for aiming his microphone beneath their backsides. 'Sorry – I forgot which end the shit came out!'

A virulently conservative commentator got halfway down an answer about gay marriage before thinking better of it and sniffing: 'I don't take questions from dogs.' 'Oh, you'll take it, bitch!' barked Triumph.

That was all the way back in 2004. Unfortunately, this is Britain, 2015, where the political class still has such a tragic hard-on for all things American that it is simply unthinkable that anyone would dream of introducing a note of wanton disrespect into the venerable institution that is the post challengers debate spin room.

Atmosphere-wise (to this outsider at least), the spin room reeks of a perverse form of chemistry as the evening wears on, a sense that something unspeakable could happen the minute the cameras are switched off. Happily, that moment appeared to be scheduled for well after my deadline, so – in time-honoured parlance – I made my excuses and left.

18 April

All hail Uber! But what about the black cabs?

ZOE WILLIAMS

I had mixed feelings about Uber, the global 'app-based transportation network' (translation: cabs you get with your phone). Then I got an Uber account and now my feelings are more mixed still. Black cabs hate them. 'Don't make this about us against Uber,' said Kevin, 52, a black-cab driver. 'It's us against TfL. They have the strictest regulations in the world, but we're the only ones who have to abide by them.'

Black cabs, anecdotally speaking so far, are really suffering. Kevin said this had been his quietest start to the year in a quarter of a century. At the end of last month, a black cab even offered to take me home from a bus stop for free, because he was bored.

From that point of view, Uber represents the classic red squirrel, grey squirrel story: the independent, sometimes fairly scarce, iconic native car-hire species edged out by a wave of sturdier, stronger, similar, creatures. So far, so bad – plus, I share some sympathy with the view that the Uber rating system, which sees both driver and passenger mark each other out of five at the end of the journey, reduces a human moment to a rateable transaction.

But then Humphrey, 51, took me to the dentist, through Vauxhall roadworks, round a byzantine one-way, for £10.04, and said: 'Me, I'm a talker. You're such a talkative lady, I'll give you a fivestar.' It might not have been the best reflection of my personality, since I was interviewing him. But I got my five-star rating and that made me feel pretty human.

All of the five drivers I spoke to had left minicab firms to join Uber, including one, Riz, 36, who had left Addison Lee, and they all felt that they were now being treated better. Way better; better to the extent that they laughed when they heard the question.

Uber has 15,000 registered drivers in the UK, in London, Manchester, Leeds and Birmingham – they launched in Newcastle on Friday. The rumour is that Addison Lee has lost 1,000 drivers; the company rejects this, saying that only 8 per cent of their business overlaps with Uber.

'I was one of these that left,' Riz said. 'They were a good company when they were owned by a cabbie, but since [Carlyle, the private equity owners] took over ... I'd do 70–80 hours a week just to survive and that meant not putting my daughters to bed, not having the energy I need to be a father or a husband. Since I finished it's been smiles all the way.'

Jo Bertram, the London general manager at Uber, said: 'We had drivers, I remember, the first Christmas bringing us presents because that's what you used to have to do with your dispatcher. That's how they'd give you the good airport slots. We had to say, "you don't have to do this. We're just going to give you the information about where the work is, you decide what you want to do".'

Riz was recommended to me by the company, but none of the other drivers knew whether Uber wanted them to talk or had to check. They all said the same. Mehari, who took me back from the dentist for £9.32, said: 'Uber might not pay tax in the UK. [Its operating firm is Dutch.] Black cabs don't want them because they're taking their jobs [Riz said a black-cab driver emptied his urine bottle on to Riz's car bonnet]. But the work doesn't stop – as much as you want, as much as you can do. Sometimes we can make £400 in a day.'

Mehari does it because he loves to travel – since he came to the UK from Eritrea, escaping the national service there which is, in effect, limitless servitude to the government with pocket money, he's been everywhere. He really likes Switzerland, for some reason that it would have taken longer than our 17-minute journey to make out.

Salih, who took me and my kid to a different dentist (this journey, at £6.27, is probably the cheapest taxi ride I've had for years), said: 'For me, it's not the money so much as the peace of mind. You don't get any hassle because there isn't any cash. I used to hate it when people tried to haggle.'

Is this the main thing, from a passenger point of view? That the act of spending is now severed from the handing over of cash – the way it was with consumables, decades ago – and so all the anxiety of getting a taxi is rubbed away? (Until you get a credit-card bill.)

Kevin, the black-cab driver, thinks that's only part of it. 'Even with Hailo [an app that calls black cabs and delivers them to you, kerbside] people are using their phones when they don't need to, there are cabs going past them. Everyone does everything by their phone.'

I love Uber; I love the way you can track your car as it approaches, the thrill when you get five stars and the sensation of going back to the 70s, the last time the cost went up in 7p increments. But then, I hate conglomerates and I love black cabs. As I say, mixed. I'm going to have to stay in until I get some moral resolution.

23 April

Tears or smiles? How to get a free Pret coffee

PAULA COCOZZA

Yesterday Clive Schee, chief executive of Pret A Manger, revealed in an interview that staff give free drinks and food to selected customers. 'They will decide "I like the person on the bicycle," or "I like the guy in that tie."'

I ride a bicycle, which gives me hope. If I go to enough Prets, will I get a free coffee?

My colleague Susan gets two free soya lattes a week. She rides a Vespa and wears her helmet in the shops. She lends me the helmet. 'Hi-i,' I say at the counter, hoisting it up. 'Can I please have one of your cappuccinos?' I am still smiling while Mario shouts 'Cappuccino!' over his shoulder. Then he turns and crushes me with the words: '£2.15.' According to Schee: '28 per cent of people have had something free.' You can find these happy people on Twitter such as Matthew Reynolds: 'Got a free coffee from @Pret Liverpool yesterday from a nice guy for no reason. Made me happy and that's all you need in life init.'

At the Islington High Street branch I approach the counter. 'Hi, how are you?' I say to Lionela. I'm not asking for coffee until we've made friends.

'Not so bad,' Lionela says. 'Yourself?'

I tell her I'm fine, and then, because I am rubbish at small talk, I say: 'Could I have a dry cappuccino, please?' Lionela asks lots of questions – do I want it in or out, would I like a receipt, but the relationship is stalling. After I have paid, I ask: 'So, do you guys really give away free coffee?'

Lionela nods and hands me the cappuccino. 'Next time you'll be the lucky one,' she says. On St John Street, the branch is quiet. The assistant takes my money. She says the freebies are 'the joy of Pret', which sounds cultish. Can she give me some tips?

'There are no tips,' she says. 'We give random coffees to anybody. Sometimes, if we see tired or unhappy customers we give them a free coffee to cheer them up.'

Pret at King's Cross station is full of lunchtime customers. This time, I am not asking for coffee, I am telling them my life story.

'Hi, I'm having a terrible day,' I say to Kamil. By now, this is not a lie. 'I need a strong coffee,' I say. 'I just lost my job.'

'What kind of coffee?' Kamil asks.

'Double espresso?' I gesture to the helmet and say: 'And now my motorbike won't start!'

Kamil is punching buttons on the till. 'Take away or to have in?' he says. Kamil has no heart. Kamil is interested only in the coffee.

'How much is that?' I say, wondering how far I will have to cycle to the next Pret, how long this must go on.

Kamil looks up and smiles. 'It is on the house.'

So there you have it. Pret does give away free coffees but you have to be lucky – or sell your soul – to get one.

With apologies to Kamil

29 APRIL

The austerity delusion (extract)

PAUL KRUGMAN

In May 2010, as Britain headed into its last general election, elites all across the western world were gripped by austerity fever, a strange malady that combined extravagant fear with blithe optimism. Every country running significant budget deficits – as nearly all were in the aftermath of the financial crisis – was deemed at imminent risk of becoming another Greece unless it immediately began cutting spending and raising taxes. Concerns that imposing such austerity in already depressed economies would deepen their depression and delay recovery were airily dismissed; fiscal probity, we were assured, would inspire business-boosting confidence, and all would be well.

People holding these beliefs came to be widely known in economic circles as 'austerians', and for a while the austerian ideology swept all before it.

But that was five years ago, and the fever has long since broken. Greece is now seen as it should have been seen from the beginning – as a unique case, with few lessons for the rest of us. It is impossible for countries such as the US and the UK, which borrow in their own currencies, to experience Greek-style crises, because they cannot run out of money. Even within the eurozone, borrowing costs plunged once the European Central Bank began to do its job and protect its clients against self-fulfilling panics by standing ready to buy government bonds if necessary. As I write this, Italy and Spain have no trouble raising cash – they can borrow at the lowest rates in their history, indeed considerably below those in Britain – and even Portugal's interest rates are within a whisker of those paid by HM Treasury.

On the other side of the ledger, the benefits of improved confidence failed to make their promised appearance. Since the global turn to austerity in 2010, every country that introduced significant austerity has seen its economy suffer, with the depth of the suffering closely related to the harshness of the austerity.

In late 2012, the IMF's chief economist, Olivier Blanchard, went so far as to issue what amounted to a mea culpa: although his organisation never bought into the notion that austerity would actually boost economic growth, the IMF now believes that it massively understated the damage spending cuts inflict on a weak economy. Meanwhile, all of the economic research that allegedly supported the austerity push has been discredited. Widely touted statistical results were, it turned out, based on highly dubious assumptions and procedures – plus a few outright mistakes – and evaporated under closer scrutiny.

It is rare, in the history of economic thought, for debates to get resolved this decisively. The austerian ideology that dominated elite discourse five years ago has collapsed, to the point where hardly anyone still believes it. Hardly anyone, that is, except the coalition that still rules Britain – and most of the British media.

I don't know how many Britons realise the extent to which their economic debate has diverged from the rest of the western world – the extent to which the UK seems stuck on obsessions that have been mainly laughed out of the discourse elsewhere. Is there some good reason why deficit obsession should still rule in Britain, even as it fades away everywhere else? No. This country is not different. The economics of austerity are the same – and the intellectual case as bankrupt – in Britain as everywhere else.

Stimulus and its enemies

When economic crisis struck the advanced economies in 2008, almost every government – even Germany – introduced some kind of stimulus programme, increasing spending and/or cutting taxes.

Normally, monetary authorities – the Federal Reserve, the Bank of England – can respond to a temporary economic down-turn by cutting interest rates; this encourages private spending, especially on housing, and sets the stage for recovery. But there's a limit to how much they can do in that direction. Until recently, the conventional wisdom was that you couldn't cut interest rates below zero. And if cutting rates all the way to zero isn't enough to cure what ails the economy, the usual remedy for recession falls short.

By late 2008 it was already clear in every major economy that conventional monetary policy, which involves pushing down the interest rate on short-term government debt, was going to be insufficient to fight the financial downdraft. Now what? The textbook answer was and is fiscal expansion: increase government spending both to create jobs directly and to put money in consumers' pockets; cut taxes to put more money in those pockets.

But won't this lead to budget deficits? Yes, and that's actually a good thing. An economy that is depressed even with zero interest rates is, in effect, an economy in which the public is trying to save more than businesses are willing to invest. In such an economy the government does everyone a service by running deficits and giving frustrated savers a chance to put their money to work. Nor does this borrowing compete with private investment. An economy where interest rates cannot go any lower is an economy awash in desired saving with no place to go, and deficit spending that expands the economy is, if anything, likely to lead to higher private investment than would otherwise materialise.

It's true that you can't run big budget deficits for ever (although you can do it for a long time), because at some point interest payments start to swallow too large a share of the budget. But it's foolish and destructive to worry about deficits when borrowing is very cheap and the funds you borrow would otherwise go to waste.

At some point you do want to reverse stimulus. But you don't want to do it too soon – specifically, you don't want to remove fiscal support as long as pedal-to-the-metal monetary policy is still insufficient. Instead, you want to wait until there can be a sort of handoff, in which the central bank offsets the effects of declining spending and rising taxes by keeping rates low. As John

From the *Guardian* project 'What Syrian refugees pack for crossing to Europe' by Patrick Kingsley and Sima Diab. In Abu Jana's bag (top) there are lemons to fight sea sickness and a laser pen to attract boats in the event of a shipwreck. Hashem al Souky's bag contains his army papers and cheese. SIMA DIAB

A Turkish police officer stands in front of three-year-old Alan Kurdi, who drowned trying to reach the Greek island of Kos in September. The image caused a public outcry over the plight of refugees. NILUFER DEMIR / DOGAN / AP

A protestor in Ferguson, Missouri in November after demonstrations sprang up across the US following the grand jury decision in the fatal shooting of 18-year-old Michael Brown. JEWEL SAMAD / AFP

In August, Isis social media released this image of their destruction of the temple of Baal Shamin in Palmyra. UNESCO denounced the bombing of the 2,000-year-old site as a 'war crime'.

Motorcyclists avoid a wide crack in the road caused by the earthquake in Kathmandu, Nepal in April. It killed over 9,000 people and injured more than 23,000. HEMANTA SHRESTHA / EPA

US presidential candidate Hillary Clinton kicks off her campaign at Franklin D Roosevelt Four Freedoms Park, New York in June. LUCAS JACKSON / REUTERS

Banknotes thrown by comedian Lee Nelson shower down on FIFA president Sepp Blatter at the Extraordinary FIFA Executive Committee Meeting in Zurich in July. ARND WIEGMANN / REUTERS

Ed Miliband, Nick Clegg and David Cameron at a service to mark the 70th anniversary of VE day on 8 May, one day after the general election.

Education campaigner Malala Yousafzai at Birmingham library after she became the youngest person ever to win a Nobel Prize.

Solar Impulse 2, powered entirely by solar energy, flies over Abu Dhabi in February. It went on to break the record for the longest non-stop solo flight in history. SOLAR IMPULSE / REVILLARD

Pro-democracy protestors in Hong Kong open their umbrellas for 87 seconds in October 2014, marking the 87 rounds of tear gas that were fired by police at unarmed protestors one month previously. ALEX HOFFARD / EPA

Christie's employees handle Picasso's *Les femmes d'Alger*, which smashed the world record for a painting sold at auction, fetching just over $179 million (£116m) in May. UKARTPICS / ALAMY

Kanye West performs on the Pyramid stage, Glastonbury. His set offered 'flickers of greatness rather than a blaze of glory', according to the *Guardian*'s Alexis Petridis. YUI MOK / PA

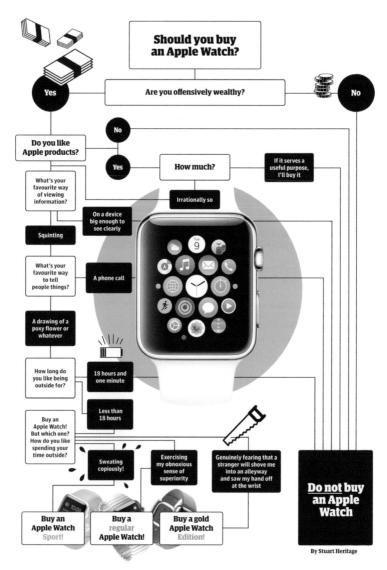

Should you buy an Apple Watch?

Are you offensively wealthy?

Yes

No

Do you like Apple products?

No

Yes

How much?

If it serves a useful purpose, I'll buy it

What's your favourite way of viewing information?

Irrationally so

On a device big enough to see clearly

Squinting

What's your favourite way to tell people things?

A phone call

A drawing of a poxy flower or whatever

How long do you like being outside for?

18 hours and one minute

Less than 18 hours

Buy an Apple Watch! But which one? How do you like spending your time outside?

Sweating copiously!

Exercising my obnoxious sense of superiority

Genuinely fearing that a stranger will shove me into an alleyway and saw my hand off at the wrist

Buy an Apple Watch Sport!

Buy a regular Apple Watch!

Buy a gold Apple Watch Edition!

Do not buy an Apple Watch

By Stuart Heritage

In March, the *Guardian* attempted to help its readers solve a pressing consumer dilemma. ANDREW STOCKS

Maynard Keynes wrote in 1937: 'The boom, not the slump, is the right time for austerity at the Treasury.'

All of this is standard macroeconomics. I often encounter people on both the left and the right who imagine that austerity policies were what the textbook said you should do – that those of us who protested against the turn to austerity were staking out some kind of heterodox, radical position. But the truth is that mainstream, textbook economics not only justified the initial round of post-crisis stimulus, but said that this stimulus should continue until economies had recovered.

What we got instead, however, was a hard right turn in elite opinion, away from concerns about unemployment and toward a focus on slashing deficits, mainly with spending cuts. Why?

Part of the answer is that politicians were catering to a public that doesn't understand the rationale for deficit spending, that tends to think of the government budget via analogies with family finances. When John Boehner, the Republican leader, opposed US stimulus plans on the grounds that 'American families are tightening their belt, but they don't see government tightening its belt,' economists cringed at the stupidity. But within a few months the very same line was showing up in Barack Obama's speeches, because his speechwriters found that it resonated with audiences. Similarly, the Labour party felt it necessary to dedicate the very first page of its 2015 general election manifesto to a 'Budget Responsibility Lock', promising to 'cut the deficit every year'.

Beyond these economic misconceptions, there were political reasons why many influential players opposed fiscal stimulus even in the face of a deeply depressed economy. Conservatives like to use the alleged dangers of debt and deficits as clubs with which to beat the welfare state and justify cuts in benefits; suggestions that higher spending might actually be beneficial are definitely not welcome. Meanwhile, centrist politicians and pundits often try to demonstrate how serious and statesman-like they are by calling for hard choices and sacrifice (by other people). Even Barack Obama's first inaugural address, given in the face of a plunging economy, largely consisted of hard-choices boilerplate. As a result, centrists were almost as uncomfortable with the notion of fiscal stimulus as the hard right.

The austerity moment

From the beginning, there were plenty of people strongly inclined to oppose fiscal stimulus and demand austerity. But they had a problem: their dire warnings about the consequences of deficit spending kept not coming true. Some of them were quite open about their frustration with the refusal of markets to deliver the disasters they expected and wanted. Alan Greenspan, the former chairman of the Federal Reserve, in 2010: 'Inflation and long-term interest rates, the typical symptoms of fiscal excess, have remained remarkably subdued. This is regrettable, because it is fostering a sense of complacency that can have dire consequences.'

Greece was the disaster austerians were looking for. In September 2009 Greece's long-term borrowing costs were only 1.3 percentage points higher than Germany's; by September 2010 that gap had increased sevenfold. Suddenly, austerians had a concrete demonstration of the dangers they had been warning about. A hard turn away from Keynesian policies could now be justified as an urgent defensive measure, lest your country abruptly turn into another Greece.

Still, what about the depressed state of western economies? The post-crisis recession bottomed out in the middle of 2009, and in most countries a recovery was under way, but output and employment were still far below normal. Wouldn't a turn to austerity threaten the still-fragile upturn?

Not according to many policymakers, who engaged in one of history's most remarkable displays of collective wishful thinking. Standard macroeconomics said that cutting spending in a depressed economy, with no room to offset these cuts by reducing interest rates that were already near zero, would indeed deepen the slump. But policymakers at the European Commission, the European Central Bank, and in the British government that took power in May 2010 eagerly seized on economic research that claimed to show the opposite.

When the coalition government came to power, then, all the pieces were in place for policymakers who were already inclined to push for austerity. Fiscal retrenchment could be presented as urgently needed to avert a Greek-style strike by bond buyers. 'Greece stands as a warning of what happens to countries that lose their credibility, or whose governments pretend that difficult decisions can somehow be avoided,' declared David Cameron soon after taking office. Concerns about delaying recovery could be waved away with an appeal to positive effects on confidence. Economists who objected to any or all of these lines of argument were simply ignored. But that was, as I said, in 2010.

By about two years ago, the entire edifice of austerian economics had crumbled. Events had utterly failed to play out as the austerians predicted, while the academic research that allegedly supported the doctrine had withered under scrutiny. Hardly anyone has admitted being wrong – hardly anyone ever does, on any subject – but quite a few prominent austerians now deny having said what they did, in fact, say. The doctrine that ruled the world in 2010 has more or less vanished from the scene.

Back in 2010 some economists argued that fears of a Greek-style funding crisis were vastly overblown – I referred to the myth of the 'invisible bond vigilantes'. Well, those bond vigilantes have stayed invisible. For countries such as the UK, the US, and Japan that borrow in their own currencies, it's hard to even see how the predicted crises could happen. Such countries cannot, after all, run out of money, and if worries about solvency weakened their currencies, this would actually help their economies in a time of weak growth and low inflation.

Yet Britain zigged just as the rest of us were zagging. By 2013, austerian doctrine was in ignominious retreat in most of the world – yet at that very moment much of the UK press was declaring that doctrine vindicated. 'Osborne wins the battle on austerity,' the *Financial Times* announced in September 2013, and the sentiment was widely echoed. What was going on? You might think that British debate took a different turn because the British experience was out of line with developments elsewhere – in particular, that Britain's return to economic growth in 2013 was somehow at odds with the predictions of standard economics. But you would be wrong.

The key point to understand about fiscal policy under Cameron and Osborne is that British austerity, while very real and quite severe, was mostly imposed during the coalition's first two years in power. Given the fact that the coalition essentially stopped imposing new austerity measures after its first two years, there's nothing at all surprising about seeing a revival of economic growth in 2013.

British economists have no doubt about the economic damage wrought by austerity. The Centre for Macroeconomics in London regularly surveys a panel of leading UK economists on a variety of questions. When it asked whether the coalition's policies had promoted growth and employment, those disagreeing outnumbered those agreeing four to one.

By this point, some readers will nonetheless be shaking their heads and declaring, 'But the economy is booming, and you said that couldn't happen under austerity.' But Keynesian logic says that a one-time tightening of fiscal policy will produce a one-time hit to the economy, not a permanent reduction in the growth rate. A return to growth after austerity has been put on hold is not at all surprising. As I pointed out recently: 'If this counts as a policy success, why not try repeatedly hitting yourself in the face for a few minutes? After all, it will feel great when you stop.'

Which brings me to the role of interests in distorting economic debate.

Scare talk about debt and deficits is often used as a cover for a very different agenda, namely an attempt to reduce the overall size of government and especially spending on social insurance. This has been transparently obvious in the United States, where many supposed deficit-reduction plans just happen to include sharp cuts in tax rates on corporations and the wealthy even as they take away healthcare and nutritional aid for the poor. But it's also a fairly obvious motivation in the UK, if not so crudely expressed. The 'primary purpose' of austerity, the *Telegraph* admitted in 2013, 'is to shrink the size of government spending' – or, as Cameron put it in a speech later that year, to make the state 'leaner ... not just now, but permanently'.

So it has been astonishing, from a US perspective, to witness the limpness of Labour's response to the austerity push. Britain's opposition has been amazingly willing to accept claims that budget deficits are the biggest economic issue facing the nation, and has made hardly any effort to challenge the extremely dubious proposition that fiscal policy under Blair and Brown was deeply irresponsible – or even the nonsensical proposition that this supposed fiscal irresponsibility caused the crisis of 2008–2009.

The closest parallel I can give from my side of the Atlantic is the erstwhile weakness of Democrats on foreign policy – their apparent inability back in 2003 or so to take a stand against obviously terrible ideas like the invasion of Iraq. If the political opposition won't challenge the coalition's bad economics, who will?

You might be tempted to say that this is all water under the bridge, given that the coalition, whatever it may claim, effectively called a halt to fiscal tightening midway through its term. But this story isn't over. Cameron is campaigning largely on a spurious claim to have 'rescued' the British economy – and promising, if he stays in power, to continue making substantial cuts in the years ahead. Labour, sad to say, are echoing that position. So both major parties are in effect promising a new round of austerity that might well hold back a recovery that has, so far, come nowhere near to making up the ground lost during the recession and the initial phase of austerity.

For whatever the politics, the economics of austerity are no different in Britain from what they are in the rest of the advanced world. Harsh austerity in depressed economies isn't necessary, and does major damage when it is imposed. That was true of Britain five years ago – and it's still true today.

4 MAY

His name is Edymandias, King of Kings (so he hopes)

JOHN CRACE

In several thousand years' time, an archaeologist will uncover a 2.6 metre (8ft 6in) piece of stone that had been lying buried for hundreds of years. Scholars will spend just as long thereafter trying to interpret its meaning. Was it the centre of a hitherto unknown civilisation based around the sun god Ed? Will future transport ministers pledge billions of pounds of public money to build an underpass to protect this national monument?

In one of the tightest elections in 50 years, which looks set to be won by the party leader the public mistrusts the least, Ed Miliband has just raised the stupidity bar still higher. It makes Neil Kinnock's 1992 'we're all right' Sheffield rally moment look almost clever.

What possessed him to imagine that carving a series of election pledges into an enormous slab of limestone to be placed in the Downing Street garden if he becomes prime minister on 8 May was a good idea? There isn't a single sentient being with connecting synapses anywhere who could think it was.

Even the title is a hostage to fortune. 'A Better Plan. A Better Future'. This stone, Ed, I'm sorry to say, is symbolic of a Totally Crap Plan. Or worse, No Plan. Then there are the pledges. 1. A strong economic foundation. When some future Arthur Evans finds this battered, broken foundation stone several hundred feet underground, his first thought will be 'My name is Edymandias, King of Kings / Look on my works, ye mighty, and despair.' Shelley will last far longer than this. As for the rest ... They read more like focus-group findings than serious electoral promises: a country where the next generation does better than the last; higher living standards for working families. Archaeologists will snigger. 'How sweet! They all say that, don't they? And now look at them ...'

If Moses had come down from Mount Sinai with a tablet of commandments as dopey as this, the whole history of religion would have had to be rewritten. The Israelites would just have said: 'That Moses – he's having a laugh.' Except Ed isn't, apparently. Unless he's secretly filming a post-election episode of *The Thick of It*. The only thing that can be said for Ed's tablet – apart from start taking different ones – is that there are only six commandments rather than the full 10. Some embarrassment saved.

If Miliband does become prime minister, it will stand in the rose garden unseen by anyone until the next prime minister knocks it down. How many members of the public will get invited to a Downing Street garden party where they will be able to admire it? Or is its sole purpose to remind Miliband of what he is supposed to be doing when he draws the bedroom curtains every morning?

And if he doesn't make it to Downing Street, the stone is history by Friday morning. Or soon thereafter, depending on how long it takes to form a coalition. The best hope is that he might be able to flog it off cheap to the Lib Dems to be recycled as a memorial for their party. From Edstone to headstone.

Now think of a stunt that might have had meaning: a stone with all the pledges that the Tories and the Lib Dems made at the election in 2010. Then place it in a prominent public place and commission a mason to chip away at all those that hadn't been kept until the morning of 7 May. By which time there would be very little left.

5 MAY

Election diary (extract)

JOHN HARRIS AND JOHN DOMOKOS

LIVERPOOL, 26 FEBRUARY
Latest *Guardian*/ICM poll: Con 36 Lab 32 LD 10 Ukip 9 Gn 7
Jack Straw and the Tories' Malcolm Rifkind face cash-for-access revelations; the Greens' Natalie Bennett reels from her on-air 'brain fade'
70 DAYS LEFT

Like a lot of worthwhile things, it all starts with fear: not just about the 11 weeks we're about to spend pinballing up and down the country, the number of times we'll hear the phrase 'hard-working families', and the efficacy or otherwise of Premier Inn's Good Night Guarantee – but the incredible complexity of what we have to cover, with the aid of only one video camera and a succession of notepads. This, after all, is the nobody-knows-anything election, with no easily predictable outcome nor any sense that, in the age of seven-party politics, most of the country is following the same electoral plotline.

So what to do? The first task is to establish what might actually be at stake from the perspective of two very different places, both the kind of ultra-safe seats the mainstream media tend to ignore: Kensington in Liverpool (poor, bleak, Labour), and its namesake in London (rich, luxurious, Tory).

We spend three days in the former, among shuttered shops and minimal human traffic, having regular conversations about what's happened to the benefits system. 'We're getting beggars back again in Kensington, because people are being sanctioned,' says Steve Faragher, a long-time resident who gives the area a voice via a small-scale setup called Liverpool Community Radio. And the election? 'No one's mentioning it, because it doesn't touch on their lives in any remote way.'

Five minutes away, though, we get a bracing sense of what this place still has to lose. Thanks to the coalition axe that has cut away 58 per cent of Liverpool city council's funding from Whitehall, Kensington's Sure Start centre is under threat of closure. Four women – respectively from Malaysia, Portugal, Cameroon and Liverpool – explain how their kids have been helped by the centre's staff and their expertise with what officialspeak calls 'special and complex needs', and there are tears (from us, not them). Without missing a beat, all of them say they are voting Labour.

In the other Kensington, local MP Malcolm Rifkind will soon stand down under a cloud of disgrace, but it matters not: a majority of people here will support the Conservatives out of pure instinct, and Ed Miliband's plans for a mansion tax and the abolition of non-dom status have surely hardened the area's deep-blue tribalism. That said, when we take the temperature here the following week, it takes no effort to pick up disquiet about some of the aspects of a thriving London economy that the Tories very rarely mention.

'What was really a family neighbourhood isn't a family neigh-bourhood any more,' one woman tells us. 'What's happened here, essentially, is that London's turned into Monaco.' In the pristine streets to the north of Kensington High Street, one thought instantly occurs: whereas Liverpool's Kensington is full of the silence of poverty and crushed hopes, its namesake in the capital has the very different quiet that comes from absentee property-owners and lives spent making huge amounts of money elsewhere.

COATBRIDGE, NEAR GLASGOW, 14 MARCH

Latest YouGov Scotland poll: SNP 46 Lab 27 Con 18 LD 4
Vince Cable says new Tory-Lib Dem coalition 'inconceivable'; Ed Miliband assures public 'we only use the smaller of our two kitchens'

54 DAYS LEFT

In Scotland, the Tory-Labour dogfight barely registers. Obviously, what matters here is the uneven scrap between what remains of the Labour party, and the insurgent, all-conquering SNP – and if you want some sense of how mind-boggling things have gotten, Coatbridge is a good place to start. Since 1982, the seat of Coat-bridge, Chryston and Bellshill has been represented by Labour's Tom Clarke, who's now 74. In 2005, his 19,000-vote majority made it the safest seat in Britain.

Now, recent polling by the Tory peer Michael Ashcroft has put the SNP 3 per cent ahead, and their candidate – 51-year-old Phil Boswell, a locally born and raised contracts manager in the oil industry – thinks he could pull off the truly miraculous and win.

The town's once-monolithic politics were traceable to its large Irish-Catholic population, and that community's deep bond with Labour (whose people once maligned the SNP as the 'Protestant party'). Coatbridge's renowned St Patrick's Day celebration, then, is the perfect backdrop to a day's campaigning in truly Baltic temperatures: the SNP doing its thing at a street stall in a shopping precinct, while round the corner in the town's St Patrick's Hall, Clarke attempts to work the room in the manner of a big-hitting US congressman.

Middle-aged women are assured of how young they look while Clarke repeats one of his stock lines: 'There's not a family in this town Tom Clarke hasn't helped.' Every time we stop at a table to talk politics, he hovers just out of shot, apparently trying to make sure that everyone stays on message.

Clarke and his comrades claim that the polls are wrong, and that they're confidently on course to win. When we return for a second bite on 21 April, we're allowed to follow him and his campaign team around the former pit village of Moodiesburn, where we ask an innocent question of a man sitting on his doorstep, about the SNP claiming to now represent the working class.

By way of a reply, he mutters something about the renowned Scot and first-ever Labour leader, Keir Hardie (who died in 1915), before Clarke jumps in. 'This man's trying to get you to say things that are anti-Labour,' he advises the fella on the doorstep, before turning to us. 'He told you from the very beginning: he's voting Labour.'

'Don't promote the SNP,' advises a Labour canvasser and, as we walk down the street, Clarke pipes up again. 'I thought you were observing,' he says, sternly. 'I didn't think you were intervening, or I wouldn't have agreed to it.'

In six years of making political videos, no politician has ever asked us to refrain from talking to the public. Clearly, it must be a sign of his imminent victory.

BOSTON, LINCOLNSHIRE, 18 MARCH

Latest *Guardian*/ICM poll: Con 36 Lab 35 LD 7 Ukip 9 Gn 4

David Cameron agrees to a seven-way debate; Ed Miliband rules out coalition with the SNP

50 DAYS LEFT

Four days later, we arrive in a completely different universe: Ukip-land, that great expanse of eastern England that stretches from the Kent coast to the pancake-flat fields of Cambridgeshire and Lincolnshire.

Our first day begins at 5.15am, watching through the morning mist as droves of migrant workers are picked up from the town's car parks and ferried to nearby fields and food-processing plants (around 75 per cent of the UK's vegetables are grown here). Boston feels tense, and prickly – swirling with concerns about the nefarious, abusive end of the local job market, pressure on schools and hospitals, and an impossible combination of high rents and low wages. Everybody we meet needs no persuasion to talk at length about immigration and who they'll vote for: Ukip – who, one market trader tells us, 'talk Boston's language'.

There is a kind of political tragedy afoot here. In 1997 and 2001, Labour came within 600 votes of taking the seat of Boston and Skegness from the Tories. But in 2004, when much of the old eastern Europe was incorporated into the EU, immigration became the focus of seething local anger – and as the Labour vote dropped, Ukip arrived to fill the void.

As in 2010, Labour's candidate in this election is Paul Kenny, a furrow-browed native of Birmingham who has lived here since 1991 and has a deep, forensic knowledge of immigration and the issues – wages, contracts, housing – around it. Ukip's hopeful, by contrast, is a 22-year-old law graduate (and 'local man', as their leaflets call him) called Robin Hunter-Clarke, who says the town's problems could be solved at a stroke by the imposition of the 'Australian-style points system' that he and Nigel Farage hold forth about until it has the same hollow ring as most of the other clichés we've heard (the sitting Tory MP, one Mark Simmonds, has decided to stand down; his replacement is a technology journalist from the *Daily Telegraph*, suggesting the Conservatives have given up).

Three weeks later, Farage is in town to address two back-to-back public meetings at the local Haven High Academy, both of which are rammed. Volunteers in hi-vis jackets usher cars into spaces like at festivals; twice over, a long queue snakes from the main entrance around the schoolyard. One man – 30-ish, by the look of him – tells us he hasn't been in work for months. 'Wages are cut,' he says. 'Gangmasters are exploiting everybody, and you can't make a living on the land any more.'

'Probably no town in England has been more fundamentally changed by open-door immigration than Boston, and I've seen the impact,' Farage half-roars from the platform. That relatively innocuous line gets thunderous applause, as does a defiant reprise of his comments about HIV patients from overseas being treated by the NHS. We leave with a very strong feeling: round here, the supposed Ukip slide in the polls has yet to happen, and they may well win.

BRISTOL, 30 MARCH
Latest Populus poll: Con 34 Lab 34 LD 8 Ukip 15 Gn 4
Diane Abbott says new Labour 'controls on immigration' mugs are

*'shameful' Nick Clegg launches Lib Dem campaign saying his party
is too 'male and pale'*

39 DAYS LEFT

The current MP for Bristol West is a Lib Dem, Stephen Williams. A recent local poll put him in third, behind Labour and a thriving Green party, whose city-wide membership has recently increased from 250 to more than 2,000 and whose plush campaign office has been paid for by that renowned rebel Dame Vivienne Westwood.

Welcome, then, to the Green surge, overseen by a pretty credible candidate: Darren Hall, a former member of the RAF ('Was I in any wars? Not really, no,' he assures us) and ex-civil servant, whose conversion to green politics came via the experience of snorkelling, when he realised that climate change was going to ruin coral reefs, and the effects of reading the famous anti-inequality screed *The Spirit Level*.

In some of the more affluent parts of the constituency, playing spot-the-Green-voter is a cinch. But at some threadbare low-rise flats in Redcliffe, one twentysomething mother-to-be doesn't know there's an election on, neither do a group of young men crowded around a stairwell, though their spirits are lifted by news that the Greens support the decriminalisation of weed.

The most interesting encounter comes when a door creaks open, a herbal aroma drifts out, and a woman looks with interest at one of the Greens' leaflets. She usually votes, she says: last time, she supported Ukip, only to have her nerves jangled by their policy of cutting benefits spending.

'This seems a bit better,' she says. And might she support the Greens? 'I might, yeah. It's a new way to vote. It all needs something else.' A pause. 'A bit of hope to vote for.'

NUNEATON, 30 APRIL

Latest Ipsos/MORI poll: Con 35 Lab 30 LD 8 Ukip 10 Gn 8

Ed Miliband says he would rather not be PM than do a deal with the SNP; polls suggest Cameron 'won' leaders' Question Time

8 DAYS LEFT

We enter the home straight with a trip to one of the 20 or 30 seats that will decide which party forms the government. The first thing we see confirms how surreal this election is becoming: 305 miles from Edinburgh, a huge billboard featuring Alex Salmond, this time dressed in a regulation burglar's black rollneck, and stealing money – English money – from someone's pocket. Oh, the subtlety and sophistication of the Tory campaign.

Labour is reckoned to have a 60 per cent chance of taking this seat back from the Tories, but in the midst of the general background noise, one message seems to have got through: that the Scots are always getting one over on the English, and some climactic Caledonian heist is now a very real prospect. Throughout the day, the same refrains repeatedly come back from people we meet: 'They wanted self-rule for their country, now they want to poke their bloody noses in ours ... Nicola Sturgeon's after as much money as possible for Scotland, and I think they have a pretty good deal already ... If the Scottish get in with Labour, we're done for.'

Nuneaton – the home town of George '*Middlemarch*' Eliot, four miles from the exact geographical centre of England – is hardly another South Bank. Instead, it bears the same scars from supposed progress as a lot of places: boarded-up pubs, fields making way for Starter Homes, and a town centre trying to make the best of it while neon-lit retail parks do a roaring trade. It all makes for a sense of low-level grumbling, compounded by a lot of complaints about benefit cheats and immigrants – and now, Scottish people. That's about as worked-up as a lot of people get: a lot of the time, mention of the election simply prompts very understandable sighs of exasperation.

As we drive away, our minds go back to a woman we met in Liverpool, the Sure Start Mum. We met her twice: once outside the children's centre, and again at an impassioned protest against the cuts at the city's Pier Head – and both times, she highlighted what sits at the heart of this election, but has rather got lost underneath all the shrill noise.

She said she'd never been on a demonstration before, and we asked her if she thought what had happened would put a rocket under public opinion, and raise people's awareness.

She looked into the camera. 'I hope so,' she said. 'And I hope they vote.

'That's the biggest one: vote.'

12 MAY

We've had the bloodletting of the Ed Wedding. Now we've got the full-fat Tory government that virtually no one predicted

CHARLIE BROOKER

It was supposed to be more complicated. After the vote, they said we'd have to get out the constitutional slide rule to try to work out who'd won. The Wikipedia entry on 'minority government' experienced a huge spike in traffic. There were more bitter arguments about legitimacy than in five seasons of Jeremy Kyle. Everyone agreed the election would herald the gravest constitutional crisis since the abdication, or that time Jade Goody slagged off Shilpa Shetty on *Big Brother*. Many said Ed Miliband was certain to become prime minister.

Yep. That's what they said.

Instead, on the night, we got what *Game of Thrones* fans might call an 'Ed Wedding'; from the shock exit polls onwards, the bloodletting never let up. Now we've got the full-fat Tory government that virtually no one predicted. And this is where we find ourselves: halfway through the Cameron Decade. The Cameron Era. Cameronian Times.

Five more years of a shiny computerised toe in a prime-ministerial suit, clonking hither and thither, a thin smile above his shiny chin. He won the election, won completely. Won the shit out of it. He's already downloaded an OS update, rebooted and entered 'phase two'. Maybe this time around he'll develop some identifiable personality traits for satirists to latch on to, beyond being a bit distant and ultimately unknowable. We can only hope.

Labour, meanwhile, have tumbled through a wormhole back to the 1980s. Some say it'll take them a decade to recover, but there's a precedent for it happening sooner. They were similarly wiped out in 1992, yet won by a landslide just five years later, fronted by a messianic warmonger. So there's that to look forward to.

The Lib Dems came out worst. As a nationwide cultural force to be reckoned with, they're now precisely as relevant as Anton Du Beke. It's clear that, in coalition they were a kind of shock absorber for the Tories – Nick Clegg, in particular, functioning as a hate-magnet, deflecting anger away from Cameron and Osborne. It was inevitable: Clegg seemed like such a blank. He was the default pre-customisation character in a video game. A photofit of a bloke you once met at a barbecue. Someone in a lift at Southampton Radio. As a consequence, he could embody whatever seemed most psychologically convenient for you at the time, which is perhaps why, back in 2010 – at the height of Cleggmania

– the public projected their hope on to him, only to replace that with scorn about a year later.

The polls, though. The polls. For a long while it had seemed implausible that Ed Miliband could ever be prime minister – surely he was too gawky, gauche and inherently comic – but the polls began to claim he was in with a shot. An early run of impressive campaign performances underlined it: they changed the way we looked at him. He suddenly appeared confident, charming even. The underdog made good. He became a quasi-ironic sex symbol. Even that insane 8ft stone pledge card couldn't completely wreck his chances. But only because they were already wrecked.

Yes, all that pre-vote buzz was ten hundred million thousand years ago, because the polls were wrong and we'd never actually thought anything good about Miliband ever. And the polls were wrong because people were lying to the pollsters. The glaring disparity between the weeks of pre-election polling and the actual result is surely useful scientific data: perhaps the most comprehensive investigation into the difference between what people claim to think and what they actually think ever undertaken. Clearly, voting Tory is a guilty pleasure some people won't readily admit to – like masturbating or listening to Gary Barlow. Or masturbating while listening to Gary Barlow. In the voting booth. Using your free hand to vote Conservative. Cameron's Britain.

'Public opinion' helps to shape countless policy decisions every day, from the colour of the wrapper on your KitKat Chunky, to whether or not we should bomb some faraway kingdom. So it's worrying to discover we might as well have decided all this shit on a dice-roll. In fact, public opinion itself might not really exist, at least not in a form that can be measured outside of a secret ballot. Traditional public opinion had everything thrown at it in the run up to 7 May. Opinion polls, opinion worms, online votes, TV news vox pops – and all of it coughed up unreliable results.

In an age where anyone can say whatever they want, online and all the time, to absolutely anybody, it's bizarre that none of us seems to know what anyone's thinking. Not without asking them to mark their opinion down using a pencil and a bit of paper, like it's 1962 or something.

If there's one thing we can get out of the 2015 election, apart from five more years of Gammonhead, and five years of Labour pacing its enclosure like a depressed polar bear, it should be an end to nervous, presumptive policy-making. Never again need any decision be guided by an opinion poll, or a focus group, or the popularity of a hashtag. Maybe that's a good thing. Or 10 bad ones glued together. I have absolutely no idea and neither do you. Because none of us knows anything.

30 MAY

Farewell, readers

ALAN RUSBRIDGER

This, if you're reading the physical paper – which you're probably not – is my last edition as editor. In just over 20 years we have put nearly 7,500 papers 'to bed', as almost no one says now. At some point in the 24-hour, seamlessly rolling digital news cycle, you'll have a new editor. I will have slipped away and my successor, Katharine Viner, will have materialised at the helm.

Since 1821 there have been just 10 editors of the *Guardian* – or 11 if you count Russell Scott Taylor, the 18-year-old who helped edit for a brief period in the 1840s. The greatest of them, CP Scott, managed 57 years in the hot seat. His son, Ted, drowned on Windermere only three years into his stint. Twenty years is, give or take, about the average.

The paper I joined in 1979 felt in some ways like a family firm, and in a sense, it still is. I started on the same July Monday as Nick Davies, who went on to become one of the finest reporters of his generation. His career led him into investigations, mine into descriptive reporting, columns and features. From the day I arrived, the *Guardian* felt like a warm bath – a place of sanctuary for free thought and writing.

And I was very firmly a writer: it never occurred to me that I would ever edit any bit of the *Guardian*, let alone the whole thing. I even left at one point. But in late 1988 the *Guardian* badly needed a *Weekend* magazine to answer the rather brilliant Saturday glossy that the *Independent* had just launched. For some reason, Peter Preston, then the *Guardian*'s editor, asked me to do it.

I had been diverted down a different journalistic path – one that would lead me, via the launch of *G2* in 1992, to take over the editor's chair on 13 January 1995. I knew enough of the *Guardian*'s history to feel utterly overawed by the responsibility. Please, please let me not drop the vase.

But, of course, the *Guardian* is bigger than any one editor. A rival kindly took me out to lunch soon after I started and reassured me: 'If I take a day off, there are six assistant editors who have a different view of what my paper should be. If you take the day off, the building itself would produce the *Guardian*.'

He was right. There is – through a combination of cultural osmosis, ownership and watchful readers – an incredibly strong shared idea of what the *Guardian* is, even if the job is to reinterpret it for each generation, 'in the same spirit as heretofore'.

My first edition appeared the next day, as if nothing had happened, with the splash headline: 'EU moves to tighten frontiers'. *Plus ça change*.

During the first 170-odd years of the *Guardian*'s life there were, of course, enormous challenges and changes, not least the move from Manchester to London in 1964. But the essentials of newspaper life were the same in 1995, when I took over from Peter Preston, as they had been in 1821, when the paper was launched in response to the Peterloo Massacre of 1819.

Stories were told in words and (more recently) pictures – still black and white, the 'proper' medium for news 20 years ago. The rhythm of the day built up to one main deadline, around 9.30pm. We knew the cost of paper, ink, printing and distribution, and could flex the price of advertising, and of the newspaper itself. The readership was overwhelmingly in the UK, and if they ever wanted to get in touch, they did so by phone or letter. It was a world of known knowns.

Twenty years later, we swim in unknown unknowns. We still tell stories in text and pictures, but the words are as likely to be in the form of live blogs as stories. We have learned to use moving pictures as well as stills. We work in audio, interactives, data, graphics and any combination of the above. We distribute our journalism across multiple channels, platforms and devices, including live discussion and debate. We're on the iWatch; we're in bed with Facebook; we're still in the corner shop.

Two thirds of our readership is now outside of the UK: we publish continuously. Virtually all our readers can themselves now be publishers and can connect with one another, and anyone else, as well as us. They contribute to the *Guardian* in ways that were unimaginable even 15 years ago.

On top of all that, we still produce a newspaper. Or, more precisely, two. The *Observer*, 30 years older than the *Guardian*, is in really good health under John Mulholland.

The economic model of what we now do is still in its infancy. Twenty years ago, no one asked a newspaper editor about their business model. Now it's one of the first questions. And, of course, the *Guardian* – though very financially secure today compared with many periods in its past – is no more immune than any of its rivals to the need to find a sustainable basis for what it does.

Some publishers have decided to erect walls around their digital content and insist on payment. The polar opposites are represented by the *Guardian* and *The Times* of London, the latter of which today claims a daily digital audience of around 281,000. In April the *Guardian* was read by more than 7 million unique browsers a day. On an equal accounting basis, we're losing (or investing) about the same amount of money. You'll have to come back in 10 or even 20 years' time to find out who judged the future best. But the *Guardian* – still the eighth-biggest newspaper in the UK – is now vying with the *New York Times* for the mantle of largest serious English-language newspaper website in the world.

So much for the numbers. While sorting through 20 years' worth of assorted papers in recent weeks – I'm a hoarder rather than a chucker – I made mental divisions for the past two decades. First came the Libel Years, during which it felt as if the *Guardian* was never out of one court or another. Almost as soon as I took over, there was a procession of MPs, cabinet ministers, lobbyists, cult-busters, quack doctors, corporations, police officers, banks and rich playboys queuing up to injunct or sue us.

There is – thank goodness – much less libel around these days, but those battles were often epic, costly and immensely time-consuming. If you won – which, mostly, we did – they could even be fun. Mostly, they were nerve-racking and exhausting. I'm not sorry to see the slow decline of the London libel industry, and hope that we, alongside other newspapers and free-speech organisations, played a small part in helping to finish it off. And a big thank you to all m'learned friends from over the years. You were expensive. But good.

Then came the first Internet Years, during which – under Ian Katz's leadership – we created a website that didn't fall into the trap of simply replicating online what we did in print. Ian and his team saw that this was a medium that was, in many important respects, quite different from print, and created a digital Guardian Unlimited that played by the new rules of the game.

Then there was an interlude with the print Format Wars – a response to the bold move by the *Independent* and *Times* to switch from broadsheet publishing to tabloid. The *Indie* even announced that it would henceforth be a 'viewspaper', not a newspaper – a startling declaration of intent that got lost in the excitement about size.

For various reasons – not least the amount of classified advertising we still took in print at that point – tabloid didn't really work for us. We needed new presses anyway – the cost of any format was neutral – and opted for the European Berliner size.

The paper that took shape in the hands of designer Mark Porter and deputy editor Paul Johnson (and, at the *Observer*, with former editor Roger Alton) was a thing of beauty and flexibility. But, even as we installed the new Man Roland presses, we knew they were likely to be the last we ever bought. In retrospect, it's not clear that the changes in printed format transformed the fortunes of anyone – big, little or medium.

The next phase was the Social Web, or Web 2.0, as it was first called. Emily Bell, by then editing our digital output and our resident seer, quickly pronounced this to be as important as the web itself. There was a fork in the road, she warned us: we could fence ourselves off from this social, economic, cultural and publishing revolution, or we could embrace it wholeheartedly. Open or closed? We went for open.

An early experiment was Comment Is Free, launched by Georgina Henry in 2006 as a way of immensely broadening and diversifying the pool of *Guardian* commentary – not just the 'above the line' writers, but the hundreds of thousands of you who flooded in to debate and argue in a way that had never previously been possible.

We had to devise new rules and conventions. A new breed of journalist – comment moderators – was born in order to handle the avalanche of opinion. We had created a new democracy of expression, which was sometimes uncomfortable, but mostly rich and absorbing, and sometimes even exhilarating. Our most recent design, overseen by our head of digital strategy Wolfgang Blau, took this still further.

And, finally, there were the stories: about crooked bungs; politicians on the take; corporations dodging tax; toxic spills; unethical policing; lethal policing; torture and rendition; female mutilation; drugs; food production; pill-peddlers and much more.

Wikileaks, in 2010, felt, and was, enormous: the biggest leak of diplomatic and intelligence cables the world had then seen. But then came phone-hacking – Nick Davies's extraordinary seven-year slog of reporting gradually shone a light on the crimes, evasions and deceptions of the most powerful news company in the world.

Davies's reporting stopped a vast, ruthless media monopoly from effectively doubling in size – with all the consequences for power, democracy, regulation and even policing that went with that. The best defence that the Murdochs – son, father and associates – could muster was that it was out of control. Any other response would have been too corporately apocalyptic to contemplate.

British journalism as an occasionally thoughtless bloodsport has as a result, I think, been checked a little, though I know not all my fellow editors either agree or approve.

And then came Edward Snowden, with his astonishing insights into the way the surveillance business had been industrialised since 9/11, so that – without any kind of meaningful informed consent – countless millions of people the world over have had their data scooped up, stored and analysed.

Judges, congressmen, lawyers, presidents, legislators, internet giants and academics around the world pored over the *Guardian* stories, so surely edited by US editor Janine Gibson. Only this month the US phone dragnet that had secretly violated the privacy of millions of Americans every day since October 2001 was shut down. This was perhaps inevitable after the programme's over-whelming rejection by Congress, and after a US court of appeal ruled that the bulk collection of telephone metadata revealed by Snowden was unlawful.

The Pulitzer prize for public service was our reward. Snowden, who made the kind of sacrifice most of us would find hard even to contemplate, must, alas, wait for his own form of absolution and just recognition.

There have been other recent successes – deputy editor Kath-arine Viner's brilliant launch of *Guardian* Australia – as part of our international expansion; Rob Evans's long, dogged campaign to drag Prince Charles's political correspondence into the open; our recent campaign to treat climate change with the gravity and impact it deserves; Maggie O'Kane's forceful crusade against female genital mutilation ... and much more.

As I've cleared my shelves and sorted through fading ephemera, I have, of course, reflected on what the *Guardian* is – and what it is to be an editor.

When John Scott, one of the sons of CP, decided to place the *Manchester Guardian* into a trust, he consulted Churchill's future Lord Chancellor, Gavin Simonds, who told him: 'It seems to me that you are trying to do something very repugnant to the law of England. You are trying to divest yourself of a property right.'

That was precisely what Scott was trying to do. Sir William Haley, later editor of *The Times*, said: 'He could have been a rich man; he chose a spartan existence. And, when he made up his mind to divest himself of all beneficial interest [in the *Guardian*], he did so with as little display of emotion as if he has been solving an algebraical problem. Most men making so large a sacrifice would have exacted at least the price of an attitude.'

The decision of the Scott family to give up all financial interest in the *Guardian* must rank high among the great historic acts of public-minded philanthropy. In doing so, they created an ownership structure with only two purposes: to secure the future of the *Guardian* in perpetuity, and to protect its independence in all situations, at all costs and against all comers.

The perpetuity bit is, of course, always a work in progress – though building an endowment of around £1bn is certainly a strong foundation for the future. The role of the Guardian Media Group – the 'commercial' wing of the operation – has been crucial.

The independence given to us by the trust manifests itself in a hundred ways. Before the recent general election, 200 of us sat in a room one lunchtime to decide which party, if any, to endorse. There was no message filtering down from above, explicit or implicit. Rightly, or wrongly, the decision was ours alone.

The same spirit is there every morning, when anyone on staff can come to the morning conference – to listen, to contribute, to challenge or to absorb. It was there when the insurers in the Aitken libel action urged our co-defendants, Granada TV, to surrender – while the Scott Trust told us to fight on. It was there when the state and assorted politicians came knocking to get them to pull the plug on the Snowden stories. The trust had the absolute answer: we can't.

It was there every time this editor needed advice from those wisest of owls, Hugo Young and Liz Forgan. It's there in the words of the centenary essay penned by Scott in 1921, in which he wrote of the balance between the material and moral existence of a newspaper – between profit and power. There was never any question for him which mattered more.

Power over profit. But even that, in a modern context, makes me a little uneasy. I end with a confession about editing, and a nagging anxiety about this business of power.

An editor, if he or she chooses, can be a very powerful figure indeed. Editors can make or break people. They dictate who gets a voice, and who remains voiceless. They can, if they want, bully and frighten whom they choose. They can impose their views on a newspaper and, through the paper, on a country and the lives of millions.

As we've seen, they can break the law while delving into private lives in reasonable confidence that no one will stop them, not even the police or regulator. They can have a disproportionate influence in shaping debates – if only by excluding any contrary arguments. One voice can dominate an entire newspaper, from the front page, throughout the reporting and the editorial columns to a select few allowed to be commentators.

People do still bend their knee to this kind of power, even in an age when the influence of mainstream media is supposed to be waning. In my modest fashion, I've experienced it at first hand. And, in a way, I'm glad of that. I want strong institutions of the fourth estate. In a world of globalised, distant, often unaccountable power, a countervailing source of scrutiny and influence is needed more than ever.

But I've never wanted the *Guardian* to be my voice – nor would my *Guardian* colleagues have wanted or allowed it. Scott saw clearly that a newspaper had to shun 'the temptations of a monopoly ... the voice of opponents no less than that of friends has a right to be heard'.

I don't know that I've always lived up to Scott's ideal in that, but it was important to me that the *Guardian* had, for instance, a

Simon Jenkins, a Max Hastings or a Matthew d'Ancona as well as writers who swam more easily with our liberal currents.

The *Guardian* has had the strength to withstand all the attacks launched in response to our journalism – and there have been many. But we drew our resilience from the power of the institution, not of any individual.

But the power of an editor has always made me nervous. Early in my editorship I gave away significant power: the power of correction. It seemed obvious to me that journalism, as an imperfect medium, will always include mistakes – and that the very last person to adjudicate on whether or not an error had been made was the person responsible for the error in the first place.

I have never forgotten this tell-it-like it is description of a newspaper by the *Washington Post*'s David Broder: '[A] partial, hasty, incomplete, inevitably somewhat flawed and inaccurate rendering of some of the things we have heard about in the past 24 hours – distorted, despite our best efforts to eliminate gross bias, by the very process of compression that makes it possible for you to lift it from the doorstep and read it in about an hour. If we labelled the product accurately, then we could immediately add: "But it's the best we could do under the circumstances, and we will be back tomorrow, with a corrected and updated version."'

And so, since 1997, anyone who thinks the *Guardian* has got something wrong can bypass the editor and appeal to someone who is himself not answerable to the editor, but to the Scott Trust. I cannot interfere in his judgments, nor edit the weekly column in which he is free to criticise the paper or expose our weaknesses.

Something like this is commonplace in American newspapers, and elsewhere, but is still not the rule in the UK. You can see why. If, as editor, you greatly savour the view from the bully pulpit, then it makes no sense at all to appoint a truly independent umpire.

More recently, I gave away more power – creating an editorial board to oversee the comment pages and leader columns. We did not completely follow the US model, in which the executive editor of, say, the *Washington Post* or *New York Times* has no say at all over the opinion pages. I remained editor of the whole *Guardian*. But I did want to create a clear divide between the business of news and comment, and to give the editorial board, headed by Jonathan Freedland, the freedom (and time) to think for themselves. Of course, CP Scott famously articulated the separation in his 1921 essay. One was free, the other sacred. As usual, he was right.

Next week, for the first time in 20 years, I will have stepped off the hamster wheel of news. The *Guardian* is in good shape, its reach, influence and endowment bigger than anything imaginable at the time John Scott made his noble and philanthropic sacrifice.

I have been blessed with wonderful colleagues, whom I shall miss terribly – only a very few of them named here. Katharine Viner will be a wonderful 11th (or even 12th) editor of the paper. Next year I will head (as well as Lady Margaret Hall at Oxford University – founded, like the *Guardian*, in the cause of reform) the institution I have come to cherish beyond all other in the media: the Scott Trust itself.

I will say goodbye to colleagues in person. But please, readers, accept this as my farewell to you, along with my intense gratitude for your support, engagement, response and argument over many years. I know many of you have now become 'members' of the *Guardian*, as we open the paper up even more to live and physical experience.

I've noticed that some of the most devoted readers tend to carbon-date themselves by editor. 'I started with Wadsworth,' an elderly loyalist might say or 'I began reading under Hetherington.'

But, in the end, we editors just pass through. We all know that you, the readers, are the real carriers of the flame.

3 JUNE

Keeping up with Caitlyn

JESS CARTNER-MORLEY

Caitlyn Jenner's *Vanity Fair* cover was expected to create a controversial, watercooler cultural moment, but it turned into something much more extraordinary. Because the image of Caitlyn Jenner – winner of an Olympic gold medal as a man named Bruce, and member of the Kardashians, the family pop culture loves to hate – brought no controversy, only applause. Kim Kardashian may have broken the internet, but Caitlyn Jenner did something even more astonishing. She united it.

Jenner, Annie Leibovitz and *Vanity Fair* produced an image that won the world over. And this, in a society where acceptance and understanding of transgender issues – while progressing – is still in its infancy. The magazine is not yet on newsstands, and while the interview is available online for digital subscribers, the overwhelming majority of comment has been based on the cover image. In it, Jenner wears an ivory satin corset, so that her cinched waist, falling just above the coverline ('Call me Caitlyn') forms the central focus. An hourglass woman's body in white, in a 1950s cut bodice, surely references Marilyn Monroe – in the minds of Leibovitz and the *Vanity Fair* art directors, anyway, if not of Jenner. Monroe stands for all-Americanism, for blue-chip Hollywood glamour (as opposed, perhaps, to the modern Kardashian brand of fame), for ultimate femininity and for vulnerability. But while Jenner's hands are out of shot, behind her back, the photo spotlights the strong muscles of her arms and thighs, reminding us of those Olympic medals, and serving as an antidote to the unguarded, exposed, Monroe-ish appeal of her corsetted waist and coy expression, half-turned from the camera.

In guidelines reissued yesterday, the media-monitoring organisation GLAAD warns against 'superficial critiques of a transgender person's femininity or masculinity. Commenting on how well a transgender person conforms to conventional standards of femininity or masculinity is reductive and insulting.' I hope it does not break these guidelines to say that the cover image draws on the iconography of strong American women. Jessica Lange, to whom many have noticed a resemblance, has had a four-decade acting career. Cindy Crawford, of whom Jenner's Coke-can curls and athletic body are also reminiscent, has sustained a modelling career since the 1980s, and most recently starred as the take-no-prisoners headmistress in the music video for Taylor Swift's 'Bad Blood'. Lena Dunham captured the spirit of the image immediately after its release, when she tweeted: 'I just want Caitlyn Jenner to take me out and teach me how to drive a stick shift in heels.'

The stylist of the shoot, Jessica Diehl, has described Jenner as 'all-American in so many ways'. Diehl moodboarded images of Lauren Bacall, and Rene Russo in *The Thomas Crown Affair* when the looks were being planned, 'and just vintage photographs of old Hollywood stars. A couple of Jackie Kennedys are never wrong.' The state of semi-undress she explains as simple openness. 'It was not meant to be risqué in any way. It was really meant to show with all honesty and purity, "This is what is going on. Here I am."' Although the ivory corset and Jenner's demure pose are not a million miles away from Kim and Kanye's April 2014 American *Vogue* cover, for which Kim Kardashian wore a strapless ivory silk Lanvin gown, Diehl sees her shoot as putting deliberate distance between Caitlyn-with-a-C and the K-word. 'Coming from a very fashion-forward family, we sort of thought that the nicest thing to do was to focus on style over fashion.'

But that is only half the story, because the Kardashians are at the heart of what happened on Monday. Caitlyn Jenner, who launched her Twitter account to coincide with the cover reveal, set a new record by reaching 1 million followers in four hours and three minutes. At the time of writing, she was almost at 2 million, having tweeted just three times. President Obama – whose five-hour record Jenner broke to reach her first million Twitter followers – responded with public support, telling Jenner 'your story matters'. Celebrities from Maria Shriver to Ellen DeGeneres, Lady Gaga to Mia Farrow, flooded the internet with messages of congratulation and welcome. It is Jenner's connection to the Kardashian family (she was married to matriarch Kris for 14 years until their divorce earlier this year) that has put a transgender woman on the cover of a glossy magazine. Kim Kardashian's tweet in support of her former stepfather – 'How beautiful! Be happy, be proud, live life YOUR way!' has been retweeted 28,000 times.

Back in February, when discussion and speculation about Jenner's transgender identity was gathering pace, the novelist Curtis Sittenfeld, author of *American Wife*, tweeted this: 'What if it turns out all along Kim Kardashian's butt has been a Trojan horse for greater compassion & acceptance of transgender people?' It was a light-hearted comment, but Sittenfeld's point is an intriguing one. The Kardashians are, arguably, the most famous family in the world. *Keeping Up With The Kardashians* is now in its 10th series, with viewing figures still over 2 million. The pop-cultural power of this is without precedent. (Imagine what Dallas would have been if the Ewings had been real people, Instagramming their Southfork barbecues.) And yet, despite their money (Kris Jenner's net worth is estimated at $125m), their fame, their connections in music and fashion (Kim is married to Kanye West; Kendall is best mates with Cara Delevingne), they have been summarily dismissed by the self-appointed keepers of pop-cultural fame as vacuous and irritating. And indeed, to date, Kardashian storylines have been trashily tabloid: sex tapes, 72-day marriages, diets and plastic surgery.

But in a plot twist that even the Dallas screenwriters could not have dreamed up, the first family of the reality-TV generation have, with the Jenner story, become catalysts for progressive social change. Brave and brilliant work for acceptance is being done by those passionate about equality, but the bald reality is that 140 characters by Kim Kardashian have more impact on cultural mores than any number of obscure activists preaching the same thing.

Less than two years ago, Chelsea Manning, the morning after being sentenced to 35 years in prison, issued a statement requesting that the media use her new name and the feminine pronoun. 'Bradley Manning says he wants to live as a woman,' reported the Associated Press; almost every major US newspaper continued to use the male pronoun. The contrast with the media acceptance of Jenner could hardly be more marked. And while the reception given to Manning's announcement reflected public ambivalence about the trial that preceded it, the acceptance of Jenner is also, surely, a direct result of the Kardashians' fame. The Kardashians, in all their eccentricities – who can forget that Kim's 14th birthday party was held at Neverland – have become part of the fabric of public life. Kim and her sisters have not only publicly celebrated Caitlyn's *Vanity Fair* portfolio, but also talked openly about their support and understanding for their mother, Kris, as she tries to reconcile memories of her marriage with this new reality. A combination of fame and social media reach means that these complex and nuanced issues around a transgender woman and her family are being explored, in real time and on pop-cultural primetime.

One person, naturally, foretold long ago that the Kardashians would one day be understood as a dynasty of great significance.

Last year, when Kanye and Kim became the first mixed-race couple to appear on the cover of *Vogue*, West said the magazine cover was the first moment at which people 'understood' his marriage, after 'two years of people not understanding an interracial relationship'. The previous year, West said in a radio interview that 'a lot of what the Kardashians do, I don't think they get enough credit for. They prep America to accept interracial relationships.' Last year, Kim Kardashian wrote on her website that 'I feel a responsibility as a mother, a public figure, a human being, to do what I can to make sure that not only my child, but all children, don't have to grow up in a world where they are judged by the colour of their skin, or their gender, or their sexual orientation.'

Like it or not, the Kardashians have done something positive, progressive and meaningful. The internet era of baring all can be a beautiful thing: prejudice can wither and fall, and acceptance and understanding blossom in its place. And I'm not just talking about Caitlyn Jenner.

4 JUNE

Charles Kennedy's death was a tragic waste of talent. Let compassion be his legacy

GABY HINSLIFF

When I think of Charlie Kennedy, it's his hands that I remember. There'd usually be a cigarette dangling from one of them; back before the smoking ban, chats in his Westminster office were usually conducted through a thick blue haze. But what really struck me, the first time I interviewed him at length, was that his hands were trembling.

I couldn't work out if it was nerves – we were discussing Iraq, the biggest judgment call of his career and one that at the time seemed to leave him dangerously exposed – or a hangover, although in retrospect perhaps the two were related. Many comedians drink to maintain the easy confidence that everyone assumes comes naturally.

But whatever it was, only the hands gave it away. The voice was calm, the arguments fluent, the judgment sharp as a knife. Charles Kennedy was a more far-sighted politician, even in drink, than many will ever be sober, and that's what's so cruelly frustrating about his death at 55; that he can never now become what he was capable of becoming. His death is a personal tragedy for family and friends, but even for those who never met him nor sympathised with his politics, there is something horribly poignant about a talent wasted.

It's easy to forget, now that the world and his dog insists they always knew Iraq didn't have WMD, what courage it took to come out against the war in 2003 when public opinion was oddly less clear-cut. Kennedy did it in the teeth of opposition from some very senior colleagues who felt he should, at the very least, sit on the fence; who sniped behind his back about whether joining stop-the-war marches was statesmanlike. He did it knowing that if the invasion turned out to be the easy success many predicted, his reputation might not recover.

Twice in his life Kennedy stood isolated on what looked like the wrong side of career-defining arguments: once in 2003 over Iraq and again in 2010, when he was the sole Liberal Democrat MP to vote against entering coalition with David Cameron. Some will say history twice proved him right but perhaps more accurately it twice proved him on the electorally successful side, which for a politician is much less grudging praise than it sounds.

When he was forced from office in January 2006, Kennedy had just obtained the best Liberal election result since 1923: 62 seats, up from 46 when he became leader. The result reflected not just his personal charm and gentleness – he had the knack of never sounding like a career politician even after 30 years at Westminster – but personal bravery too. Few could have felt it more acutely when so many of those left-leaning voters he won over from Labour abandoned the party in 2010, reeling in disgust from the decision to go into coalition. It is anyone's guess when, or if, his party will regain that lost ground.

Yet while his death will cast a long and emotive shadow over the current Liberal Democrat leadership contest, it's too crude to draw from him the lesson that the party succeeds simply by tacking relentlessly left. What marked Kennedy out from Paddy Ashdown before him or Nick Clegg after him (poor Menzies Campbell did not last long enough to be marked for much) was a deep suspicion of getting too close to either main party – whether in the sort of grand reunion of the left proposed by Tony Blair, or in right-wing coalition with Cameron. He believed fiercely in liberalism as something quite distinct from any other political creed; found ways to dramatise those differences which were right for his particular time; and above all was unafraid to defy a public mood which is often shallower than the public will admit.

And yet the worst thing about the messy, graceless way he was ousted early in 2006 is that it had become inevitable. Kennedy was always cheerfully shambolic and, when I spent a day with him on the campaign trail a few months earlier, I wasn't surprised when he pitched up so late for our early morning train to Norfolk that we nearly missed it.

But he seemed oddly hunched, withdrawn, going through the motions. Something felt wrong. Things started to happen that couldn't be easily explained – absences from high-profile appearances, erratic behaviour – and friends grew uncharacteristically irritable when pressed about that, as if searching for ways to protect him without lying. Too many people came under too much pressure to cover up for him and when Cameron, the first electorally credible Tory leader in a decade, succeeded Michael Howard in December 2005 his party's patience with its leader swiftly ran out. He got the big career judgments right; it was everyday life that defeated him.

Many Liberal Democrats, I suspect, will be wondering today if there wasn't some possible intervention they missed, or at least a better way in future of ensuring that politicians don't self-destruct. As the SNP's Alex Salmond has pointed out, Westminster is the worst place in the world for anyone with personal demons, combining a late-night boozing culture (although it's infinitely more sober now than it was in the 'two-bottle lunch' days of 1997, when I started out as a reporter) with loneliness, exhaustion, intense pressure and being far from home. Depression, divorce and dependency can engulf even old hands – and when Kennedy was elected, he was a 23-year-old from a remote Scottish farming community who'd only been to London twice before. While all of this is more openly discussed now than a decade ago, thanks partly to individual MPs bravely speaking up about their experience of mental illness, the Commons could do more to support vulnerable members – particularly when they lose their seats.

But it's not just about the House of Commons, is it? All those people getting cheap laughs on social media out of Kennedy's last erratic performance on the BBC's *Question Time*, or rejoicing in his defeat on election night, were just a visible example of a culture which not only stigmatises people with mental health problems but treats public figures – politicians or otherwise – as if they were somehow less than human. If Charles Kennedy's death leads one or two to pause before unleashing mob scorn or fury, if it prompts an ounce more compassion for people whose lives might well be more complicated than they look – well, a fine liberal legacy that would be.

4 JUNE

Fall of the Sepp Blatter dynasty: how Qatar became a frontier too far

MARINA HYDE

They call Afghanistan the graveyard of empires, but history may judge Qatar to have been Sepp Blatter's fatal act of expansion. In awarding the 2022 tournament to the tiny desert kingdom, his Fifa might be argued finally to have strategically overreached itself. For those more comfortable with conspiracies than complexities, that picture of Blatter holding the open envelope to reveal the word 'QATAR' will be forever read as a come-and-get-me plea to the US authorities, America having been among the disappointed World Cup bidders.

Was that when it went ineluctably tits up, if you'll forgive the reliance on one of Edward Gibbon's stock phrases? It's certainly pretty to think so – which is to say, miles too glib. But one thing on which we might all agree on is how astonishingly quickly empires can fall when they do. By way of a consolation sop to Blatter's vanity, let's stick the outgoing Fifa president on a par with the Ming Dynasty, which ruled for 276 years and collapsed in barely a decade.

As someone who physically resembled the man behind the curtain even when he was the great and powerful Oz, Sepp Blatter did not appear unrecognisably different as he delivered his surprise resignation speech on Tuesday evening. And in one sense, nor did the house he ran for 17 years and helped shape for four decades. The ultimate machine politician may be gone but the machine remains, and investigating it will seem like a picnic compared with reforming it.

Nevertheless, it already feels as if something about Fifa has changed irrevocably with his departure, just as something about Rupert Murdoch's empire changed forever when the latter was forced to close the News of the World. What had so long felt like an unassailable hierarchy suddenly no longer did, and for all that other imperial business was got on with as usual, there was an immediate and enduring sense that the high water mark of a certain culture had passed. A spell had been broken. One minute Rupert was the most feared power in the land, who could stalk into Downing Street via a haunted mirror whenever he wanted, and then ... well, he wasn't. It just wasn't the same.

And so with Fifa. Not long ago it was riding so high that it appeared able to do anything: appropriate any funds, dictate any terms, override any country's constitution, ignore any criticism. Only on Saturday I was waffling on about how Blatter's victory against the backdrop of the FBI probe recalled Nixon's landslide re-election during the middle of the Watergate investigation, and speculated whether he'd make it the full two years that the former US president managed before he was forced to resign. The morning after victory, Blatter declined any attempt at striking a note of humility, telling a TV interviewer: 'I forgive everyone, but I do not forget.'

Four days later, he was on the way out (leaving himself a few months to 'not forget' a few enemies, one imagines – even as reports suggest that FBI investigators are hoping some of his enemies will decide it is in their interests not to forget him). The vast structures of Fifa are still systemically corrupted, but the authorities are pursuing it as never before. If anyone goes to see *United Passions* – the preposterous vanity movie Blatter commissioned about his works – when it gets its US release this week, they will do so wearing the grins usually reserved for those posing with the tacky statuary in a very recently deposed dictator's palace.

Of course, it wasn't really that sudden – and the FBI criminal probe, while being the most devastating, was not the only malfunction of Fifa's system. Whichever way you shake it, something odd was happening by the time of the Confederations Cup in Brazil two years ago, as mass public protests against the government began explicitly linking the language of Brazil's bid for the following year's World Cup – 'Fifa standard' – to the comparatively hopeless state of the country's public services. I was only being half-facetious when I described this as Fifa's Arab Spring, which saw even members of his fabled 'football family' such as Romário turning on a governing body they declared parasitic. Blatter did not explicitly cast the dissenters as insurgents, but it was difficult to avoid the sense that his once-unquestioned imperium was failing to smooth all in its path.

'When we say football connects people,' blathered Blatter of these protests, 'it connected people in the stadium. Perhaps unfortunately it also connected people in the street.' He may find instead the social media network did that – the same new technology that has made consent harder to manufacture than once it was. That same network does not permit, for instance, the deaths of hundreds upon hundreds of nameless migrants building Qatar infrastructure to be a missable footnote, as once they would have been.

Fifa's presentational challenges have metamorphosed. By way of one example, these days a single graphic comparing Qatar 2022 construction deaths to those incurred for other mega-events is not simply shared, but reproduced around the world, used to attack sponsors, taken up by America's hottest comedy show. Different hierarchies are at work, and Sepp Blatter's regime lacked a strategy for dealing with them.

Of course, there are sadnesses to his demise. It is too early to say for sure, for instance, but it's possible we'll now have to rule out his receipt of the longed-for Nobel for bringing peace to the Middle East via the medium of football. But a spell has been broken, and it is impossible not to take heart that things aren't just the same.

15 JUNE

Talking posh isn't enough

STEPHEN MOSS

As the working-class son of a steelworker and a pub pianist from south Wales, moving up to Oxford in the mid-1970s was a bit of a shock to the system. I was about as far away from posh as it was possible to be. I recall that tipping the 'scout' – the man who cleaned my room and made my bed – was a source of particular concern. I suddenly had a servant, but how much was I supposed to give him at the end of term? I'm sure the pathetic amount I coughed up soured our always-uneasy relationship.

The combination of not having taken a year off – most of the students from public schools did the Oxbridge entrance exam in their post-A-level year – and being from a background that was the antithesis of posh made it hard to adjust. I tended to hang around with sporty types who talked mainly about cricket averages.

Nobody ever told me it would be a good idea to go to lectures not just in modern history – the subject I was studying – but ancient history, art, philosophy and politics, too. The difference between comprehensives and public schools is that the latter give you the space to develop as a rounded person early. They encourage free thinking. For me, the jump from A-level spoon-feeding to self-directed learning was huge and, by the time I was getting to grips with it, the course was more or less over. Education really is wasted on the young, at least on this young person.

I must have been conscious of my lowly social origins because I changed my accent more or less overnight, abandoning my Welsh lilt in favour of a form of received pronunciation so extreme that, when years later I met a theatrical voice coach, she said it was redolent of Oxford in the 50s rather than the 70s. I make Prince Charles sound common, though, if you listen closely, you can tell it's not the genuine article. Some people think I'm South African, so clipped are my vowels. The literary editor Karl Miller thought I'd been to Sandhurst.

The disguise sort of worked. I did a passable posh accent (for a while the Welshness used to reassert itself when I was tired), got a first because I was very good at passing exams, and got a job in publishing. I was a moderately successful ersatz posh person.

Except you never really become posh. For all the carapace of poshness, you remain what you are. Or rather, you end up not fitting anywhere: too posh for the working class, too working-class to be truly posh. This is why I ended up being a journalist: an observer, an outsider, restless and self-doubting.

Those who are born posh enjoy the benefits of a social capital in early life that can never be replicated later. You just can't manufacture that ease, that assumption that the world exists for your benefit. We had a 'buttery' at Oxford where students, almost invariably the posh ones, would gather with dons for pre-dinner drinks. I never dared go in there. Even though we were all supposed to be equal, somehow it didn't seem that way.

I've been rereading Anthony Powell's great novel sequence *A Dance to the Music of Time* recently. Powell (he pronounced it 'Pole') is the archetypal posh Englishman: Etonian, military family, steeped in art and literature from a very early age, certain in his judgments, critical of error and fuzzy thinking, alert to the many shades of social class, preoccupied by lineages and hierarchies, and – in the character of his narrator Nicholas Jenkins – all-seeing, all-knowing and in complete control.

The sympathetic characters in *Dance* are doomed posh romantics – Charles Stringham and Hugh Moreland, especially. The arch-villain is Widmerpool, another Etonian, but one whose father made his money selling liquid manure. Widmerpool is a parvenu who devotes his life to climbing the greasy pole, imposing his will. Powell dislikes the imposition of will, the out-and-out triers. He admires easy talent and selfless service he identifies with people who punt their way through life.

Being unposh, I have spent my life trying to be Stringham – to have his style and ease, his contempt for the worldly and workaday – but I know that my autodidactical destiny is to be Widmerpool. The dance is an ungainly one.

17 JUNE

Jeremy Corbyn: 'I don't do personal'

SIMON HATTENSTONE

A couple of hours ago, Jeremy Corbyn secured his 35th nomination at the last possible moment – just enough for him to make the shortlist for the Labour leadership race. If you were expecting him to be all swagger and selfies, whoops and high-fives, think again. This is Jeremy Corbyn, man of the people, five-time winner of parliamentary beard of the year (when beards weren't trendy, mind), veteran leftist, the obsessive campaigner who has signed up to virtually any issue worth signing up to over the past 40 years.

'Congratulations!' I say, enthusiastically.

'Thank you,' Corbyn says, warily. 'I'm slightly surprised that we made it through, but there we are.'

Corbyn is such an unlikely leader, so devoted to the collective that he can't even bear to refer to himself in the first person. It's always we – and there's nothing royal about it (he is a devout republican). 'We' turns out to be a subset of lefties who wanted an alternative to the Stepford candidates standing for the leadership. If he were elected leader of Labour, you half expect the first thing he would do is get rid of the top job and replace it with a co-op.

So why has he stood? 'We had a discussion among a group of us on the left about how we might influence future developments of the party. All of us felt the leadership contest was not a good idea – there should have been a policy debate first. There wasn't, so we decided somebody should put their hat in the ring in order to promote that debate. And, unfortunately, it's my hat in the ring.'

Why did it have to be his hat? 'Well, Diane [Abbott] and John [McDonnell] have done it before, so it was my turn.' So he took some persuading? 'Yeah. I have never held any appointed office, so in that sense it's unusual, but if I can promote some causes and debate by doing this, then good. That's why I'm doing it.' He offers a tiny smile. Blink and you miss it. 'At my age I'm not likely to be a long-term contender, am I?'

If this were a job interview, Corbyn would have already been shown the door. And not just because of his age – 66. Corbyn is the anti-Blair, in every way. Whereas you cannot be unaware of Blair when he is in the room (he is all charisma), you might well not notice Corbyn arriving or leaving. And despite the smears by association in yesterday's newspapers, he could not be more different to the preening George Galloway. He is a silver mouse of a man with extraordinarily committed politics. His history of campaigning is on display on the shelves in his Commons office – in file after ancient file of carefully documented paperwork. Here's the Guildford Four, there's the Birmingham Six, Afghanistan and Iraq, a delegation about Chechnya to Moscow, Mordechai Vanunu, who was imprisoned in Israel for giving away its nuclear secrets, Palestine, the World Social Forum 2004 in Mumbai, the legality of war conference of the European left, Stop the War (of which he is chair), CND (vice-chair), the Antarctica Act 1996, and on it goes. He is an international socialist, so there are modest gifts from the Black American Workers Association celebrating his 25 years in parliament and multicoloured tequilas from Venezuela, 'which I don't actually drink'.

The thing about Corbyn is that he is nearly always proved right – after the event. So when he insisted on embracing Gerry Adams and Sinn Féin decades ago, many people thought he was mad. Ditto when he campaigned for the Guildford Four and the Birmingham Six, whose innocence was later proved. And we've not even started on apartheid ...

The wall behind his desk is dedicated to more personal stuff – a poster celebrating the centenary of Arsenal, a drawing of his grandson (he has three grown sons, one of whom works with John McDonnell), photographs of his beautiful wife and a historic Islington Trade Council banner (personal is all relative with Corbyn).

You would expect Corbyn to have charisma by the bucket-load and a leonine ego, but he doesn't. He is kind and gentle, yet almost invisible – as if he has sacrificed his personality to the cause. He reminds me of the actor Jim Broadbent, who once told me he wanted to strip himself of individuality, be a clean sheet, so he could build himself up afresh for every part. He still has a touch of Citizen Smith about him (without the laughs) and even his biggest fans admit he can't open his mouth without expressing the need for peace, justice and solidarity.

Corbyn has been MP for Islington North for 32 years and last month secured his seat with a whopping 21,000 majority. It is one of the most socio-economically and ethnically diverse constituencies in the country, and he feels many of their views are not being heard in today's Labour party. 'Politically active people felt more and more disenfranchised, particularly during the ultra-New Labour years.'

Within seconds, he segues into one of his current favourite topics. 'I've just had an interesting discussion on the TTIP.' The what? 'Ah, sorry – the Transatlantic Trade and Investment Partnership. This is a negotiation between the US and European Union to develop a way in which investment would be protected, and a way in which governments must not make life difficult for investors. The fear is that it's a race to the bottom, with the lowest common denominator on both sides of the Atlantic becoming the norm. Hence a government that tries to enforce special conditions on a company, such as wage levels and working conditions, could then be threatened with legal action by a newly created trade court.' This is a good example of why many people believe it is important to have a candidate like Corbyn because it is unlikely we would hear much about the TTIP from the three other candidates (Andy Burnham, Yvette Cooper and Liz Kendall) in the leadership race.

Not surprisingly, Corbyn doesn't buy into the idea that Ed Miliband's Labour had moved too far to the left. 'It certainly wasn't an ultra-left manifesto,' he says. 'What was it proposing? A limited amount of public ownership of the national railways, which is actually very popular, quite good stuff on the minimum wage and so on, but on the economy, it wasn't fundamentally redistributive, which is what we need to be putting forward. We live in a very unequal society.'

The biggest problem, he says, was that Labour allowed the Tories to set the agenda on the economy and never offered an alternative narrative. 'We're very bad at asserting certain things. After the 2010 election and Liam Byrne's note in the Treasury, it became in the public mind a fact that Labour spent too much and this became repeated all the time, unchallenged. And by the time we actually got round to an election five years later, there was an assumption that we admitted we'd spent too much. Actually, what did we spend too much on? The banking system collapsed because of a combination of a sub-prime mortgage crisis and deregulation. There was a lot of money spent buying out bank shares and buying out banks, a lot of money spent on quantitative easing to keep the money supply going, and now Osborne is selling off RBS shares at a loss and calling it a triumph for him and his government. So I think we have to be much more assertive as to what actually happened.'

But he is unimpressed with the attacks on Miliband by New Labour's old guard. 'I obviously didn't agree with everything he did or said in the campaign, but he stood up well and worked very hard and should be thanked for that. I'm not joining in personal attacks ... I don't do personal attacks.' It's true, he doesn't. Try as you might to get him to badmouth an individual politician, he won't. Everything is about the policy.

Would there be a role for Ed Miliband in a Corbyn-led shadow cabinet? 'I hope there will be a very good role for Ed. He's a very intelligent person, was a great environment secretary, and I hope he does those kind of issues in the future.'

Corbyn grew up in a politicised family in Shropshire. 'Mum and Dad met campaigning on the Spanish civil war. Both were active peace campaigners. They died in 1986 and '87. Dad would be 100 now.' His brother Piers, a weather forecaster who denies that climate change is a product of human activity, was even further to the left of Corbyn when they were growing up and joined the Communist party. He couldn't be more opposed to Piers on global warming, but he refers to him affectionately. 'We talk quite a lot. Don't always agree. It's a family, you know.'

As a boy, he liked working on local farms and making things (nowadays, he has an allotment, on which he grows all sorts). He went to a good grammar school, was a poor student and left at 18 with two A-levels, grade E. 'John Major said I was better qualified than him. He got O-levels.' Was he lazy at school? 'I liked reading about things, doing my own course of study in that sense.' I ask what politicised him. 'Peace issues. Vietnam. Environmental issues. Then I did VSO in Jamaica when I left school. An amazing two years.' Typically, there are no anecdotes, nothing personal – just a list of issues and events. On his return from Jamaica, he worked for trade unions, eventually becoming national organiser of Nupe.

One of the few cited stories about Corbyn is that the former Labour MP-turned-Ukip MEP Robert Kilroy-Silk tried to hit him but Corbyn ran away. 'I had been on a programme on television the day before talking about why Militants shouldn't be expelled from the Labour party. He thought they should, and he was extremely abusive, threw me against a wall in the voting lobby. His quote was: "I'm an amateur boxer, I can sort anybody out," and somebody said to me what do you do in your spare time, and I said: "I'm an amateur runner," which is true. I do enjoy running.' So he did run away? 'No. I walked off. You can hardly run through the voting lobby. He thought it was a great triumph for his macho prowess.'

There is something of the ascetic about Corbyn. At the time of the expenses scandal, it was reported that he had the lowest claim in the Commons – £8.95 for a printer cartridge. Actually, he'd like to come clean on this one, he says – he'd screwed up his expenses. 'You had to pay within a certain period for things, and somewhere along the line we claimed for one print cartridge, but the rest of the stuff was slightly slower going in so that went into the next claim period, which was a much more realistic claim. A more typical Corbyn claim might run to 'a few hundred quid each quarter'. He rents his office from the Ethical Property Company. 'Fine people. Hosanna to the Ethical Property people.' He raises his mug of coffee by way of a toast.

You have described yourself as parsimonious, haven't you? 'Probably, yes.' How? 'Well, I don't spend a lot of money, I lead a very normal life, I ride a bicycle and I don't have a car.'

Corbyn seems so distant from modern Labour. Has he ever been close to leaving? 'I've often been extremely frustrated by the Labour party, particularly over Iraq and, earlier, on Vietnam. Then you think what the Labour party has achieved, and that it is the electoral home to millions of people, so I'm still in it. Always have been. I remember discussing this with Tony Benn many times, and he said: "You know, comrade, we're just in it, aren't we?" Tony was a very close friend.'

Could he imagine having a relationship with somebody who wasn't on the left? 'No. At the end of the day, it's the question of your values. They get in the way.'

In 1999, he and his first wife (a Chilean very much on the left) divorced. Is it true that the marriage collapsed because of a row over their children's schooling (he wanted the local comp; she insisted on a grammar school and won)? There is a tense silence. He looks me in the face. 'I hated that period. I hated the publicity for it. I hated the pressure put on my kids as a result of it, and it was very unpleasant and very intrusive. We divorced. We have three kids; we get on very well; we talk to each other; and I don't like dragging personal things into my political life. And I think it's very sad when that happens. I don't criticise anybody else for what happens with their children, and I don't expect people to interfere with my children's lives.'

But it was an issue of principle? 'I feel very strongly about comprehensive education, yes.' He pauses. 'It's gone, it's past and people should leave personal stuff out of it if they can.'

It says so much about you, I say. But he shuts the subject down. 'Well, I've got three boys and love them dearly and we get along great.'

We talk about the key plank of his leadership bid. Corbyn talks in generalities rather than costed specifics. Yes, he would redistribute, and, yes, the wealthier would pay more tax, he says. 'Austerity is used as a cover to reconfigure society and increase inequality and injustice. Labour needs to offer a coherent economic alternative.'

What does he say to those who call him an anachronism? Nothing, he says. 'It's not personal. It's about a political idea. It's about ensuring there is a debate, about ensuring that the best traditions of Labour are still around.'

What is his greatest weaknesses as a potential leader? He thinks. 'I tend to see the best in people all the time. Is that a weakness? I don't know.'

Like the rest of the country, Corbyn doesn't think he has a chance of winning. But these are funny times in politics. Just think of the SNP in Scotland, I say. 'Well, Scotland is part of the UK,' he replies, enthusiastically.

How would he feel if he actually won? 'Interested,' he says calmly. 'And hopeful that we could bring about some changes in Britain.' Would it scare him? He closes his eyes, as if imagining himself as Labour leader for the first time. 'Scare me?' He smiles. 'It would be a challenge.'

25 June

The sisters of Isis

NABEELAH JAFFER

Karen sat in a hotel room in Istanbul, grappling with a difficult decision. She had spent about $3,500 (£2,220) on the round trip to Turkey from her home in the US but, when she had bought the ticket, she had had no intention of flying home. The return bookings were for appearance's sake. Her SMS mailbox was filled with promises for the future: messages from an Islamic State fighter who had promised to marry her. But as she sat in that Istanbul hotel room, something didn't feel quite right.

Her prospective groom's insistence on absolute secrecy had not seemed strange at first. Karen had met him through the swarm of Isis-friendly social media. They started by chatting on

Twitter and Ask.fm, then moved to encrypted messaging apps such as Kik, Surespot and Telegram. Paranoia runs through most of the online interactions – no one's identity is clear, and anyone could be bluffing. But the hint of danger was part of the glamour and Karen thought she was being careful. She was in her late teens and had recently graduated from high school, where she had been a lonely girl interested in *Star Trek* and computer programming.

She had converted to Islam less than a year before her journey, after watching the news and deciding to learn more about the religion. She had been inspired by Isis's apparent authenticity – they were as far removed from the west as it seemed possible to be. Her Christian parents worried about whether she would be safe walking down the street wearing a hijab. She kept her real plans well hidden. Online, she disguised her identity by using a kunya – a traditional Arab title. Karen had created several of these, but mostly she went by Umm Khalid – 'mother of Khalid'. The name derived from Khalid bin Walid, a military commander known as the 'Sword of God' in early Islam. Umm Khalid was also the name of a Palestinian village that was evacuated in 1948 and swallowed up by the Israeli city of Netanya. The name has its roots in violence inflicted and violence suffered.

When she met the Isis fighter Abu Muhammad online, she took the chance to bring her new identity to life. As she planned her trip, she asked him to put her in touch with some of the women who had already joined Isis from the west. She wanted to know that she could trust him. He promised that he would, but made an excuse the next time she asked, and the time after that. This made her uneasy, but so did the prospect of delaying the trip.

All the other Isis supporters she had met online said that it would only become more difficult and dangerous to get to Syria as time passed. Things weren't easy at home: her parents 'had a fit' when she tried to wear a niqab. And so she boarded the plane to Istanbul, hoping for the best.

Later, Karen did not like to talk about all the promises Abu Muhammad had made to her: it was embarrassing to think about how naive she had been. He had told her to board the bus from Istanbul to Urfa and make the 18-hour journey alone, as many others had done. At the other end he, or one of his friends, would be waiting to hear from her. They would come at once, and would help her to cross into Isis territory immediately. But to her, the plan seemed risky and rushed. He had told her so little. Things came to a head on the final day, when the tone of his texts became more sexual. When she confronted him, he argued that there was nothing wrong with doing, as she later called it, 'things'. They were, he pointed out, just 24 hours from being married.

This was not, to Karen's mind, how pious and devoted jihadis were supposed to behave. Unlike some girls, who flirted with fighters online, she had never obsessed about true love. Marriage was a practical consideration – a means to a life with Isis. But she would talk, from time to time, about wanting to be a good wife to a good husband – one who behaved like a perfect Muslim. Sexting was not part of the picture.

I later contacted Karen in private on encrypted apps, and eventually she opened up. She had flown home to the US after two days in Turkey ('with great photos of Istanbul', she added, 'lol.'). One final piece of information had clinched her decision to call off the Isis marriage. She had heard about a woman similar to herself being kidnapped in Urfa by the PKK, the Kurdish nationalist group, then arrested. The PKK is listed as a terrorist organisation by the US and the EU, but is also at the forefront of the fight against Isis on the ground. She began to wonder if Abu Muhammad was really who he claimed to be. 'Talking to him, I realised that things weren't right,' she said. She became convinced that Abu Muhammad was not from Isis but the PKK. It was by the grace of God, she told me, that she was still alive and free.

She had broken no laws, and no longer intended to do so. Others in Isis have since offered to help her to come over, but she trusted no one enough to take the risk. She issued some sharp advice. 'Brothers lie to get a wife.' Like the three schoolgirls from Bethnal Green, Karen was from a lower-middle-class background and had a decent education. Almost all the women I came across looked and sounded not unlike myself at 16. They were conservative Muslim girls, whether recent converts or the daughters of Muslims, who took their faith seriously. Although their interpretation of Islam rarely agreed with mine, the women I spoke to were driven in part by religious ideals. But few of these women were willing to engage thoughtfully with a variety of Islamic religious texts, traditions and interpretations. They hated disorder and ambiguity; the clear-cut doctrines issued by jihadist ideologues appealed to their political sensibilities. Opposing the west was their measure of religious authenticity.

'It's time for action'

'The sickest thing I've ever done in my life is cross that Turkish border,' said Umm Umar on Twitter. She was using 'sick' to mean 'best'. 'I'll never forget that night.'

She was already in Syria and was the widow of an Isis fighter. In our private conversations, she tried to influence me with her single-minded energy. 'It's time for action,' she wrote. 'Your Eemān [faith] will get sooo high during the border crossing,' she promised. 'Big adrenaline rush.' After some thought, she added: 'It's sinful for u to be staying in UK whilst there is a khilāfah [a caliphate].'

Umm Umar was just 16 when we started talking. She was born in Britain but her parents were Bangladeshi. She walked out of her parents' home in the middle of the night, leaving a letter on her bed explaining her actions. She seemed pleased to be able to share her experiences. 'Creep out,' she told me. 'If u can take out a student loan pls do so.' What about our religious duty to repay loans? 'No,' she said, without missing a beat. 'The kuffar [non-Muslim] wealth is halāl [permitted] for us.'

Umm Umar did not enjoy her childhood in Britain. 'Man I hated UK so much,' she told me the first time we spoke. She grew up in a part of the country where there were few migrants, and even fewer Muslims. Other kids often beat her up at school when she was small, she said, and spat at her on the bus when she was older. She was desperately lonely and alienated.

Her strongest bond was with her mother. 'Give my mother happiness,' read a prayer she retweeted. 'If sadness still lingers in her eyes, give her whatever happiness is left of mine.' But Umm Umar's sentimentality was shadowed by a violent streak. When I asked her about hurting her parents, she reassured me that it was 'halāl'. 'I did it and I'm sure everyone else did it,' she wrote. 'Right now we are in a state of war.'

Like most of the girls I spoke to, Umm Umar's marriage to an Isis fighter in Syria had largely been a pragmatic affair. 'Life without a mahram [close male relative] here can get quite difficult,' she told me. She had been matched with a fighter who was British Bangladeshi, just like her. His family were even from the same village in Bangladesh, she told me, relishing the coincidence of fate that had brought them together. He had been 'so so sweet and caring', but had been killed just a couple of months earlier. She was now the wife of a shaheed [martyr] and was being honoured. She seemed proud of her husband's success, and never spoke a word of grief or sadness. Another western woman in Syria I spoke to – Umm Zahra – was almost envious when she discussed Umm Umar's status. 'U dnt hav 2 pay 4 ANYTHING if u r wife of a shaheed,' she told me. But she was careful not to seem discontented. All women, she promised me, were looked after. 'U will still get money each month.'

Umm Umar had travelled to Syria because she wanted to join a perfect Islamic state. Like the other women, she painted a picture of an Islamic utopia. This was for the sake of propaganda and, I suspect, to reassure themselves that they had made the right decision. To all these women, Isis was simply dawla [state], as if no other country existed or mattered. 'U can come here and study btw,' Umm Umar wrote to me once. 'Study fiqh [Islamic legal interpretations], hadeeth [sayings of the Prophet], medicine, etc.'

I once asked Umm Umar about al-Khansaa – the rumoured women's brigade that enforces Isis's harsh interpretation of sharia law on the women living there. 'Yes u can do hisbah [join the religious police],' she said. 'But if ur married your husband will want u to stay at home lol.' She added: 'lots of ajar [reward for good deeds].' She had taken part in the hisbah patrols after being married, while her husband was away fighting. After he was killed, she had entered the traditional three-month mourning period. She had just a few days remaining when we last spoke, and planned to 'resume my job insha'Allāh [God willing]' at the end of it. I asked her if she had a happier life in Syria than she had in the UK. 'Yep I do,' she answered, adding a smiley face.

Karen, the American, also reflected from time to time about a 'perfect' Islamic state – although she had become more jaded since her decision to return to the US. 'I'm an 18-year-old cynic who still dreams of an Islamic utopia,' she wrote once, 'which won't ever exist on this planet.'

She argued that no 'government with humans in charge' could ever avoid corruption and 'truly implement sharia'. Karen's newfound cynicism was rare among the women I talked to, most of whom really believed that they were going to help create an

Islamic utopia. 'Sharia is a perfect system who protects all,' wrote one female supporter on Twitter, 'not just about cutting hands and stoning fornicators ... like Saudi.'

Dr Katherine Brown of King's College London compares the women who have travelled to Syria to join Isis to 'individuals who went out to join the Soviet Union in the 1950s and 60s, who weren't looking to fight, but were looking to become new citizens of the Soviet state. What's interesting is that they believe it's possible ... Islamic State is saying: "You can have this perfect world – you just need to try a little bit harder."' There is a totalitarian impulse behind this. By joining the state, these women think they will become, in Brown's words, 'perfect people'.

Melanie Smith of the Institute for Strategic Dialogue calls the 'caliphate utopian ideal' one of the common 'key pull factors' that draw women over. They imagine a world in which there is little poverty and inequality, governed with perfect fairness under clear-cut, divine laws that work to the advantage of all. It is a vision that makes no allowances for the ambiguity and variety of traditional Islamic legal interpretations, or for the disorder of real life.

But there are also 'push factors', says Smith, that drive women away from their homes in the west: often loneliness and alienation. Isis propaganda is designed to appeal to people who feel like outsiders in their own homes. 'Islam began as something strange and it will revert to being strange,' reads a hadith [teaching] that is popular among Isis supporters online, 'so give glad tidings to the strangers.'

'I miss my mum'

Umm Abbas came to my attention when she retweeted some popular advice:

'Feeling alone and alienated? Stop sinning.' When I asked her how she had found life in the UK, her answer was terse: 'Stress depression.' She was a British woman in her 20s with Pakistani parents.

Where Umm Umar was open and easy to talk to, Umm Abbas was brisk and wary. On Twitter, she talked enthusiastically about her journey to Isis. 'The most amazing ... experience of my life,' she wrote, 'was crossing with a family of over 10 members who had a newborn baby with them! :)'

Like Umm Umar, Umm Abbas was relentlessly positive about life with Isis.

I asked her what happened to girls who found themselves with abusive husbands: 'Dawla has the best of men,' she promised, 'and the sharia court here protects you from all types of violence.' There was a process, she and Umm Umar explained, for unmarried women to be matched with a husband.

After being placed in a maqar [a shared house for 'sisters'], a woman writes down what sort of 'brother' she wants to marry. The emir of the area matches her with someone and sets up a brief meeting, after which, if both parties are agreeable, the marriage quickly takes place. 'They will still contact ur dad,' Umm Abbas told me.

But if the woman's father refused, the emir would go ahead and marry them anyway.

Chinks of unhappiness sometimes appeared. Umm Abbas's marriage was much more difficult than Umm Umar's had been. 'Life throws all types of trials,' she wrote to me. 'The biggest is listening n obeying to your husband.' She wouldn't say anything more except that her marriage was 'sometimes tough'. She saw this as a test, requiring sabr [patience] on her part.

She wasn't alone in her unhappiness. Umm Umar would occasionally issue quiet pleas for comfort and reassurance. 'I miss my mum ...' she tweeted once. Umm Zahra shared her jealousy of a possible co-wife, and even of hooris [the famous '72 virgins' that martyrs are said, in jihadist propaganda, to receive in heaven]. I pointed out that the Qur'an does not actually specify the gender of hooris or of those who receive them, nor restrict them to martyrs. She stopped answering my messages.

Complaints about difficulties in daily life were often couched in positivity. 'Candlelight dinner with the akhawāt [sisters],' tweeted Umm Umar, '#CozTheElectricityWent #ItsAllPartOfTheStruggle.' Sometimes complaints were hidden in advice. 'No good makeup,' Umm Abbas told me, 'n clothes too. I brought 2 suitcases.' A recent issue of *Dabiq*, the Isis magazine, addressed itself specifically to the concerns of western women within Isis. The article urged those who had lost their husbands to 'be patient', and to 'be wary of thinking of going back'. Dawla is not without its doubters, and utopian dreams are not easy to sustain, but few will be able to return home any time soon. 'People risk their lives to bring you in,' Karen said to me once. She was still suffering from guilt at being a 'coward' for not going through with her journey to Syria. But she knew that, once there, no Isis fighter would risk his life to get her out again.

For each of the estimated more than 500 western women who have travelled to Syria to join Isis, there are more sitting at their computers at home, voicing their support online. Most won't make the journey, but they will go about their lives with the quiet fantasy of one day being citizens of dawla.

There is a code that Isis supporters use to communicate online. Going to Syria is 'taking a holiday'; 'green birds' and 'dusty feet' are references to hadiths about martyrs. A single finger pointing upwards represents the Isis brand of monotheism and a commitment to death and victory. But Umm Kulthum disapproved of all this. 'We've turned [jihad] into a kind of fad,' complained a post she shared on Tumblr, warning against 'trivilising' violent jihad. 'We hold up our index fingers ... like we're all part of some uber-cool club.' She had other things in common with the various women I spoke to. Many spoke of being constrained by everyday life, and of longing to be part of something bigger. 'You can't just live life waiting for the next weekend to come,' Umm Kulthum wrote once. 'Your aspiration should be greater than that.' She shared one important trait with the bulk of online Isis supporters: a belief that a global war between 'true Islam' and 'the kuffar' was taking place, and that Muslims had to choose a side.

Umm Kulthum knew that Isis was associated with brutality. Some of the women I spoke to argued that the violence was exaggerated by the western media. Others defended it by arguing that the kuffar did worse, while a few, including Umm Kulthum, actively relished it. She shared pictures of Isis fighters with guns. In private, she was remarkably sweet and tender. She called me her 'beloved sister'.

She was Libyan but had spent much of her life in England, and received her secondary education in a state school. She had been lonely there, and spent some time on antidepressants. By the time we spoke, she was back in Libya with her parents and siblings, hoping to have the chance to travel to Syria herself. But Britain still loomed large in her mind. It was there that she had been converted from the 'jaahiliyyah' [ignorance] that she saw in her Muslim parents to 'true Islam'.

Umm Kulthum was fixated on stories of Muslim oppression. Her social media accounts were a montage of Muslim suffering – Syrian children killed by Bashar al-Assad; Palestinian youths burned alive by Israelis. For Umm Kulthum, this justified almost any brutality in return. She felt all Muslims had a duty to 'protect their siblings in Islam'; she was convinced that only violent jihadists took this seriously. 'Jihad is our right even as just human beings, not Muslims,' she said once. 'Do we not have the right to defend ourselves?' For all her hostility to the west, her western education had helped to shape her. Like the other women, she used the language of 'human rights' and 'girl power'. She shared stories of women in niqabs, with weapons, charging into battle.

Special contempt was reserved for Muslims who she thought were colluding with the west by failing to support violent jihad. Such people are known in Isis circles as 'coconuts' – brown on the outside, white on the inside. The word has its roots in the anti-colonial movements of the 20th century. When I mentioned I had non-Muslim friends, Umm Kulthum was stern. 'Habibti,' she wrote, 'do not take kafir as your friend.' Umm Umar was pitying: 'U have to understand that these kuffar are our enemies,' she wrote to me. 'And they will never stop fighting us until we follow their ... way.' Others were harsher. After the shootings of three Muslim students in Chapel Hill, North Carolina, Umm Abbas retweeted: 'and muslims think that the west cares about them. you are a joke by Allah.'

For these women, there is no room for an ambiguous multicultural identity. No Muslim, a recent issue of *Dabiq* argued, has 'any excuse to be independent' of Isis, which is waging 'war on their behalf'. All Muslims in the west must make their choice to either live as 'inauthentic' coconuts or to redeem themselves in death.

'It hurts to think right now'

Theological ambiguity was also difficult for these women. They believed that Islam was defined more by opposition to today's western world than by any religious ideal. After the Chapel Hill shootings, one female Isis supporter argued that candlelight vigils for the victims were un-Islamic because they involved 'imitating the kuffar'. All believed that 'pure Islam' lay in whatever was as anti-western as possible.

Umm Kulthum presented democracy as the binary opposite of a utopian caliphate. 'The law of Allāh should not be voted over,' she said, quoting Anwar al-Awlaki, the jihadist propagandist who was killed in 2011. I tried, occasionally, to argue that there are many different interpretations of sharia law, and that Islam has contained some democratic ideas – the first four Sunni caliphs did not inherit their positions, and the idea of community consensus in legal interpretation has a long tradition. The response was usually confused or hostile. 'You're a muslim and love democracy???' one of Karen's online friends said, 'hmm.'

What troubled me most was not that these women didn't agree with my interpretation of Islam. It was that none of them seemed willing to form independent religious opinions at all. Brown of King's College pointed out that few of the women seemed 'empowered to find faith on their own terms'. When I asked each of the women about their beliefs, they told me to read Anwar al-Awlaki, or to watch popular jihadist ideologues on YouTube. Whenever I asked Karen why, on religious grounds, she supported Isis's interpretation of sharia law, she avoided answering. She was busy, or had a headache. 'It hurts to think right now so I won't,' she said.

Each of these women struggled with ambiguity or disorder – in theology, in identity and in life. Each was convinced that there could be only one valid interpretation of Islam and of sharia law, and that it lay in whatever appeared to be as anti-western as possible. To find it, they had to erase their western identities. Joining Isis offered them an opportunity to do so.

'We don't fit in here or there'
For some women, erasing the western part of them was a struggle. Converts 'have different battles to born Muslims', Umm Raeesa said once. 'Muslims thinking u r a fake Muslim.' She was one of Karen's closest online friends. They had bonded over their shared difficulties: both women had been accused by other online Isis

supporters of being spies. Their only recourse was to emphasise their religiosity on social media.

Umm Raeesa was vicious towards critics of Isis, affectionate towards her online friends and professional in her daily life. She was 25 and worked in finance in Australia. She had converted to Islam two years earlier, but she wore just a headscarf and left her face uncovered. 'I'd prefer to wear niqab at work,' she told me once, 'but would have zero chance of a job lol.' She had been raised a Catholic, but didn't connect with the faith. She supported Isis vehemently online, but had no imminent plans to make the journey. 'This area is unstable,' she told me. 'I think it needs to settle down.' For the time being, she was content to fight for Isis online without having to give up her life in Australia.

More than anything else, Umm Raeesa craved human connection. She had a deep yearning to belong. I woke up to fresh messages from her almost every morning. 'Asalaam Alaikum dear sister,' she always wrote. 'How r u?' Sometimes she wanted to talk about Isis or about Islamophobia, sometimes she just wanted to chat about her day or to ask me about mine. Many of the women I contacted sought affection and praise in the arms of the Isis sisterhood.

Smith and Brown describe this as another 'pull factor' that can draw women away from their homes and towards a greater sense of belonging. To Umm Kulthum, I was always 'habibti'. Karen often tweeted about the 'baqiyah sisterhood': 'Muslimah's of the Ummah make sure you got each other's backs!'

All these women knew what to expect of life under Isis. They warned me that their days would revolve around being a wife and a mother, and would be spent largely indoors. One of Karen's online friends was once asked, on Twitter, why she didn't just go back to her home country if she didn't like the west.

'We don't fit in here nor there lol,' she replied. When I last spoke to Karen, she had decided to remain at home, in the US, for the time being. But she worries that she is being a 'coward', and still considers a possible future with Isis. 'Sometimes I wish I could just leave this place,' she tweeted once. She still might.

All names have been changed

28 JUNE

The Greeks for whom all the talks mean nothing – because they have nothing

JON HENLEY

On a steep, gardenia-scented street in the north-eastern Athens suburb of Gerakas, in one corner of a patch of bare ground, stands a small caravan.

Plastic mesh fencing – orange, of the kind builders use – encloses a neat garden in which peppers, courgettes, lettuces and beans grow in well-tended raised beds. Flowers, too.

The caravan is old, but spotless. It is home to Georgios Karvouniaris, 61, and his sister Barbara, 64, two Greeks for whom all the Brussels wrangling over VAT rates, corporation tax and pension reforms has meant nothing – because they have nothing, no income of any kind.

Next Sunday's referendum – which, if the country stays solvent that long, will either send Greece back to the negotiating table with its creditors or precipitate its exit from the eurozone – is unlikely to affect them much either.

'I do not see how any of it will change our lives. I have no hope, anyway,' said Georgios, sitting in a scavenged plastic garden chair beneath a parasol liberated from a skip.

After seven years of a crisis that has left 26 per cent of Greece's workforce unemployed, 30 per cent of its people below the poverty line, 17 per cent unable to meet their daily food needs and 3.1 million without health insurance, it is hard to see how anything decided in Brussels or in Athens in the coming week will do much to change the lives of a large number of Greeks any time soon.

'Those that were already on the margins have been pushed right to the very, very edge, and those who were in the middle have been pushed to the margins,' said Ioanna Pertsinidou of Praksis, a charity that runs day centres for vulnerable people and offers legal and employment advice.

'So many people – ordinary, low-to-middle income people with jobs and homes and their lives on track – have seen their lives go down the drain so fast,' Pertsinidou said. 'People who never dreamed that one day they would not be able to pay their electricity bill, or feed their children properly.'

As it has scrabbled for every last cent to satisfy its creditors and ward off bankruptcy, Greece's government has taken cash wherever it could – local authorities, healthcare, pensions, social services have all been tapped. In a country of 11 million people, public spending is now €65bn (£45.6bn) less than it was in 2010. 'There is no safety net left,' said Pertsinidou.

No one need tell that to the Karvouniaris family. Georgios is a stern man, still strong, smartly shaven and dressed in a clean green polo short and jeans. His sister, remarkably jovial, wears black for their younger brother Vangelis, who died of nobody will say exactly what two years ago next month, aged 52. He spent a brief week in hospital before his death, for which his siblings recently received a €2,000 bill – which they managed to get written off.

Until March 2013, the three lived in an apartment a mile or so away that they had shared since 1980. None of them had ever married. It worked well. Georgios, a welder and mechanic before becoming a bank security guard, and Vangelis, a salesman, shoe repairer and, latterly, gardener, were the breadwinners. Barbara cooked, cleaned and looked after her brothers.

Quite early in Greece's crisis, Vangelis lost his job. Then in February 2011, Georgios lost his at the Agrotiki bank, where he had worked for 12 years. After leaving school at 12 and working ever since, Georgios got €465 unemployment benefit for eight months, then €200 for a year, then nothing.

The rent on the apartment was €250. 'We spent all we had,' he said. 'Our savings. We sold Barbara's jewellery, for half its worth. We tried to sell this patch of land but no one would buy it. For the first time in 30 years, we didn't pay our rent. By the end we couldn't even afford food.'

If the Karvouniarises are not now sleeping rough, it is because a neighbour saw them sitting in tears outside their apartment building, formally threatened with eviction and all packed up but with nowhere to go. They had not eaten for three days.

It took time, but Despina Moragianis – a relative of that neighbour – and her friends, Ann Papastavrou and Niki Festas, women in their 60s, rallied their women's group in Halandri.

Twenty-odd people, none wealthy, pitched in to buy the 15-year-old caravan, which was towed to the Kourvaniaris family's small plot, once intended as Barbara's dowry.

For 13 months there was no water, but a campaign by the women persuaded the Gerakas town hall to fit a standpipe in May last year. Later, the group raised €1,000 to have it plumbed into the caravan and a septic tank dug, so the toilet works. The next target is a solar panel for electricity.

Every month the group holds a raffle, the proceeds of which buy fresh fruit and vegetables – apples, oranges, beans, potatoes – which Moragianis and her friends bring up to the caravan once a week. Fresh meat is once a week. Non-perishables – spaghetti, rice, flour, condensed milk, tomato sauce – come from the food bank.

And so the Karvouniaris siblings survive. Georgios digs, recycles what he can find on the streets, takes long walks and dreams of fresh milk. No electricity means no fridge. Barbara cooks – there is a gas stove – cleans, washes clothes and tends her garden.

The couple have no money – a friendly town hall official paid their latest €18 water bill out of his own pocket – and no hope of any until Georgios qualifies for his pension at 67. 'I'd hoped it might be 65, in four years' time, but they've just recently decided to raise the age limit,' he said.

He is not sure how much he will get even then. Pensions have been a major stumbling block in Greece's aid-for-reforms talks with its creditors, who want further savings from a system whose benefits have already been cut by 45 per cent, leaving nearly half of Greece's pensioners below the monthly poverty threshold of €665.

It is not just pensioners in penury. Under a limited relief programme promised by the Syriza party during its election victory in January, more than 300,000 of the poorest Greek households applied last month for food aid, a small rent allowance and to have their electricity reconnected for free.

So far the government has found the money to pay a small housing benefit to precisely 1,073 people, the social solidarity minister, Theano Fotiou, admitted. The €70 a month grocery voucher Georgios and Barbara were promised under the scheme – 'We have no house and no power, so there was nothing else we qualified for,' said Georgios – has yet to materialise.

Barbara's face briefly clouds. How does she feel about the way they have been treated? 'Disgusted,' she said, quietly. 'Just

... disgusted.' She smiles again. 'But we've been lucky. There are people who have nowhere to sleep at all.'

According to a University of Crete study earlier this year, there are now 17,700 people without proper and secure housing in Athens alone. Some sleep rough or in cars, others camp with friends or relatives, or live in squats and hostels.

A majority are in their own homes, threatened with imminent eviction because they are among the estimated 320,000 Greek families who have fallen behind with a mortgage or other payment to their bank.

Two are in a small donated caravan, living on food donated by a group of Greek women. Georgios is grateful, but he also gets angry sometimes. 'I have worked all my life. I've paid my taxes all my life,' he said.

'I'm 61 years old and if it wasn't for the generosity of people who three years ago we had never met, we would be sleeping on a bench. You do what you can. But it doesn't seem right.'

Summer

Farewell to America (extract)

GARY YOUNGE

For the past couple of years, the summers have had names like hurricanes. Not single names like Katrina or Floyd – but full names like Trayvon Martin or Michael Brown. Like hurricanes, their arrival was both predictable and predicted, and yet somehow, when they landed, the effect was still shocking.

We do not yet know the name that will be attached to this particular season. He is still out there, playing *Call of Duty*, finding a way to feed his family or working to pay off his student loans. He (and it probably will be a he) has no idea that his days are numbered and we have no idea what the number of those days will be.

The precise alchemy that makes one particular death politically totemic while others go unmourned beyond their families and communities is not quite clear. Video helps, but is not essential. Some footage of cops rolling up like death squads and effectively executing people who posed no real threat has barely pricked the popular imagination. When the authorities fail to heed community outrage, or substantively investigate, let alone discipline, the police, the situation can become explosive. An underlying, ongoing tension between authorities and those being policed has been a factor in some cases. So, we do not know quite why his death will capture the political imagination in a way that others will not.

But we do know, with gruesome certainty, that his number will come up – that one day he will be slain in cold blood by a policeman (once again it probably will be a man) who is supposed to protect him and his community. We know this because it is statistically inevitable and has historical precedent. We know this because we have seen it happen again and again. We know this because this is not just how America works, it is how America was built. Like a hurricane, we know it is coming – we just do not yet know where or when or how much damage it will do.

Summer is riot season. It's when Watts, Newark and Detroit erupted in violence in the 1960s, sparked by callous policing. It's when school is out, pool parties are on and domestic life, particularly in urban centres, is turned inside-out: from the living room to the stoop, from the couch to the street. It's when tempers get short and resentments bubble up like molten asphalt. It's when, to paraphrase Langston Hughes, deferred dreams explode.

This is not my desire; it is my prediction. You can feel it building with every new Facebook post, viral video and Twitter storm. You can hear it from conversations with strangers at post offices, liquor stores and coffee shops. It is an unpleasant prediction to make because, ultimately, these riots highlight a problem they cannot, in themselves, solve; and it is an easy one to make because, as one bystander in Baltimore put it when disturbances flared there earlier this year: 'You can only put so much into a pressure cooker before it pop.'

This is the summer I will leave America, after 12 years as a foreign correspondent, and return to London. My decision to come back to Britain was prompted by banal, personal factors that have nothing to do with current events; if my aim was to escape aggressive policing and racial disadvantage, I would not be heading to Hackney.

But while the events of the last few years did not prompt the decision to come back, they do make me relieved that the decision had already been made. It is why I have not once had second thoughts. If I had to pick a summer to leave, this would be the one. Another season of black parents grieving, police chiefs explaining and clueless anchors opining. Another season when America has to be reminded that black lives matter because black deaths at the hands of the state have been accepted as routine for so long. A summer ripe for rage.

I arrived in New York just a few months before the Iraq war. Americans seemed either angry at the rest of the world, angry at each other, or both. There has barely been a quiet moment since. First there was the jingoism of the Iraq war, then the re-election of George W Bush in 2004, Hurricane Katrina, disillusionment with the Iraq war, the 'Minutemen' anti-immigration vigilantes, the huge pro-immigrant '*Si se puede!*' protests, Barack Obama, Sarah Palin, the economic crash, Occupy Wall Street, the Tea Party, Obama's reelection and the current rise in anti-racist activism. Being a foreigner made all these phenomena intriguing. Politically and morally, I picked sides. But, when reporting, it was more like anthropology. I saw it as my mission to try and understand the US: why did poor white people vote against their economic interests? How did the descendants of immigrants become xenophobic? Why were people disappointed in Obama when he had promised so little? The search for the answer was illuminating, even when I never found it or didn't like it.

But the cultural distance I enjoyed as a Briton in a foreign country felt like a blended veneer of invincibility and invisibility. I thought of myself less as a participant than an onlooker. While reporting from rural Mississippi in 2003, I stopped to ask directions at the house of an old white couple, and they threatened to shoot me. I thought this was funny. I got back into my car sharpish and drove off – but I never once thought they would actually shoot me. How crazy would that be? When I got home, I told my wife and brother-in-law, who are African American. Their parents grew up in the South under segregation; even today, my mother-in-law wouldn't stop her car in Mississippi for anything but petrol. They didn't think it was funny at all: what on earth did I think I was doing, stopping to ask old white folk in rural Mississippi for directions?

Yet, somewhere along the way, I became invested. That was partly about time: as I came to know people – rather than just interviewing them – I came to relate to the issues more intimately. When someone close to you struggles with chronic pain because they have no healthcare, has their kitchen window pierced by gunfire or cannot pay a visit to their home country because they are undocumented, your relationship to issues like health reform, gun control or immigration is transformed.

But my investment was primarily about circumstances. On the weekend in 2007 that Barack Obama declared his presidential candidacy, our son was born. Six years later, we had a daughter. I have only ever been a parent here – a role for which my own upbringing in England provides no real reference point. One summer evening, a couple of years after we moved to Chicago, our daughter was struggling to settle down and so my wife decided to take a short walk to the local supermarket to bob her to sleep in the carrier. On the way back there was shooting in the street and she had to seek shelter in a local barbershop. My days of being an onlooker were over. I was dealing with daycare, summer camps, schools, doctor's visits, parks and other parents. The day we brought my son home, an article in the *New York Times* pointed out that in America 'a black male who drops out of high school is 60 times more likely to find himself in prison than one with a bachelor's degree'. Previously, I'd have found that interesting and troubling. Now it was personal. I had skin in the game. Black skin in a game where the odds are stacked against it.

Obama's ascent, I was told by many and frequently during his campaign, would change these odds. Whenever I asked 'How?'

no one could say exactly. But his very presence, they insisted, would provide a marker for my son and all who look like him. I never believed that. First of all, one person cannot undo centuries of discrimination, no matter how much nominal power they have. Second, given the institutions into which Obama would be embedded – namely the Democratic party and the presidency – there would only ever be so much he could or would do. He was the most progressive candidate viable for the presidency, which says a great deal, given the alternatives, but means very little, given what would be needed to significantly shift the dial on such issues as race and inequality.

Pointing this out amid the hoopla of his candidacy made you sound like Eeyore. I was delighted when he won. But somehow I could never be quite as delighted as some people felt I should have been. The symbolic advantages of Obama's election were clear. For two years I pushed my son around in his stroller surrounded by a picture of a black man framed by the words 'Hope' and 'Change'. A year or so after Obama came to office, my son had a playdate with a four-year-old white friend who looked up from his Thomas the Tank Engine and told my son: 'You're black.' It was a reasonable thing for a child of that age to point out – he was noticing difference, not race. But when my son looked at me for a cue, I now had a new arrow in my quiver to deflect any potential awkwardness. 'That's right,' I said. 'Just like the president.'

But the substantial benefits were elusive. Obama inherited an economic crisis that hurt African Americans more than any other community. The discrepancy between black and white employment and wealth grew during his first few years and has barely narrowed since. In 2010, I used this anecdote in a column by way of pointing out the limited symbolic value of having a black president. 'True, it is something,' I wrote. 'But when Thomas is safely back in the station and the moment is over, it is not very much.

Because for all the white noise emanating from the Tea Party movement, it has been black Americans who have suffered most since Obama took office. Over the last 14 months the gap between my son's life chances and his friend's have been widening.'

This last statement was as undeniably true as it was apparently controversial. I had not claimed that my son was likely to do badly, simply that his odds for success were far worse than the kid he was playing with, and that they were further deteriorating. A study in 2014 found that a black college student has the same chances of getting a job as a white high-school dropout. 'As the recession has dragged on,' the *New York Times* pointed out just a couple months before my son's playdate, the disparity between black and white unemployment 'has been even more pronounced for those with college degrees, compared with those without.' But insisting that racism would have a material effect on my son's life ruffled some readers' feathers.

'Nonsense,' wrote one commenter. 'Your middle-class status means his future will have more in common with his white friends than any poor black kid.' Another – a *Guardian* contributor, no less – also chimed in: 'For you to claim shared victimhood on skin colour alone is highly disingenuous. Your son is highly likely to do OK, to say the least. He has most of the advantages in the world.'

Such responses betrayed complete ignorance about the lived experience of race in a country as segregated as the United States. Class does make a big difference, of course: this is America. We have healthcare, jobs, university educations and a car; we live in a community with reasonable schools, supermarkets and restaurants. In short, we have resources and therefore we have options.

We do not, however, have the option not to be black. And in this time and this place that is no minor factor. That is not 'claiming shared victimhood', it is recognising a fact of life. Class offers a range of privileges but it is not a sealant that protects you from everything else. If it was, rich women would never get raped and wealthy gay couples could marry all around the world.

To even try to have the kind of gilded black life to which these detractors alluded, we would have to do far more than just revel in our bank accounts and leverage our cultural capital. We would have to live in an area with few other black people, since black neighbourhoods are policed with insufficient respect for life or liberty; send our children to a school with few other black students, since majority-black schools are underfunded; tell them not to wear anything that would associate them with black culture, since doing so would make them more vulnerable to profiling; tell them not to mix with other black children, since they are likely to live in the very areas and go to the very schools from which we would be trying to escape; and not let the children go out after dark, since being young and black after sunset makes the police suspect that you have done or are about to do something.

The list could go on. None of this self-loathing behaviour would provide any guarantees, of course. Racism does what it says on the packet; it discriminates against people on the grounds of race. It can be as arbitrary in its choice of victim as it is systemic in its execution. And while it never works alone (but in concert with class, gender and a host of other rogue characters), it can operate independently. No one is going to be checking my bank account or professional status when they are looking at my kids.

Trayvon Martin was walking through a gated community when George Zimmerman pegged him for a thug and shot him dead. Clementa Pinckney, a South Carolina state senator, was in one of Charleston's most impressive churches when Dylann Roof murdered him and eight others.

I have not only never met an African American who thought they could buy themselves the advantages of a white American;

I have yet to meet one who thinks they can even buy themselves out of the disadvantages of being black. All you can do is limit the odds. And when one in three black boys born in 2001 is destined for the prison system, those odds are pretty bad. Having a black man in the White House has not changed that.

When I interviewed Maya Angelou in 2002, she told me that the September 11 attacks of the previous year were understood differently by African Americans. 'Living in a state of terror was new to many white people in America,' she said. 'But black people have been living in a state of terror in this country for more than 400 years.' It is that state of terror that has been laid bare these last few years.

The American polity and media episodically 'discovers' this daily reality in much the same way that teenagers discover sex – urgently, earnestly, voraciously and carelessly, with great self-indulgence but precious little self-awareness. They have always been aware of it but somehow when confronted with it, it nonetheless takes them by surprise.

It is as though the centuries-old narrative of racial inequality is too tiresome to acknowledge, except as a footnote, until it appears in dramatic fashion, as it did after Hurricane Katrina or the protests in Ferguson. At that point the bored become suddenly scandalised. In a nation that prides itself on always moving forward, the notion that they are 'still dealing with this' feels like an affront to the national character. That's why Obama's candidacy had such a simple and uplifting appeal to so many Americans. As the radical academic and 1970s icon Angela Davis explained to me in 2007, it represented 'a model of diversity as the difference that makes no difference, the change that brings about no change'.

This most recent episode of racial awakening has lasted longer than most. For the last couple of years the brutal banality of daily life for some people in this country has become visible and undeniable to those who have no immediate connection to it. But nothing new has happened. There has been no spike in police brutality. What's new is that people are looking. And thanks to new technology (namely the democratisation of the ability to film and distribute), they have lots to look at. As a result, a significant section of white America is outraged at the sight of what it had previously chosen to ignore, while a dwindling but still vocal few still refuse to believe their eyes.

'Terror,' the anthropologist Arjun Appadurai writes in his book *Fear of Small Numbers*, 'is first of all the terror of the next attack.' The terrorism resides not just in the fact that it happens, but that one is braced for the possibility that it could happen to you at any moment. Seven children and teenagers are shot on an average day in the US. I have just finished writing a book in which I take a random day and interview the families and friends of those who perished. Ten young people died the day I chose. Eight were black. All of the black parents said they had assumed this could happen to their son.

As one bereaved dad told me: 'You wouldn't be doing your job as a father if you didn't.'

5 JULY

A man called Y

IAN COBAIN

This is a true story.

One January morning, Y went to the cashpoint near his home to draw out some money. When the machine swallowed his card, he went into the bank, where he was told he needed to contact the card provider.

He arranged to visit a local branch of his own bank, where he was introduced to the manager. Y noticed that the manager appeared to be slightly nervous. A man and a woman walked over to Y, asked him to confirm his name, then asked him to accompany them to another office at the bank. Inside, six or seven policemen were waiting. Y was informed that he was being arrested as a suspected terrorist. He was handcuffed, and led away.

That was in 2003. Since then, Y has been convicted of no criminal offence – 'not so much as a parking ticket', he says – yet has spent years behind bars. When allowed out of prison, he has faced extraordinary restrictions on his movements.

Y is told in which house he must live. At one point, he was told in which town he must reside. On first arriving at his new home, he is given a map of the neighbourhood, on which is marked a boundary beyond which he cannot stray. If he crosses the boundary, he may be sent to jail. He is told how long he can remain outside his home: initially, he was allowed out for just two hours each afternoon. He must wear an electronic tag, which is linked to a sensor in his home, and must telephone the company that operates the tag every morning and every evening. If he fails to make the call, he may be sent to jail.

Y cannot meet anyone without the prior permission of the government. Any prospective employer must agree to be vetted by the government and, as a result, few are prepared to give him a job. If he returns to education, the government will decide what he can study.

Visitors are not permitted to remain in his home overnight. He has recently been given permission to buy a computer, but he must connect to the internet by cable, and is barred from using email, Skype or any form of social media. If he attempts to do so, he may be sent to jail.

And then there is the little matter of his name. When Franz Kafka wrote *The Trial*, his story of a young man who is subjected to a bewildering legal process that he can never influence, the novelist at least gave his protagonist, Josef K, a first name.

By order of a court, the *Guardian* cannot publish Y's real name. We may identify him only as Y. If we breach the order, I may be sent to jail.

All this is happening in Britain in 2015.

Y was born 45 years ago in a town in western Algeria, where he worked for many years as a tax inspector. He was a supporter of the Islamic Salvation Front, an Islamist political party whose imminent victory in the general election of January 1992 was annulled by a military coup. After the coup, members of the party were arrested or murdered, and the country slid into civil war. Y was detained and severely beaten: he still carries the scars. The Algerian government says he is a terrorist. It is an allegation he denies.

In 1998, he left Algeria for Spain, and, in 2000, he arrived in the UK. In Algeria, meanwhile, he was tried in absentia, convicted of criminal association, and sentenced to death.

In the UK, Y claimed asylum and, in 2001, was given indefinite leave to remain. He settled in north London and helped to run the bookshop at the mosque in Finsbury Park, which would later become infamously and inextricably linked with the preacher Abu Hamza.

In early January 2003, as the countdown began to the invasion of Iraq, police raided a flat above a pharmacy in nearby Wood Green and arrested six men on suspicion of attempting to use the seeds of castor oil plants to make ricin, the highly toxic protein.

The media went into overdrive. The *Mirror*, for example, gave over its entire front page to a graphic showing a skull and cross-bones over a map of Britain, below the banner headline: 'IT'S HERE'. The BBC reported that sales of gas masks were soaring.

Tony Blair said 'the find' highlighted the dangers of weapons of mass destruction, while the then US secretary of state, Colin Powell, referred to the 'UK poison cell' while making the case for the invasion of Iraq to the UN.

It was against this background that Y was arrested: his fingerprints were found on a ricin recipe discovered at the Wood Green flat. The only problem with the ricin plot was that there was no ricin. None. There never had been any, but there was no public admission of this until 2005, when a government scientist was compelled to reveal the truth while giving evidence at the Old Bailey, where Y and the other men were on trial, accused of conspiracy to murder.

Clearly somebody at the flat had been up to no good, in a bumbling sort of way: there were a small number of ingredients that could be used in an attempt to manufacture ricin, plus the recipe. And one of the defendants, Kamel Bourgass, was extraordinarily dangerous: while on the run after the Wood Green raid, he stabbed to death a Manchester police officer, Stephen Oake.

Y's defence was that he operated the photocopier at the mosque bookshop, and that his fingerprints would be on thousands of documents he had never read; he said he had never met Bourgass. At the end of the trial, Bourgass was convicted of the lesser charge of conspiring to cause a public nuisance. He had already been jailed for life for the murder. Y and three other defendants were cleared – the jury was unanimous – and the prosecution of four further men was abandoned.

Y, who had been held in Belmarsh high-security prison in south-east London, was a free man, but that did not last long. The Home Office gave notice that it was going to attempt to deport him to Algeria, regardless of the death sentence hanging over him, and a few months later he was detained, pending deportation. He is almost philosophical about this turn of events: 'It was after 7/7 and the home secretary – I think it was Charles Clarke at that time – had to show that he was doing something.'

The jurors were furious, however. Two of them, who had subsequently befriended Y, wrote in the *Guardian* that a government 'that seems bent on chiselling away at civil liberties' was ignoring their verdict.

And Y was about to have his first dealings with the Special Immigration Appeals Commission, or Siac, a place for which the adjective Kafkaesque could have been created.

Siac is the extraordinarily secretive court that deals with appeals against government proposals to deport people believed to pose a risk to national security. Aptly, perhaps, it convenes underground, in the basement of a building off Chancery Lane in central London. There is a curtain around the witness box from which unseen members of MI5 give evidence, and a screen down the centre of the court to shield government observers from the gaze of the public or the press.

Not that many journalists attend Siac. One of the few who does, the BBC home affairs correspondent Dominic Casciani, says: 'It's the only court I can think of where I can be told there is a case of national importance, only to find the doors locked and no clear indication of when they are going to open.'

It is not only the journalists who are turfed out of court on a regular basis: so, too, are the appellants and their lawyers. Whenever the government deploys what it euphemistically calls 'closed evidence', the appellants can be represented only by government-appointed barristers known as 'special advocates'. And once the special advocates have seen the government's secret evidence, they cannot talk to the appellants to take instructions.

As a consequence, Y cannot know the evidence that the government relies on at Siac. It is clear, however, that MI5 believes the Old Bailey jury reached the wrong verdict, and, in 2006, after seeing the secret evidence, Siac concluded that he did pose a risk to national security.

Y was released on bail from Belmarsh and went to live in the house of a man in east London, a peace activist who wished to help. 'The problem was that he had to keep his computer locked in a box, and his daughter had to get permission from the Home Office to visit him. Even his cleaner had to get permission to come inside the house.'

Y told the Home Office he wanted to move and was found a new home in north London. At this point, he was allowed out of the building for two hours each day, between midday and 2pm. The house was on a road opposite a park, but he was forbidden to enter: the boundary on the map that he was given ran down the middle of the road. 'Why were the boundaries drawn that way? I was never told.'

Later that year, when the government began to believe it had a chance of deporting Y, he was detained once more so that he could not abscond. This time he was sent to Long Lartin maximum security prison in Worcestershire. Bail was refused – for 'reasons which can only be given in closed', said the Siac judge – and Y began receiving treatment for depression. It was almost two years before he was released, and this time he was told he must live in a house in a small town 45 miles north of London.

'On my second day there I was late returning to the house. It was a Friday, I had been to the nearest mosque, but it was on the other side of the next town and I missed the bus on the way back. I ran, but I was late. The following Monday lots of plainclothes police from London arrived. I was driven straight to Belmarsh, and was back up before Siac in the morning. The judge let me go back to the house.'

Over the years that followed, Y's case continued to ping-pong back and forth between Siac, the high court and the supreme court. It still does: he's due back before Siac next month. In theory, he is on Siac bail pending deportation. In reality, he is living a life controlled by the government. He is not alone: seven other men are also on Siac bail.

That life is getting easier. In 2011, Y was allowed to return to London, and now lives in a house in the north of the city that is provided by the Home Office. 'It's got two bedrooms and a garden. It's quite nice. I'd have been happy with a flat.'

He receives £74 a week in income support benefit, and works as a volunteer at a local Roman Catholic church, carrying out small repairs. As well as being allowed to use a computer at home, he is permitted to carry a simple mobile phone. He assumes his calls are monitored.

Y's curfew conditions have been eased, and he is required to be at home only between midnight and 8am. His map is bigger too: today, Y's world stretches all the way from Euston Road on the edge of central London, to the North Circular Road, six miles away. There is one street in the middle that remains out of bounds. 'Don't ask me why.'

In addition, he is permitted to go to the British Museum or the National Gallery, providing he gives 48 hours' notice. He can also apply for permission to travel further afield and, on occasion, it is granted. He recently travelled to Canterbury, for example, although the Home Office warned him that he was permitted only to visit the cathedral and museum, and not the city itself. 'They also said I couldn't stop for a coffee at the railway station.' He shakes his head. 'Someone's sitting there in an office, making up these conditions.'

Y had been engaged before his 2003 arrest, but the relationship could not survive the strictures of Siac bail. 'We split up. She would have been subjected to all the same conditions, and she couldn't live with all these conditions.'

His relatives live in Algeria and many of his friends eventually fell away. He finds it all but impossible to make new ones. Prearranged meetings need to be agreed with the Home Office. 'And people from my community, the Algerian community, when they hear the words Home Office, they run: they're scared of the Home Office. It's hard, making friends.'

One of the few who has befriended Y is Bruce Kent, the former Catholic priest and vice president of the Campaign for Nuclear Disarmament. It was while sitting with Kent in a Costa Coffee shop, not far from Y's home, that Y was pointed out to me.

He seems to be a patient man, and has not lost his sense of humour. From time to time he laughs out loud when describing some of the more absurd curbs that he has faced. At other times he uses the word 'normal' to describe the restrictions. 'Well, they're normal to me now. I've been living with them for 12 years. They've become the norm.'

He still suffers from depression, however, and takes a range of antidepressants as well as sleeping tablets. 'And I'm getting forgetful. Maybe it's the stress. I'm really worried that one day I will forget to make the phone call to the tag company. And then I'll go back to jail.'

7 JULY

I feel like a wally for believing George Osborne's flashy promises of a northern powerhouse

HELEN PIDD

I'm fed up of London getting all the cool stuff. That wild outdoor pool in the heart of King's Cross or the garden bridge across the Thames, however flawed and vain the conceit. I'm fed up with London getting the sort of serious investment that has transformed the capital's schools from the shame of the nation into the envy of Europe. I'm sick of having to drive to Bradford because the trains from Manchester are so slow and rubbish. I hate the fact northern museums have to beg to stay open while their London counterparts build grand new wings. And I'm narked that George Osborne has made me look like a wally for believing in his northern powerhouse just before the whole concept was thrown into question by the cancellation – 'pause', whatever – of the Manchester–Leeds trainline upgrade.

I'm not the only one who had drunk the powerhouse Kool-Aid. Considering Manchester hasn't had a Tory MP since 1987 and all 96 seats on the council are currently Labour, the city bought into the idea of being anchor tenant in Osborne's groovy utopia in a major way. 'WE ARE ALL WINNERS' yippeed the front page of the *Manchester Evening News* in December. The Conservative chancellor had just lavished goodies on his pet city in his pre-budget autumn statement, including £78m for a superduper arts centre called the Factory, while rubber-stamping a devolution deal with Greater Manchester.

The vain side of me started to rather like the idea of living at the heart of a powerhouse. Having initially dismissed Osborne's plans as empty electioneering, by the time the Tories had won an outright majority despite voters in almost every northern city showing them the finger, I had begun to think the powerhouse was an actual thing that might really happen. Sure, the details were a bit vague – James Wharton, the youthful MP for Stockton South who was appointed minister for the northern powerhouse in May, admitted recently that the government did not even have a working definition of where exactly the 'north' was. And the whole foisting-a-mayor on places which had specifically voted against one was a bit dodgy. That's before we even started on what the whole thing meant for everywhere in the north that wasn't Greater Manchester, particularly the north-east. 'But,' I started telling people, 'at least the Tories appear to have a plan for the north of England. Where's Labour on devolution?'

Yes, Osborne was cutting billions from the budgets of northern councils while promising a 'revolution in the way we govern England' by devolving power to these increasingly penniless town halls. But why is he still wanging on about it with five years until the next election if he doesn't mean it? After seeing him addressing constituents at hustings in Knutsford in April, I believed he saw it as his legacy. Hearing many of them get worked up about some minor planning wrangle, Osborne referenced *Cranford*, the novel written about the town by Knutsford native Elizabeth Gaskell. Reminding them that the plot revolved around a campaign to stop the construction of a railway line to Manchester, he said: 'Development is always controversial and there are always reasons people give for stopping it. But I don't want to be part of a generation of Britons who gave up, who said, "We're not going to build anything any more," who accepts it was in the past, when we built our roads, our railways that powered our economy forward and gave people a decent living.'

Transport was always a key pillar of the powerhouse project. Osborne kept telling us he had earmarked £13bn to improve our trains and roads, scrapping the pacers – the 'buses on rails', which had been rejected by Iran as too shonky – and speeding up journey times along the crucial TransPennine route. Then the transport secretary, Patrick McLoughlin, stood up in parliament last month and admitted that promised electrification work on the notoriously unreliable Manchester–Leeds route was being 'paused', while the Great Western railway, which runs from London to Bristol and beyond, was a 'top priority'. I felt duped and stupid, like after I'd gone around telling people that of course Lance Armstrong didn't dope because nobody could be so cynical as to give cancer victims false hope by pretending it was all about the bike rather than the drugs.

The *Manchester Evening News* was not impressed either. 'GET US BACK ON TRACK GEORGE' yelled the front page last Friday, demanding a firm commitment that electrification will go ahead and a promise that London's Crossrail 2 will not take priority. That was before the *Observer* revealed on Sunday that £5bn of the promised £13bn transport dosh is made up of the standard allocations to local councils for projects such as pothole filling.

That's why if Osborne is to prove that his northern powerhouse is more than just rhetoric, he has to put the north of England at the heart of tomorrow's budget. He can't carry on making flashy promises that the powerhouse will add £44bn to the northern economy, or £1,600 per person living there while a) not showing his working out to prove such claims and b) slashing local budgets so many times more than those in the southern Tory shires. He also has to prove that the money he pledges is new, rather than a repackaging of already allocated funds. Come on, George. Don't go Lance on me now.

11 JULY

Omar Sharif – a true exquisite who brought foreign glamour to Hollywood

PETER BRADSHAW

Sharif, who has died at the age of 83, was not your regular corn-fed Wasp dreamboat idol. His saturnine looks and foreign glamour made him to Hollywood of the 1960s what the French star Charles Boyer had been to an earlier generation.

He had a touch of class, part of an aristocracy of international sophistication, at once raffish and rather conservative, a style that was becoming a little *démodé* even in the era that saw Sharif achieve his great celebrity. It is interesting that when the ageing Turkish actor and hotel-keeper in Nuri Bilge Ceylan's 2014 Cannes Palme d'Or-winning film *Winter Sleep* wants to impress people, he drones on about having once met Omar Sharif .

Sharif's professional passion for contract bridge and the demi-monde of the casino – a vocation he pursued in parallel to the movies – gave him the allure of a gambler and man-about-town. If producers of the time took a more adventurous line in casting, Sharif might have made a brilliant 007.

His great success was created by David Lean, who made him a star in two of the epics which were 'sweeping' in a way only Lean could manage – *Lawrence of Arabia* (1962) and *Dr Zhivago* (1965). Lean conferred upon Sharif a certain orientalist charisma, and gave him one of the greatest entrances in movie history.

In Lawrence, he is Sherif Ali, the Arab tribe leader who befriends Peter O'Toole's Lawrence, appearing almost like a force of nature or a djinn, in the shimmering haze of the desert in a mysterious, fascinating, daringly drawn-out continuous camera shot. If Sharif had less dash and style, the rest of his performance in that film would have been an awful anti-climax. It wasn't, though he was very much the subordinate player to that other sensational newcomer: O'Toole.

He was upgraded to leading-man status with *Dr Zhivago*: unlike Lawrence, this movie had women in it, and Sharif's Egyptian provenance was an approximation of Russianness. He was the soulful, romantic lover in the pre-revolutionary age, for the movie version of Pasternak's 1957 novel. Sharif and Julie Christie made a very handsome couple, though the film's alleged slushiness and its resemblance to a kind of eastern *Gone with the Wind* meant it was not much liked by the critics and marked the beginning of the decline in Lean's fortunes.

Three years later, Sharif starred in a movie which cemented his image of card-playing raffishness: *Funny Girl*, again providing the good-humoured ballast of experience to a newcomer – fledgling musical star Barbra Streisand.

All too often Sharif became simply a place-marker of foreignness; and the most egregious example of this was when he was cast as Che Guevara in *Che!* (1969), with Jack Palance as Fidel Castro. It was a toe-curling example of a Hollywood movie attempting to grab something that was very modish – Guevara had died only two years before – and attempting to cram it into a traditional commercial formula. Sharif simply went through the motions, and this rather politically old-fashioned guy was not a natural fit as Che.

Sharif earned plaudits towards the end of his career as *Monsieur Ibrahim* (2003) in François Dupeyron's heartwarmer about the elderly Turkish shopowner who befriends a lonely Jewish boy in 1950s Paris, and twinklingly dispenses wisdom and quotations from the Qur'an.

Sharif's career is that of an extremely intelligent and capable actor who had built up a substantial following in the Egyptian film world before breaking into a Hollywood English-language industry which perhaps didn't know quite what to do with him: not sufficiently clean-cut to be a conventional romantic lead, too charismatic to be a second-string character-player, and maybe too engaging to be the bad guy. He had enormous style – a man born to be captured by a movie camera.

16 JULY

Inspect a gadget: Egg Master

RHIK SAMADDER

What? Vertical grill encased in silicone housing. Ingredients are poured into the plastic tube and heated by an embedded, wraparound element. When ready, food spontaneously rises from the device.

Why? Because there is no God.

Well? This week's gadget describes itself as 'a new way to prepare eggs', which is accurate in the way chopping off your legs could be described as a new way to lose weight. Let's start with that name, its unsettling taint of S&M, an overtone consistent with the design. In hot pink and stippled black rubber, Egg Master's exterior screams cut-price, mail-order adult toy; its funnelled hole suggests terrible uses. It has a traffic light on it, for some reason. 'Spray non-stick agent into container' the box advises, which definitely gets the tummy rumbling. As instructed, I crack two whole eggs into the hot tunnel, trying to ignore the gurgling sound from within. It's impossible to see what's going on, but it smells bad. I squint into the dark opening. A bulging yellow sac peers back at me. Minutes pass; the smell does not. Then without warning, a flaccid, spongy log half jumps from the machine, writhing like an alien parasite in search of a host body. It's like a scene from *The Lair of the White Worm*. I can't look at it, let alone eat it. To stall, I consult the badly photocopied handbook, which suggests other treats this baby is good for. Egg Master Egg Crackers, mixed-up crackers, egg and cheese; Egg Master Egg Dog; PB&J Egg Master (peanut butter and jelly); the tantalising Cuban Egg Master. It's a dossier of culinary hate crimes (Barbecue Pork Egg Master has two ingredients: 'biscuit dough and three teaspoons of precooked pork'). Nervously, I try the sulphuric, sweating egg mess before me. The taste is ... not the best. As I dry heave into the sink, I try to remember if I read about this machine in the Book of Revelation. Why is it in the world? Who created it? Maybe no one. Perhaps soon, sooner than you think, we will all bow to the Egg Master.

Redeeming features? It's quite space efficient, being so dense with evil. Box contains free wooden skewers, to defend yourself from your food, and a pipe cleaner to swab the device. Though no holy water.

Counter, drawer, back of the cupboard? Under the floorboards. 0/5.

19 JULY

The witch-hunters are ready to reform the BBC to death

STEWART LEE

Due to its legendary nose for news, last week's *Sunday Times* was first to reveal the 'eight experts' chosen by culture secretary John Whittingdale to 'help decide the BBC's future', the Murdoch empire barely able to wait to share its horror at the venerable institution's latest humiliation.

And what a golden shower of talent Whittingdale has stitched together, a veritable human centipede of business-minded entities, in order to safeguard the nation's cultural heritage.

Dawn Airey is the former head of Channel 5, the launch of which in 1997 marked a colourful new chapter in British broadcasting. Some might say that asking a former head of Channel 5 to decide the future of the BBC is a bit like asking someone who draws ejaculating penises on the inside of public toilet cubicle doors to curate the National Gallery, but she is sure to bring an interesting perspective to the negotiating table.

Dame Colette Bowe sits alongside her, chief press officer to the late Leon Brittan in the 1970s, and currently chairwoman of the Banking Standards Board. She must be brilliant, as bringing standards to banking is a tough job. Apparently there's a Conservative MPs' Scruples Committee as well.

Darren Henley is a former managing director of Classic FM, which is like Radio 3 with all the problematic programmes filleted out, the perfect playlist to keep people calm while they wait on hold for hours for someone in a call centre to answer their phone. 'Just one Cornetto! Give it to me! Delicious ice cream. From Italy.'

Andrew Fisher is the executive chairman of Shazam, a smart-phone app which identifies unknown songs, and with which he has made the world a much duller place, bereft of mystery; crushing the richness of human experience for economic gain, giving you what you want, right here, right now. Perhaps Andrew can now develop an app that can identify what someone has had for dinner from the smell of their farts?

His co-committee member, Alex Mahon, is a former chief executive of Elisabeth Murdoch's Shine Group, connecting her to the exciting world of government-friendly media businessfolk, Cotswold kitchen-supper snafflers, and police horse-sharers, and to those most likely to monetise the vacant space left in broad-casting should she and her colleagues have, regrettably, to reform the BBC out of existence.

In an atmosphere reminiscent of a medieval witch trial, where the three-nippled woman with all the cats is bound to be found guilty of whatever she can be tortured into confessing to, everyone knows the BBC has been doing something wrong, and must be punished, just as soon as some appropriate crimes can be agreed upon.

But no one so far seems to know what kind of BBC they want. Our metrosexual prime minister believes it should concentrate on the kind of HBO box-set programming he and Sam enjoy when chillaxing at home, and which he imagines emerges fully formed from a salami-making machine in Los Angeles.

Others complain the BBC makes shows that are 'too commer-cial', and clearly it would be better if the job of making popular shows, and indeed all television, was left up to Sky, since they are so good at it. But who could ever have dreamed that a show about an old man travelling through time in a phone box, a laugh track-free sitcom set in a paper company office, complete with cutaways to photocopier in-trays, and a motoring review show in which vehicle analysis is interspersed with actionably inappropriate banter, would become commercial hits?

True creativity isn't an exact science. But is there anyone on the culture secretary's panel of business-friendly bean-counters who understands this? Indeed, the actual creative talents who have made the BBC the globally respected brand it is of late are notably absent from the negotiations.

Where is Armando Iannucci, a BBC-nurtured polymath now making box-set content for HBO? Where are Russell T Davies, Mark Gatiss, and Steven Moffat, who between them made massively successful brands of genres viewers maintained that they loathed – nerdy science fiction, sexless literary detective stories and hardcore gay action? Where are Dick and Dom or *Horrible Histories*, educating children by stealth, and David Attenborough, who did the same to generations of adults? And where am I?

Like it or not, and I am not sure that I do, I am objectively the most critically acclaimed British TV comedian this century, and every one of my BBC series of the last decade has been either nominated for, or won, multiple Bafta, British Comedy and Chortle awards. Any panel on the future of the BBC that includes a phone app bloke over me is clearly not worth the beer mat it was hastily drawn up on.

The sad truth is, the reason none of the above artists, writers and communicators are welcome on the culture secretary's committee is because they see culture as inherently valuable in and of itself, not simply as a branch of business that is too naive to know how to maximise its profit margins. And there is no place for them in his process.

Last Sunday, after I read in the *Sunday Times* of the culture secretary's plans, I was stuck in traffic on the north circular with the kids. A new young writer called John Osborne, who I hadn't heard of before, came on Radio 4 and told a half-hour story about childhood holidays that left all of us, aged four, eight and 47, spellbound. The kids noticed I was crying and asked why.

I explained it was not just the quality of the work, but also that the government were dismantling the only broadcaster that would ever commission it. My eight-year-old said that if David Cameron did that he would send him a collage of hundreds of photographs of dog muck. You cross creatives at your peril.

I've been watching a lot of spaghetti westerns of late. I developed a taste for them in the late 80s when Alex Cox used to rave about them on BBC2's *Moviedrome*, informing me, educating me, and entertaining me, as he did. Their big, simple gestures tell me everything I need to know. Robert Hossein's revenge tale *Cemetery Without Crosses*, from 1969, has just been cleaned up for commercial release by Arrow films.

Maria (Michele Mercier) arranges for the daughter of her husband's killer to be raped. But in a haunting, dialogue-free scene, her uncertain expression appears to convey a hint of regret that she let her desire for vengeance get the better of her conscience.

23 JULY

Best summer reads digested: *Go Set a Watchman* by Harper Lee

JOHN CRACE

The unwanted, unloved elder sibling of To Kill a Mockingbird

It was an elegantly written first sentence worthy of the most earnest unpublished first novel. Jean Louise settled back into a sophisticated New York silence, breathing in the fragrance of the heavy southern air as the train reached Maycomb.

'Please can we just sit down and talk about how you defended the Negro Tom Robinson 20 years ago, Atticus,' she said. 'It's not ringing any bells.' Only the singing of a few startled finches broke the heavily pregnant silence.

The next morning a desperate Negro came running to the door.

'My son has run over and killed a white man. Please help.'

'Sure.' Jean Louise's heart filled with joy. Atticus was a good man after all!

'Thing is, Scout,' Atticus said later. 'It's far better for me to come along and take the case than leave it to some civil rights lawyer. Them lawyers are causin' a whole heap of trouble round here.'

'If you won't defend a Negro properly then come to the aid of an 89-year-old lady who has had a stroke and is almost totally deaf and blind. Poor Miss Nelle was determined not to let anyone read another word she'd written and now her lawyer and publishers have decided to cash in on a pisspoor, first-draft manuscript.'

Atticus yawned. His rheumatoid arthritis was tiring him out. 'It's not one for me, Scout. I hate geriatrics even more than I hate Negros. Now, if you don't mind, I've got a Klu Klux Klan meeting to go to.' Racialism was more difficult than Jean Louise had initially thought.

4 August

David Cameron used 'swarm' instead of 'plague' in case it implied that God had sent the migrants

FRANKIE BOYLE

Last week a proud, beautiful, beloved African creature, who'd lived the last years of his life in a fenced compound, was killed by a train in the Channel tunnel. That's the British for you: criticising people fleeing genocide for pushing their children over a perimeter fence, when we'd do it for a 40 per cent discount off an Asda telly.

If you feel more emotion looking at a picture of queuing lorries than a picture of desperate humans living in a lay-by, you need to check your bedtime routine for someone beating you round the head with a meat tenderiser. Only the British could experience great pain at the thought of a traffic jam – a place where you can sit alone with your radio on without being expected to do any work. Aren't traffic jams unbearable? By the time you get home, you need to sit alone in a comfy chair with your favourite music on just to calm down.

Can you think how desperate these refugees must be? I appeal to women to understand this – not because they are more compassionate, but they'll understand that getting into a van driven by a bloke from Kent is something you'd never do by choice. Can you imagine stowing away in the back of a van? To survive cholera, genocide and starvation, only to be killed by a sleeping bag covered in chlamydia. Migrants are desperately fighting to get into the backs of vans that drowsy nightclub goers are desperately fighting to get out of.

David Cameron has offered France dogs, fences, and car parks – dealing with a humanitarian crisis like a primary school kid emptying his pockets for the bullies. I've mused before about whether he might be a psychopath and it's worth noting that he has left reassessing the processing and treatment of genuine asylum applications until after his three-week holiday in Portugal. Cameron used the phrase 'promiscuous swarm of foreign peoples'. Oops, my mistake, that was Hitler – but you get the general idea. Cameron's use of the word 'swarm' was carefully thought out; he avoided the word 'plague' in case it implied God had sent them.

The *Daily Mail* (catchphrase circa 1938: 'German Jews Pouring Into This Country') has revelled in the kind of reporting that can only be the sign of a decadent society in freefall. No doubt Rome, in its later days, was also full of people who held very firm opinions based on little evidence, I simply can't be bothered to find out. One headline reported on terrible food shortages. You might think: 'How wonderful to see the *Mail* reporting on one of the driving forces for people leaving their countries,' but, of course, they meant no frankfurters for Hampshire. At least Calais has replaced the *Mail*'s hideous stories about how drowning migrants are ruining British people's holidays, presumably because it's now impossible for Brits to lay their bloated, burnt bodies down on the beach without locals trying to give them the kiss of life.

Of course, these poor migrants are being used as a distraction by a media and political class (I now use this term instead of government, because the government and opposition seem to be in consensus) that know Calais is an insignificant element of illegal immigration, and suspect that many of the refugees have a good claim to asylum. It's silly season and they want to spin out a story that is essentially about aggressive hitch-hiking until the bread and circuses of the new football season and *The Great British Bake Off* get into their stride.

That's not to say it isn't hellish for the people living it. We invade their countries and justify it by saying that our way of life is better, then boggle at the idea they might think living here is great. We pay no attention to how our actions in other countries have precipitated this situation. There has to be something wrong with a world where the best employment option for a farmer in sub-Saharan Africa isn't being a farmer in sub-Saharan Africa, but crossing the Mediterranean on a punctured lilo, only to spend days dangling under a lorry so that he can end up selling lollipops in a nightclub toilet. Our indifference is staggering. For a lot of these people, their best chance of survival may be to dress up as a leopard and hope to get Twitter onside.

Of course, the true existential threat to us might come from ourselves. If we can look at another human being and categorise them as 'illegal', or that chilling American word 'alien', then what has become of our own humanity? To support policies that dehumanise others is to dehumanise yourself. I think most people resist that, but are pressed towards it by an increasingly sadistic elite. If you're worried about threats to your way of life, look to the people who are selling your public services out from under you. The people who will destroy this society are already here: printing their own money, printing their own newspapers, and responding to undesirables at the gates by releasing the hounds.

13 AUGUST

Puritanism is everywhere. But where's the socialism that involves sharing life's joys?

SUZANNE MOORE

I love the story that John Mortimer used to tell. He was in his 80s when he revealed to some interviewer his habit of having a glass of champagne at 6am. 'How long has this been going on?' was the horrified reaction. 'Ever since I could afford it,' came the reply. There is something here about what the good life might be, though, God knows, none of us is allowed to say it any more. Of course the anecdote changed over the years. Repeating it on TV in front of a member of a boyband who had just got out of a detox centre, Mortimer was asked: 'Are you having counselling?'

'Champagne socialist' is now an insult – not merely a description of a lifestyle. To enjoy oneself without publicly checking one's privilege is some fuzzy betrayal of a thing that was hitherto never quite spoken out loud. The thing now is named as austerity. Belts must be tightened, budgets reduced, frugality applauded. One of the reasons I don't support Corbyn is an innate political distrust of asceticism. I can't help it. There is no need to rehearse the solid arguments against him. They have been had and, by now, the process of enshrinement is beginning. In personal terms, everyone describes him as an extremely decent man. Politically, though, Corbynism now represents a kind of purity. And, on the left, purity always shades into puritanism, an unbecoming exercise in self-flagellation that is curiously indulgent.

It is entirely unfair to judge a man, or indeed his movement, by a vest, but life isn't fair and that's why we have politics. If Corbyn now reigns as the King of Unspin, the real deal, the arbiter of authenticity, then presumably he will appeal to exactly the sort of working-class voters whom Labour needs back. Let's see!

The anti-austerity movement is real and necessary, but the need of middle-class people to pretend to live austere lives is beyond me. It demonstrates a fantasy of class difference fuelled by guilt that I don't share. If you have been poor, you don't want to be again. Now a peculiar re-enactment of poverty is available to all in the name of being Green or even healthy. Entire conversations revolve around people who, unprompted, will list the things they are depriving themselves of, with a further 10 minutes on their fascinating 'intolerances'. The rise of the individual detox sits alongside the rise of food banks, whose users have no choice about the manner of their deprivation.

So, in Labour we now have an entire party going into some spaced-out detox mode. It may feel itself more energised, invigorated even. If it bores on long enough, maybe it can sell that detox to the workers? After all, it works well for the shiny young women who tell us that unadorned raw vegetables are 'a treat'.

I am not convinced, because the perennial political question – 'What do people want?' – has a very simple answer. On the whole, the same things we all want. Security and nice things. Pleasure-giving things. Part of the political disconnect is do with the perceived joylessness of machine politicians: Nigel Farage and Boris Johnson broke through because of a joie de vivre that the right is less contemptuous of. Poor Yanis Varoufakis, Greece's former finance minister, got into trouble for posing while laughing with salad on his terrace with his lovely wife. If you are preaching anti-austerity, how dare you even have a terrace? Or salad tongs?

This strand of thinking on the left is generally clueless about culture and clueless about its value. The arts are a good thing if they dissent in the correct way. Corbyn's statement on the arts is typically top-down party stuff about protecting the theatre and the BBC. Kill me now.

It is deeply unfashionable to talk of the disruptive power of pleasure, or the power of culture to change this status quo because everything is currently reducible to the economy or inequality. Yet there is a whole other strand of left thought, from Robert Tressell to Raymond Williams, which argues that culture is itself both 'ordinary' and brilliant and that everyone must have the greatest parts of it. The purpose of socialism is to spread all of it out more evenly and give everyone more choice. The liberal horror of 'bling' is a snobbery about how those you choose to represent may choose to represent themselves.

The current wave of puritanism is everywhere, from the policing of language to the denunciation of food groups, so it is no surprise that it should surface politically. It's all about denial and self-denial. Ascetism may be morally laudable and a real contrast to the excesses of the political class – but it is a dead-end for the left.

Remember how Nye Bevan insisted that council houses should be bigger and have two bathrooms, which was considered an unnecessary luxury for working-class people? Remember how Bevan swilled his champagne and was told off for it? Remember how we used to talk of the good life for all and now it's all about individual wellbeing? It's so dull. Where is the vision of socialism that involves the sharing of life's joys as well as life's hardships? Where is the left that argued that nothing is too good for ordinary people – be it clothes, buildings, music.

So you have your Bennite tea, I shall continue to demand the finest wines known to humanity.

24 August

From launch to burnout in five years: One Direction's withdrawal was inevitable

TIM JONZE

The writing had, as they say, been on the wall for One Direction. Quite possibly adorned with emojis and then posted to an obscure social network that nobody over the age of 15 can fathom, but on the wall nevertheless.

In November last year, an Instagram video emerged of Liam Payne meeting fans and posing for what looked to be like his 9,264,754th and 9,263,755th selfies. The rapid, mechanical way in which he worked his way down the line of fans, combined with the dead-eyed stare he relaxed into between each forced grin, told the whole story: here was a man who had long stopped enjoying this kind of fame.

Earlier that month, the *Guardian* had gone to interview the band, intrigued by stories of a group who – band in crisis cliché alert! – travelled even tiny distances in separate cars. The writer, Tom Lamont, found five young men who – despite the grinding schedule of world tours, awards shows and promo – furiously denied any hint of exhaustion. 'It's not a question of burnout,' insisted Payne. Four months later, Zayn Malik quit the band, saying he just wanted to 'be a normal 22-year-old'.

But life could hardly be normal. One Direction were a group who formed in the public eye, as part of the 2010 series of *The X Factor*, in which they finished third – the oldest of them, Louis

Tomlinson, was only 18. They found themselves catapulted to instant fame in the UK, which rapidly spread worldwide, and their success made them the darlings of the UK music industry – they won five Brit awards, four MTV video music awards, 11 MTV Europe music awards and 19 Teen Choice Awards. Their four albums and series of tours have made them rich – last year, Forbes named them the second-highest earning celebrities under 30 – and made others rich, too. They're more a list of notable stats than a group – more than 50 million record sales, 91 worldwide number 1s, more than 7.5 million concert tickets sold.

Now One Direction seem to be calling it a day, even if their rumoured split has been reported as a 'break' rather than 'break up'. Should we be surprised? Five years is a decent stint for any boyband to remain at the very peak of commercial success – it's roughly the same lifespan as Take That achieved, and though the likes of New Kids on the Block and Backstreet Boys lasted longer, their careers were bookended by slow rises and rapid falls. In fact, anyone who has seen the script laid down by countless other teen pop sensations will not be treating the news as a shock.

The Spice Girls and Take That had both lost a member by this stage of their lifespans. The 1D boys have already been on as many tours (five) as the Backstreet Boys and N-Sync had before serious cracks appeared, and put out at least as many albums (four) – or more than – all the aforementioned groups.

The truth is, a boyband can't expect to last much longer than this. On a basic level, life in one can be unrelentingly tough. This statement might not go down especially well with anyone currently manning a cash-strapped NHS ward or riding out the daily lottery of a zero-hours Sports Direct contract, but it's true. Payne and Malik, along with Harry Styles, Louis Tomlinson and Niall Horan, have spent half a decade having all their financial, sexual and egotistical needs looked after several times over. But the work-rate required to keep a pop group's wheels turning, and the global fanbase sated, should not be underestimated.

Scott Robinson of 5ive once recalled a life in which he rarely had time to eat, and would often use the 10-minute periods he spent in a make-up artist's chair to catch up on his shut-eye: 'I'd wake up looking like a pop star. But I promise you I didn't look like a pop star before I sat in the chair,' he told the BBC.

The four members of Little Mix once told me of a schedule so packed that they had to book advance slots into their timetable just to be able to wash their hair. 'If we do *Daybreak* we have to get up at, like, 2am. It's ridiculous,' said Jesy Nelson. At the time, the girls were still in their early days, when even the most gruelling aspects can seem exciting, but anyone working under this kind of routine for a sustained period of time will inevitably start to go a little loopy, no matter what the rewards.

Life in a pop group is one in which you get little control, from the minute you're formed. Kevin Yee from failed 90s boyband Youth Asylum recently told a Reddit AMA that he had to surrender virtually every aspect of his life to higher powers, from his hairstyles to his opinions. Scared that the teenage girls they were being marketed at might be put off if they found out Yee was gay, his management allegedly took him to a grocery store and taught him how to 'walk "straight", up and down the aisles'.

Such a life might have felt suffocating two decades ago, but nowadays there is the added glare of social media to contend with, in which every aspect of your behaviour will be analysed for potential 'scandal'. Payne will know all about this from his selfie lapse. Likewise Malik, whose engagement to Little Mix's Perrie Edwards was called off shortly after a relatively innocent Instagram photo emerged of him with his arm around the midriff of a blonde fan.

Malik has recently re-emerged, of course, having seemingly decided against the idea of living like a normal 22-year-old (maybe he listened to Noel Gallagher, who said: 'Pfft! Who wants to be a normal 22-year-old?! They're fucking shit-for-brains!') and decided to sign a solo deal with RCA. On Twitter, he declared his desire to make #realmusic – a genre of music so authentic that it can only be described using a hashtag – which brings us to another reason why boybands rarely last forever. They long to be taken seriously as artists, which isn't easy when you're required to perform songs called things like 'Best Song Ever', 'Kiss You' and 'Summer Love' for months on end.

Just ask Charlie Simpson, who, depending on your point of view, either courageously or foolishly turned his back on future pop star millions in Busted in order to devote himself to emo punk project Fightstar. 'Every day at work, I was in a fucked-up situation,' he told the *Guardian* back in 2006. 'I was in a music career, which was amazing, and I hated it because it wasn't fulfilling me in any sense of the word. I kept thinking, imagine if this was a band I really liked, I'd be loving it. It was like torture.'

Signs that One Direction have been craving credibility are certainly there. A recent *X Factor* performance saw them performing 'Where the Broken Hearts Go' with the Rolling Stones' Ronnie Wood on guitar. Niall Horan has declared himself a massive fan of the Who – which must have made it all the more galling when Roger Daltrey blasted the group, saying: 'Here we are with the world in the state it is in, and we've got One Direction.' Malik, meanwhile, has been hanging out with Malay, producer of Frank Ocean's Channel Orange, and there have been hints too of a possible hook-up with Odd Future's Tyler the Creator.

The notion of packing it all in to show the world your real talent might seem deluded, yet there's enough evidence of it paying off: Robbie Williams, Justin Timberlake, Beyoncé Knowles all turned boy-band- or girl-group-member fame into stratospheric solo success.

Whatever happens to 1D during their period 'focussing on solo projects', though, there's no escaping the fact that this news was always inevitable. The clue is in the name: boyband. As the members develop chest hair and stubble and permanent hang-overs they look increasingly awkward and out of place serving their original audience. They're just not designed for the long haul. In effect, the writing was on the wall for One Direction from the very moment they formed One Direction.

27 August

Why I ate a roadkill squirrel

GEORGE MONBIOT

The first hour of the day, before the sun is over the horizon: this is the time to see wildlife. In the spring and summer, when no one else is walking, when there is no traffic and the air is dense, so that the sounds of the natural world reverberate, when nocturnal and diurnal beasts are roaming, you will see animals that melt away like snow as the sun rises.

Whenever I stay in an unfamiliar part of the countryside, I try to wake before dawn and walk until the heat begins to rise. Many of my richest experiences with wildlife have occurred at such times. In this magical hour, I too seem to come to life. I hear more, smell more, I am more alert. I feel that at other times my perceptions are muted, my senses dulled by the white noise of the day.

Last weekend, I camped with my family at a barn-raising party on the western foot of the Quantock hills, in Somerset. On

Saturday I crept out of the tent at 5am, when the faintest skein of red cloud netted the sky. Below me, mist filled the valley floor. I slipped through the sagging fence at the top of the field and found myself in a steep, broad coomb, covered in bracken.

I climbed for a while, as quietly as I could, until a frightful wail shattered my thoughts. I crouched and listened. I could see nothing on the dark hillside. It came again, from about 50 metres to my right, half-shriek, half-bleat, a wild, wrenching, desolate cry, a cry that the Earth might make in mourning for itself.

My mind spooled, discounting possibilities until only one remained: a fawn calling for its mother. I waited, and soon I heard her answering bark, coarse and coughing, like a dog with bronchitis. Then, to my left, I heard others bark, and soon I realised that I was standing between two halves of a herd of red deer, ranged across the hillside above me. Upwind, they were unaware of the intrusion.

The high ground, as in almost all English upland conservation sites, was sheepwrecked: swarming with the white plague, reduced to low heather and gorse and bracken with scarcely a tree in sight, supporting as a result just a sparse selection of the species that might have lived there. There are some magnificent woods a little further to the east, which number among the few native forests permitted to grow above 600 feet in Britain; sessile oaks writhed and wind-bitten into fantastic shapes. But elsewhere in the Quantocks the landscape pornographers (people who insist on seeing the uplands naked) who dominate British conservation still stamp their fetish on to the hills.

As the sun turned from red to yellow to white, I followed a path down into the enclosed pastures of the lower slopes. Here I found field mushrooms poking through the dew, their gills as pink as raw flesh. I picked some and wrapped them in my shirt. Wild mushrooms collected at dawn and eaten for breakfast are sweet, nutty, faintly tinged with aniseed. They bear no resemblance to those on sale in the shops.

Walking without a map, I reached the valley floor too soon and found myself on the main road. In some places there were no verges and I had to press myself into the hedge as cars passed. But on such early walks, almost regardless of where you are, there are rewards. Just as I was about to turn off the road, on to the track that would take me back to the barn, I found a squirrel hit by a car that must have just passed me, dead but still twitching. It was a male, one of this year's brood but fully grown. Blood seeped from a wound to the head.

I picked it up by its hind feet, and though I had played no part in its death, I was immediately gripped by a sensation so discrete, so distinct from all else we feel, that I believe it requires its own label: hunter's pride. It's the raw, feral thrill I have experienced only on the occasions when I have picked up a fresh dead animal I intend to eat. It feels to me like the opening of a hidden door, a rent in the mind through which you can glimpse a ghost psyche: vestigial emotional faculties that once helped us to survive.

The portal is one of the oldest literary motifs, a staple of metaphysical narratives for thousands of years: the gateway through which a hero passes into another world. I have come to believe that portals are mythic representations of these perceptual openings, fissures that allow us to see, though briefly and darkly, the ancient soul of humankind. To me, this ancient soul is the psychological equipment, abandoned but not absent, with which we once navigated a world where we were both hunters and hunted. To judge by my own fleeting experiences, the land beyond the portal is an enchanting, electrifying place, in which senses and sensations are tightened and stretched, tuned as at no other time to the inner and the outer life.

All this, in response to a dead squirrel. Well, I'm sorry, it's how I felt. Unless you have felt it too, it doubtless sounds as if I'm raving. But I am trying to describe something that I believe to be fundamental; an essential yet neglected component of our being.

I showed the squirrel to the small tribe of children that had formed in the campsite, girls and boys between the ages of three and nine, and asked them if they'd like to watch me prepare it. As I expected, they clustered round, enthralled. How wrong we are to assume that children will be repelled and horrified by dead animals. On the contrary, they want to see as much as they can. What tends to repel and horrify them is the suffering of live animals. In this respect, they often seem to me to have a keener ethical sense than adults do.

I borrowed an axe and sharpened it on a stone, told the children what I was about to do, in case any of them had qualms, then chopped off the head, tail and feet. Immediately, a lively argument erupted over who was to claim these trophies. As I opened the abdominal cavity with my penknife, they pored over the guts, fascinated by the anatomy. They asked me to cut open the heart, to see what it looked like inside. I showed them the tiny atria and ventricles, in which the blood had clotted. Then I skinned the squirrel and stretched and salted the skin on a piece of plank, whereupon another dispute arose about who would take it home.

While the flavour of squirrel meat is excellent, it is also tough; and on previous occasions I have stewed it. But that wasn't possible at the barn, where there was only a barbecue and a camping stove. So I spatchcocked it and marinated it in lemon juice for a couple of hours, before we cooked it slowly on the barbecue. It was exquisite: tender and delicately flavoured.

I've eaten plenty of roadkill. I'll take anything fresh except cats and dogs (my main concern is for the feelings of the owners, rather than the palatability of the meat, though it would require an effort to overcome the cultural barriers). But I was never before foolish enough to mention this eccentric habit on social media. I noted on Twitter how good the meat was and was greeted by protests.

Alongside the various 'yucks' and concerns about disease and fleas – none of which seem valid to me if the meat is properly cooked – were comments questioning the ethics of what I had done.

'Disappointed, what a strange thing to do, you should have just buried it.'

'... we should treat animals as equal until they are. Eating it demonstrates that it is worthless.'

'I thought I could look up to you, you monster ...'

'The big question is what makes a squirrel different from a human. Very few people would consider it OK to eat a dead person.'

'... all that good stuff you've done and then you skin a squirrel and eat it, huge fall from grace.'

I asked one of these respondents why she felt the way she did, and she was good enough to give me some answers. She told me I should 'have respect for the life and feel sorrow it has been killed. Not think skin it and eat it'. I asked her whether she would find it more or less upsetting if I had eaten some chicken or pork. She answered: 'I'm not a veggy! Please just don't scrape things off the road and skin them. Your time better spent highlighting eco/politics.'

On one level, I think I can understand these comments. We have become so far removed from the realities of meat production that anything which reminds us of where it comes from and how it is processed (let alone reared) is disturbing and dissonant. So it should be, given the realities of factory farming and slaughterhouses. But it seems to me that some people have confused what is customary with what is ethical.

Familiarity can render any kind of horror invisible and the common modes of livestock production are no exception. It is the unfamiliar that attracts opprobrium, even if it inflicts no harm.

The great majority of farmed meat, in my view, is unethically produced. The treatment of farm animals, particularly intensively produced pigs and chickens, is a suppurating open secret, sustained by tacit consent in a nation that purports to love animals and lavishes affection on dogs and cats. Pigs are just as intelligent and capable of suffering as the pets we treat almost as if they were children.

While free-range production tends to be kinder to the animals, its environmental impacts can be much worse. Free-range chicken and pig farms pollute groundwater and rivers. Outdoor pig farming has often caused soil slumping and erosion, resulting in muddy floods downstream, some of which have repeatedly inundated people's homes. A friend describes the worst examples as 'opencast pig mining'. Sheep ranching across most of our uplands inflicts environmental damage out of all proportion to the tiny amounts of meat it produces, as the sheep seek out any seedlings that rear their heads, ensuring that trees are scoured from the hills.

And most of the farmed animals in this country are fed on either soya or maize, whose impacts on the living world are terrible. A new paper in the journal *Science of The Total Environment* reports that 'livestock production is the single largest driver of habitat loss'.

Perhaps you can dismiss these problems from your mind. But the overuse of antibiotics by livestock farms, that can lead to resistant strains of pathogens, and the competition for scarce arable land between the production of animal feed and grain for human consumption must surely trouble anyone with a concern for other people.

Even organic, low-input, high-welfare production could be described as ethical only if we ate less meat. Then, if manure production were in balance with crop production, it would make sense. But we are swimming in animal manure in this country (sometimes, given the state of our rivers and coastal waters, literally). We need less of it, not more. In the context of over-consumption across the spectrum, and the vast land-take this requires, any form of meat production exacerbates the problems.

I don't regard the eating of meat as wrong in itself; it is contingent on circumstance. I don't have a problem, for example, with eating wild rabbits, pigeons or deer. All live here in great abundance, as they benefit from the way we manage the land. Deer are, by any reckoning, overpopulated, due to the absence of predators.

I see rabbit, pigeon and deer meat as by-products. The animals are killed primarily for pest control and will continue to be killed, like the squirrel on the road, whether or not we eat the meat. Suppressing their populations does not damage ecological processes; in the case of deer it tends to enhance them. If some of the millions of grey squirrels killed every year in this country were sold for meat, it would be no bad thing. The same does not apply to pheasants laid down by shooting estates or grouse slaughtered by driven shoots. In both cases, their management, designed to boost their numbers, causes grave environmental problems, and any purchases that help to make these industries more viable contribute to the damage.

Perhaps if we engaged more with the natural world and developed a better understanding of our evolutionary history and our psychological place within it, we might spend more time thinking about what we eat. In doing so, I believe, we would enrich our lives, as well as the life of the more-than-human world. To seek enlightenment, about ourselves and the world around us: this is what makes a life worth living.

4 SEPTEMBER

Can images change history?

IAN JACK

Like many people – or perhaps just many people of a certain generation – I first saw pictures of Alan Kurdi [initially misreported as Aylan] in the old-fashioned way, sitting on the sofa at home watching the BBC's *10 O'Clock News*. The sequence began with a still that showed a Turkish policeman at the sea's edge cradling the three-year-old Syrian boy in his arms. Brief footage then showed the policeman carrying the dead boy up the beach and disappearing behind a rock.

Fergal Keane's report told us that the boy's mother and five-year-old brother were also among those who died when two boats of migrants (a term the BBC prefers to 'refugees') sank soon after they set out on Wednesday at around 6am local time to make the crossing from the Turkish mainland to the Greek island of Kos. Of the 23 people on board, only nine, including Alan's father, Abdullah, are thought to have survived.

The BBC warned its audience that the report contained distressing images. In fact, news editors thought to moderate our distress by omitting an earlier picture in the sequence that shows the dead child lying face down on the sand with his head in the sea. The policeman stands a few feet away in a posture that suggests he may be texting or photographing the body with his mobile.

Among national newspapers, only the *Guardian* and the *Independent* published this image unaltered. The websites of the *Mirror*, the *Express* and the *Mail* used versions that pixellated the body or (in the *Daily Star*'s case) obscured the head. The *Telegraph* and the *Financial Times* made the same decision as the BBC and omitted the image from their selection.

Was it particularly shocking? Those of the policeman holding the child are certainly softer images – they have compassion and even an ambiguity: could the child be alive? They suit a finer idea of humanity. Separated from the living, alone with his face in the sea, Alan represents the less comfortable proposition that death reduces even the liveliest child to a heap of flesh and bone. Pixellation does nothing to help – if anything, it increases the notion of Alan as an object, a cadaver – but perhaps it spares him a final indignity. At least I imagine that is its purpose, which isn't a bad one.

Until recently, those who died in calamities beyond Europe and North America were rarely identified unless they were European or North American. The western media felt easy about using pictures of them as anonymous bodies drowned in a flood or mutilated by war. The Iraqi soldier burned to a crisp by an American air bomb in the first Gulf war; the little girl's face staring up from her grave after the Bhopal gas disaster in 1984: we never felt the need to know who they were. The Kurdi family have been named. That and the pixellation represent a step on the journey to thinking of them as like ourselves; to go the whole way we would need to extend to them the reticent coverage that we accord our own dead, which is never to picture them outside a coffin.

Even so, newspapers felt the need to justify publication – on the grounds (to quote the *Independent*) that the images served 'as a stark reminder of the impact of the refugee crisis'. Something uncomfortable happens when a newspaper decides to explain its decisions – something unpersuasively pious (mea culpa, in my time as an editor) – and here I felt it had no reason to. Like most people, I think I can imagine a little of the reality summoned by the words 'Several children drowned yesterday when ...' and these pictures didn't take me far beyond that.

The *Daily Beast* published more disturbing ones online the same day, from a beach in Libya rather than Turkey and accompanied by a piece of over-pitched irony by the American writer and editor Christopher Dickey: 'Do not look at the photographs here. Do not look at them at all. They will, in an instant, inspire revulsion, anger and calls to "do something now!"' Five pictures showed the bodies of five children in the shallows. All had their faces pixellated. There was no sign of decomposition or disfigurement. One wore what looked like a disposable nappy and had his arms bent above his head, as if sleeping. A Victorian Christian might have said these children looked at peace. But here, unlike the sight of the policeman carrying Alan, the photography looked intrusive.

Images such as these may well inspire the revulsion and anger desired by Dickey, though the results of 'shocking' documentary photography are hard to judge. The first photographs of starving people to be published in newspapers were probably those taken to accompany reports by British special correspondents travelling in India during the 1880s; famines, however, persisted far longer. The Iraqi photograph by Kenneth Jarecke, mentioned above, did nothing to prevent the second Gulf war that the US entered so blithely, despite Jarecke chalking a message under the Iraqi soldier's blackened skull: 'If I don't photograph this, people like my mom will think war is what they see on TV.'

But other pictures, especially of children, have awoken consciences or shaped public attitudes in lasting ways. In 1972, Nick Ut photographed a naked and severely burned girl, nine-year-old Kim Phuc, running away from a napalm attack. It deepened the unpopularity of the Vietnam war and became one of the last century's most enduring images. (Richard Nixon wondered if it had been 'fixed'.) Three years earlier, Don McCullin visited a school compound in Biafra and found a nine-year-old albino boy holding an empty tin of corned beef; he looked hardly able to stand. The rights, wrongs and horrors of the war in Biafra have been largely forgotten outside Nigeria, but the picture has never lost – may never lose – its ability to provoke sympathy, distress and charity.

The children in these two pictures were both alive (Kim Phuc still is; she survived her burns and lives in Canada). To manage a picture of a dead child that doesn't cause offence is a harder proposition; and yet Raghu Rai's photograph of the Bhopal gas disaster was published throughout the world without any moralising justification or, so far as I'm aware, any criticism. The day after the explosion, Rai had visited a graveyard where a man, in the act of burying his young daughter, had scraped the earth from her face for a final farewell. There could hardly be a greater intrusion into private grief, but picture desks everywhere, including India, simply recognised it as memorable picture. Pixellation, had it then been available, would have destroyed it.

What all three pictures have in common, and what separates them from Alan's, is an aesthetic, owed partly to their monochrome reproduction but mainly to the skill of the gifted, professional photographers who took them. This may not matter.

Artless but honest pictures can still change our perceptions of the world. The self-delusion is to imagine that our own prejudices and desires play no part in their creation or their power. Wouldn't images of young men with their heads blown off have ended the first world war sooner? Should we have seen pictures of the 116 dead children as they were pulled from the mudslide of Aberfan? Why aren't there well-known images of the thousands of children who were charred in Dresden and Hiroshima? We pick and choose among the images that might horrify us, always believing that our intentions are good.

8 September

We can all learn lessons from these school dinner ladies' fight for fair pay

ADITYA CHAKRABORTTY

About 300 women in a pocket of inner London have just won a big victory in one of the most important battles of our time. They are Camden's school catering workers or, as I used to call them in my days of ballpoint-pen-smeared shirts, dinner ladies. After months of protest they are finally earning the London living wage. That means a pay rise of £2.55 per hour, which, for the majority of the part-time staff, equals around £1,500 extra each school year. For a good number of them, that's the difference between their families eating properly or going hungry.

I want to pass on their story because it's a good one, and funny in parts. But most of all because it's surprising – had you met these women even a few months ago, you might have considered their cause to be as good as lost.

Back then, Camden's dinner ladies were on just above minimum pay. They ranked among the 4.9 million employees in this country who the Resolution Foundation describes as earning less than a living wage – a group that has swollen in size since the banking crash. Analysts and trade unionists often depict low-paid work in strikingly similar terms: it's low-skilled, and done by people who aren't in a union, and who work for an outsourcing firm that offers its clients low prices and gives its staff miserly pay. In this way, the position of low-paid workers in Britain is first described, then euphemised and finally rationalised. Meanwhile, the super-salaries paid to the richest 1 per cent are usually passed off as the just reward for top talent.

However highfalutin the excuses made by a society for paying a few people millions and many, many more below subsistence, it doesn't change the reality of living on crap wages. Ask Annie-Rose Barnes, central to the dinner ladies' fight in Camden. Her mother is chronically ill, while her husband's shoulder injury stops him plying his trade as a carpenter. With her poverty-pay job the family's main source of income, Barnes had to support her teenage boy through school: 'Uniforms, books, trips. He's got size 10 feet and shoes don't come cheap.'

She racked up debts, fell behind on rent and stinted on her meals. Stress and a poor diet meant she dropped from a size 10 to a size six within two years. And still, she says, household basics became unaffordable discretionary items. 'Sanitary towels,' is one example. 'I'd use toilet tissues instead.'

It says something about 21st-century Britain that it can expect workers to leave their homes and slog it out in a hot kitchen and come back without enough money for a pack of Always. Still, according to the usual calculations, Barnes's position would normally be deemed hopeless. She and her colleagues worked for an outsourced school-meals firm, Caterlink, which was under no contractual obligation from Camden council to pay staff any more. The women weren't in any union – Barnes remembers that at the outset some hadn't even heard of trade unions. Oh, and let's not forget that they were all women – which in our jobs market makes you much more likely to be on crap wages. Game, you might say, over.

Except one thing really annoyed Camden's dinner ladies: they knew that Caterlink also provided school meals to Islington, the borough next door, and that the council there had insisted all staff get London living wage. Which meant that in schools just a few minutes' walk away, women doing the same jobs were earning hundreds, thousands more.

This is where things get even more interesting – as the impossible slowly became first achievable, then a done deal. Barnes went to the library, began reading up on workplace rights and ended up joining a union. The women's campaign for better pay cranked into gear late in 2013, and over the next year and a bit the number of dinner ladies signing up with Unison climbed from fewer than 25 to well over 100. This was the outcome of hundreds of face-to-face conversations with dinner ladies across the borough, some of whom took convincing that union activism would not jeopardise their jobs (for the record, no one I've spoken to has said Caterlink managers attempted to dissuade the women from joining a union – but the fear was still there). Four of them ended up taking a week's training in how to become shop stewards.

In dealing with the union, Caterlink argued that the contract didn't allow it to pay the London living wage. Yet at the same time its parent company, Westbury Street Holdings, was buying champagne bars for a reported £25–30m. This is where two other elements become very important. First, the local newspaper, *Camden New Journal*, began campaigning hard for the dinner ladies – including sending a reporter and snapper to the Berkshire mansion of Westbury's chairman and chief executive for a classic bit of name-and-shame. Each story dented the reputation of Caterlink, which is trying to grow its school-dinner business across the UK. Second, the Labour-run Camden council had made a big deal of campaigning for equality.

By early spring of this year, the dinner ladies had won concessions but not the immediate grant of a living wage. Then came a rally at the Town Hall, at which the staff first banged pots and pans then told councillors how they served roast beef to school-children while feeding their own kids jacket potatoes. With the general election imminent, the council and Caterlink agreed to the demands. The dinner ladies won.

You might at first think this story heartening – but unique. After all, how many other Annie-Roses are going to sit in a reference library? How many other union branches will try a bit of direct action, or local freesheets be willing to annoy the council that gives them so much advertising?

Yet the more I turn it over, the more I think this tale tells us something bigger: that what we're told is political and economic common sense can be shown up as nonsense. We've grown used to compromises and accommodations, to accepting whatever's deemed realistic, even if it's useless – whether that be bad wages or an opposition party with a permanent cringe. And then 300 women get it together and show that it needn't be so.

So Camden dinner ladies deliver the first lesson of the academic year: crap jobs can be made better. And the very act of refusing what's doled out to you can work wonders. Barnes has just moved from her old school job, but plans on getting involved in organising her new workplace. 'I've already got my eye on a couple of new campaigns,' she says, and cracks up laughing.

14 September

On David Cameron's visit to Lebanon

STEVE BELL

15 SEPTEMBER

Refugees scramble for ways into Europe as Hungary seals borders

PATRICK KINGSLEY

For a few fleeting minutes, there was some humanity in the darkness. It had turned midnight on the Serbian side of the Hungarian border, the time that Hungary had said it would close its borders for the final time to refugees. A fortified border fence had finally been finished. At the fence's weakest point, where refugees had for weeks walked into Hungary along a set of disused railway tracks, police had blocked the way with the carriage of a freight train.

Yet even after the clock struck 12, Hungary seemed to soften, letting a few hundred stragglers enter its territory via a legal foot-crossing that lies in Horgoš, a mile to the west of those train tracks. At 10 minutes past midnight, there were still families running, limping and panting up the road that leads to the border gate. More than 160,000 people had crossed this line so far this year and no one wanted to be the first to be turned away.

'I'm hoping, hoping, hoping,' said Badr, a 47-year-old Syrian engineer, as he neared the final stretch. 'We lost everything in Syria – homes, friends, and family. We need to pass through this border.'

So began a day in which Fortress Europe began to pull up the few drawbridges still open. First Hungary blocked its southern border with Serbia, putting into action its much-heralded fence, declaring a state of emergency in two southern counties, and arresting dozens of people for attempting to cross the border under new laws unveiled last week by the prime minister, Viktor Orbán.

Next Hungary announced plans to seal its border with Romania, a move denounced as 'not a fair gesture' by the foreign ministry in Bucharest. Then Serbia warned it could not become the dumping ground for Europe's refugees – or, as its foreign minister put it, 'a collection centre'. And finally Austria introduced security checks along its border with Hungary, a measure it said could be extended to those with Slovenia, Italy and Slovakia if needed.

The collective display demonstrated European leaders' continued belief that the biggest mass migration since the second world war is a possibility to be avoided, rather than a certainty to be better managed.

But they appear to have reckoned without the desperation of people like Badr. Following him into Hungary were mothers with babies on their backs and fathers with children strapped to their fronts, all of whom have faced far worse than a closed border. There were grandmothers from Iraq and grandfathers from Afghanistan. There were Syrians fleeing the remains of Aleppo and Palestinians running from Yarmouk, a generation after their parents first fled from Israel to that now-desolate Damascus suburb. There was a man in a wheelchair. And an Iraqi on crutches – 22-year-old Mostafa from Baghdad, one of the very last few to heave his way across the border. Asked how he felt to have got there in the nick of time, a breathless Mostafa said: 'Happy.'

And then the gates clanged shut. At around 12.20am on Tuesday, Hungary finally blocked the main route used by refugees to reach the safety of the European Union, leaving about 100 people stranded in the dark. Later in the night, Hungarian police erected a flimsy second fence behind the main barrier of the crossing, just in case anyone hadn't cottoned on.

Perhaps they hadn't. A few metres away, Radwan – a 38-year-old printer from Yarmouk, and one of the first to be turned away from Hungary – struggled to compute what was happening.

Having brought two babies and three older children all the way from Syria, he was trying to find a new home just a few decades after his parents' generation fled from Israel. Now even Europe had shut its doors to them.

'We're Palestinian-Syrians, where else are we supposed to go now?' Radwan asked, cradling his three-year-old son Abdallah, who hasn't spoken since leaving Syria two weeks ago. 'We're coming from destruction and killing. I shouldn't have to take five children all the way here for us to be shut out here.'

Radwan and his wife Mayada slumped on the tarmac next to the gates of Hungary – exhausted, shocked, and unsure what to do next. But of one thing they were certain: even this setback would not put off a Syrian population fleeing from a fate far worse. 'This won't stop people,' Mayada said, rocking her youngest baby to sleep. 'For example, my sister and her husband and their three children will leave Syria soon. I have told them that it is difficult, but they will still come.'

That determination was clear on Tuesday as people confronted by the Hungarian fence at Horgoš considered whether to take a different route – through Croatia, Bosnia or Romania. At least one drifted into the night, hoping to cross the Croatian border. Back in Belgrade, one smuggler offered a ride to Sid, a town on the cusp of Croatia. Loitering in the shadows of Horgoš, another hinted at alternative routes through the Hungarian border. 'We have other ways,' the smuggler said, vaguely. 'This was the easiest, but we have other ones.'

But with the fence now fully fortified, it is a tough barrier to cross undetected. Sixty were caught in the act overnight. So most people kept their faith in the legal crossing point at Horgoš – and by mid-afternoon on Tuesday, thousands had gathered alongside Radwan and Mayada forming a vast tent city on the border. Either the many newcomers hadn't heard about the latest developments, or they hoped for a last-minute change in Hungary's plans.

'Maybe tomorrow you won't see me, maybe tomorrow I'll go to Croatia,' said Abu Hossam, a business graduate from Homs, a city wrecked by the Syrian war. 'But I don't know. Our city is destroyed. We can wait here for one week or one month until they open up this country.'

As numbers swelled, so did the chaos and the rumours. Huge crowds of dehydrated Syrians and Afghans rambled up and down the razor-wire fence in the heat, responding to the latest Chinese whispers. Someone said people could in fact cross into Hungary along a nearby road, so everyone scurried there. That rumour turned about to be false, so hundreds just sat down on the tarmac and blocked a queue of lorries. People chanted: 'No food, no water – let us cross the border', while someone hung a cloth from the fence that simply read: 'Europe Shame'. Then came word that people could claim asylum in a set of cubicles that lined the border, a few hundred metres away. But once they got there, they found the doors to those cabins almost never opened.

'They said the Syrians should enter from there, and others from here – but no one's been let in,' said Heba, a water engineer, ambling about in a daze. Shady, Heba's husband, summed things up: 'We are all lost.'

So, too, were two representatives from the International Organisation for Migration. What is going on, a journalist asked them. 'Can you tell us?' one of them replied.

It took a pair of 12-year-old twins, Khalid and Fahed Kashkool, wearing matching checked shirts and turquoise trainers, to try to make sense of the madness. Having procured a document written in incomprehensible Hungarian jargon, the young Syrians told a crowd of compatriots that anyone who signed it, and then claimed asylum in the cubicles, would not be returned to Serbia.

Hungary's government spokesman, Zoltán Kovács, suggested otherwise. Refugees arriving from Serbia should have claimed asylum there, Kovács said, because it's a safe country. 'If someone has already claimed asylum in Greece but moved on, it is possible that Hungary, with the confines of European solidarity, will handle their case,' Kovács said from Budapest. 'Also minors travelling without adults.'

But the vast majority of people who reach Hungary from Serbia will probably have their application rejected. Indeed, by midafternoon on Tuesday, at least 16 had already had their requests for asylum turned down. One, Zahir Habbal, an electrician from Damascus, told the *Guardian* that interrogators made no attempt to find out about his circumstances in the few minutes they took to reject his application. 'They didn't ask anything about my life,' Habbal said. 'It wasn't interesting to them.'

Hungary's behaviour was condemned by the UN, who said asylum-seekers shouldn't be expected to rely on Serbia's virtually non-existent reception system. 'Serbia is a safe country of origin,' said Babar Baloch, a UN refugee agency spokesman, but it has no asylum system for refugees from other countries.

For this reason, Serbia's leaders began to speak out on Tuesday. For months the Serbian government has allowed refugees to cross its land, unbothered by a flow of people who do not wish to linger long within Serbia's borders. But with the refugees' exit now blocked, and tens of thousands more expected to arrive in Serbia in the coming weeks, Serbia now fears turning into a dumping ground for Europe's unwanted. 'The idea of returning all migrants to Serbia, with others flowing in from Greece and Macedonia, is unacceptable, because we would then become the centre of arrivals,' the foreign minister, Ivica Dačić, told reporters on Tuesday. 'Serbia cannot handle this.'

Similar statements can be expected from Serbia's neighbours, should the refugee route shift towards Romania or Croatia, and the Balkan states beyond.

As refugee after refugee said in Horgoš on Tuesday, border closures will never be an effective deterrent to people fleeing experiences that are far more traumatic. It was the Kashkool twins who put it best. They grew up in Ghouta, Khalid said, where civilians have been subjected to chemical weapons. On their way to school, they were shot at by snipers. There's no way they could return there.

'This closing border isn't going to stop Syrian refugees, because of the war,' continued Fahed, standing a metre from the Hungarian fence. 'Syrian refugees are going to come and stay here. And if they don't get in, they'll go to Slovenia, and from Slovenia they'll make their way to Austria, and then from Austria they'll go to Germany.'

But on the other side of the barbed wire, a Hungarian translator, along with most of Europe's political class, hadn't got the message. 'Go away from here,' he later shouted in Arabic. But the Syrians laughed. Where else were they supposed to go?

15 SEPTEMBER

All hail the Bearded One! The first 100 days of Jeremy Corbyn as Prime Minister

CHRIS MULLIN

Thursday 7 May 2020. The polls have closed and, to general astonishment, a BBC exit poll is predicting a narrow victory for Jeremy Corbyn's Labour-Liberal Democrat-Green alliance.

From the outset, it is clear that there has been a huge increase in turnout among the young and the disaffected. As one commentator puts it: 'Generation Rent appear to be taking their revenge on middle England.'

As usual, Sunderland South is the first seat to declare, less than an hour after polls close. Unsurprisingly, the Labour candidate is returned, but the swing is modest, causing commentators to suggest that perhaps the exit poll is mistaken.

The first sign that the earth is about to change places with the sky comes just after midnight when Labour begins picking up home counties seats it hasn't held for a decade. Ipswich, Harwich, Harlow, Dover, the Medway towns and Plymouth Sutton fall in quick succession. Two Brighton seats and one in Bristol go Green, along with the hitherto safe Tory seat of Totnes.

At dawn, the result remains unclear. Most of the traditional Tory strongholds have held firm. In Surrey, Sussex, Hampshire and North Yorkshire, Tory MPs are returned with increased majorities. The outcome hangs on what happens in the 40 seats in which Labour, the Liberal Democrats and the Greens have agreed not to oppose each other.

2am: All eyes are on Islington. Upper Street has been blocked since early evening by crowds chanting 'Jeremy, Jeremy' and 'Jez we can'. Of the Bearded One, there are only intermittent glimpses: at the declaration of his own result and, later, when he appears on the steps of Islington town hall. His demeanour, as ever, is downbeat and, as is his habit, he joins in the applause. 'We must await events,' is all he says, before disappearing back inside. A large screen outside the town hall relays the results. The cheering and the chanting intensify with each new gain. By dawn, a delirious crowd is blocking the entire street from Highbury Corner to the Angel tube station. Large screens relaying the results have been erected at intervals along the entire length of the street. The atmosphere is more Glastonbury than Islington.

Meanwhile, commentators who only hours earlier had been predicting a Labour meltdown are now opining knowledgably on the causes of the earthquake. There is general agreement that the Tories overdid austerity. The collapse of just about all non-statutory services, the outsourcing of parks, the boarded-up theatres and youth clubs and the sporadic outbreaks of inner-city rioting have finally triggered a political backlash beyond the Labour heartlands. That, plus the growing realisation that an entire generation of young people have been priced out of the housing market by overseas investors and ruthless buy-to-let landlords.

There is general agreement, too, that attempts by the Tories and their tabloid friends to paint Corbyn as an agent of Hamas and Hezbollah have spectacularly backfired. Not least as a result of the revelation that MI6, with ministerial approval, has been talking to Hamas all along.

The tabloid press has gone bananas. 'BRITAIN VOTES FOR LUNACY', screams the *Sun*, without waiting for the final result. 'STARK RAVING BONKERS' is the *Mail*'s considered opinion. The broadsheet press is only mildly less hysterical. The front page of the *Telegraph* is headed 'CIVILISATION AS WE KNOW IT: THE END'. There is much talk of assets being evacuated. Florida seems to be the preferred destination.

From Chelsea to Chorleywood come reports of panic buying. Cue TV cameras panning empty shelves in the King's Road branch of Waitrose.

Only on Friday morning, when the rural results come in, is the outcome clear. Former Lib-Dem strongholds in Devon, Cornwall and Northumberland have returned to the fold, along with Richmond Park and Twickenham, which declared overnight. Corbyn's controversial decision not to contest these seats has paid off.

By noon, it has become clear to everyone that Corbyn is in a position to form a government. In Tatton, Cheshire, an ashen-faced George Osborne is shown on TV conceding defeat. 'I have just telephoned Mr Corbyn to congratulate him,' he says through gritted teeth. A statement from the Scottish Nationalists, who have retained all but three of their seats, welcomes the outcome and says they look forward to working with the new government.

An hour later, Corbyn, looking cheerful and well-rested makes his way with difficulty by bicycle through the crowds in the Mall to the palace, where he is to be anointed. In deference to the occasion, he is wearing a smart sports jacket with a red-flag lapel button, but no tie. His majesty, unlike many of his courtiers, is said to be not too distressed by the outcome. In fact, say some, he is positively gleeful. Indeed, there are rumours that he has for some months been engaged in private correspondence with the Labour leader on a range of issues.

The sun shines. From all over the country there are reports of impromptu street parties.

Friday, 1pm: Corbyn, hotfoot from the palace, enters Downing Street pushing his bicycle. By now, he has acquired a police escort that, with difficulty, carves a path through the crowds to the door of No 10. 'The dark days of austerity are at an end,' Corbyn says, before chaining his bicycle to the railings and disappearing inside.

News of his government trickles out slowly over the weekend. Many of the names are unfamiliar, but there are some surprises. Chuka Umunna is to be chancellor of the exchequer. Immediately the share index, which had been plummeting, stabilises.

Hilary Benn is to be foreign secretary. Dan Jarvis, a former major in the Parachute Regiment, defence secretary. The Green MP Caroline Lucas will be secretary of state for the environment. Tom Watson becomes deputy prime minister and secretary of state for culture, media and sport. John McDonnell, who two years earlier had been dramatically deposed as shadow chancellor in what came to be known as Corbyn's night of the long knives, takes education while Diane Abbott gets local government. The ever affable Charlie Falconer, a veteran of the Blair administration, is to lead the Lords.

It is, however, the subsequent non-political appointments that cause the most comment. The US economist and Nobel laureate Paul Krugman is to be governor of the Bank of England. The new head of Ofcom, the media regulator, is to be the former Lib Dem MP Vince Cable.

The name of Jeremy Corbyn appears in the in-tray of President Trump at 8am Washington time. The president at once convenes an emergency meeting of his closest advisers. He is not a happy bunny. 'I thought you assholes told me that this couldn't happen ... So, what's your advice? Sanctions? Do we send in the marines?'

The head of the CIA replies: 'Cool it, Mr President. It's early days yet.'

This result is the following statement by the White House press secretary: 'The United States respects the will of the British people and looks forward to working with Mr Corbyn.' Her facial expression suggests otherwise, however. Later, it emerges that the US ambassador to London has been recalled for urgent consultations.

Having named his cabinet, the new prime minister spends Sunday afternoon tending to his allotment. Monday brings the first trickle of policy announcements and they prove popular with middle England. The proposed high speed railway, HS2, is to be abandoned in favour of investment in existing railway lines and the reopening of some scrapped by Dr Beeching. The expansion of Heathrow and Gatwick airports is also to be abandoned. 'Demand management, rather than predict-and-provide, is the future of aviation policy,' says the accompanying statement. Squeals of outrage from the vested interests are largely lost in the accompanying celebrations. Suddenly, Corbyn has friends he didn't know he had, in deepest Buckinghamshire and parts of Sussex hitherto off-limits to the Labour party.

Week one: In a statement to the House of Commons, the new defence secretary, Major Jarvis (as the press have taken to calling him), announces that plans to renew the Trident missile system are to be scrapped, resulting in a saving to the public purse of many billions. Part of the proceeds will be invested in equipping and expanding conventional forces. He is at pains to emphasise that there are no plans to leave Nato. Major Jarvis adds that a modest expansion of the armed forces is to be undertaken in anticipation that British forces will have an increased role to play in UN peacekeeping. Immediately, a retired field marshal and a number of retired generals pop up to say that this represents a long overdue outbreak of common sense. Which largely trumps the howls of outrage from the military wing of the Tory party.

Week two: the King's speech. Some observers affect to notice a spring in his majesty's step. Among the highlights is a media diversity bill that places strict limits on the share of the British media owned by any single proprietor. As expected, the railways are to be taken back into public ownership, at no cost to the public purse, as the franchises expire. A state energy company will be established to compete with those in the private sector and a state investment bank will be set up with a mandate to invest only in productive and environmentally friendly activity. Plans to renationalise the energy companies are to be put on hold 'for the time being'.

The flagship of the legislative programme is to be a housing bill reintroducing rent controls, and encouraging local authorities to build affordable housing. There is to be an indefinite moratorium on the sale of public housing.

Finally, a bill to enact reform of the House of Lords. Life peerages will be converted to terms of 12 years; likewise, the remaining hereditary peerages will be converted to a fixed term, allowing the hereditaries to die out. To sweeten the pill, former peers are to be allowed life access to the club facilities. Resistance, however, will not be tolerated. If necessary, up to 1,000 new peers will be created to force through the new arrangements.

Week three: the new chancellor's pre-Budget speech. Words such as 'caution' and the phrase 'fiscal responsibility' feature frequently. Behind the scenes, there are reported to have been some differences between the prime minister and his chancellor, but come the day they are all smiles.

The new chancellor devotes some time to mocking the efforts of the previous administration to deal with the deficit. 'The right honourable gentleman,' says Chancellor Chuka as he points an accusing finger at the former prime minister Osborne, 'promised to pay down the deficit in five years, then in nine, then in 10, and all he succeeded in doing is collapsing much of the public sector while leaving half the deficit unpaid.' Osborne shifts uncomfortably. Gone is his trademark perma-smirk.

Then, radiating calm, the chancellor proceeds to announce a 'carefully managed' programme of quantitative easing to help revive the main public services. 'I am advised that this will result in a small increase in inflation, but – to coin a phrase – that will be a price worth paying in order to repair the damage that the right honourable gentleman and his friends have inflicted on our social fabric.' He goes on: 'There will be no more deficit fetishism. The remaining deficit will be ringfenced and paid down over 20 years, as one might repay a mortgage.' At every point, he is careful to announce that he has acted in close consultation with the new governor of the Bank 'and other leading economists'.

To the relief of the southern middle classes, the chancellor announces, with a sideways glance at Corbyn, whose expression is studiously neutral, that there is to be no increase in the top rate of taxation. And plans for a mansion tax have been abandoned. Instead, there will be 'two and possibly three' new council tax bands, raising much-needed revenue for local government.

The budget is well received in most quarters. In the City, relief is the prevailing sentiment. Share prices remain buoyant. The pound regains some of its earlier losses against the dollar. Talk of relocation to the far east has faded. Only the Barclay brothers, following news of a review of their tax arrangements, announce that they will be abandoning their rock in the Channel Islands and relocating to Tuvalu.

As for the Tories, they remain shell-shocked. George Osborne has announced his resignation. A long and bloody leadership election is anticipated.

To general astonishment, among the early visitors to Downing Street is a grim-faced Rupert Murdoch. He is closeted with the new prime minister for more than an hour, at the end of which the following announcement is made: 'Mr Murdoch has asked the government to allow 21st Century Fox to extend its holdings in Sky plc. I have agreed to this subject to two conditions. First, that the Broadcasting Acts are amended, requiring Sky to compete on a level playing field with the main terrestrial TV channels. And secondly, that he relinquishes control of all his British news-papers which will, in future, be managed by a trust in which no single shareholder will have a controlling interest. Mr Murdoch has accepted these conditions. Our discussions were amicable.'

And so it came to pass that Jeremy Corbyn, serial dissident, alleged friend of Hamas, scourge of the ruling classes (to say nothing of New Labour), was seamlessly translated into a saintly, much-loved figure. Much to the new prime minister's embarrass-ment, mothers began to name their sons after him. Corbyn-style beards became fashionable among men of a certain age and waiting lists for allotments shot up, following a much-praised appearance on *Gardeners' World*. How long the honeymoon would last was anyone's guess, but it was wondrous to behold.

Most astonishing of all, in an interview to celebrate 100 days of the new administration, was this testimony: 'I guess I was wrong about Jeremy. Perhaps we all were.' The author? No less a figure than Tony Blair.

Index